AF271670

Nantucket Vistas

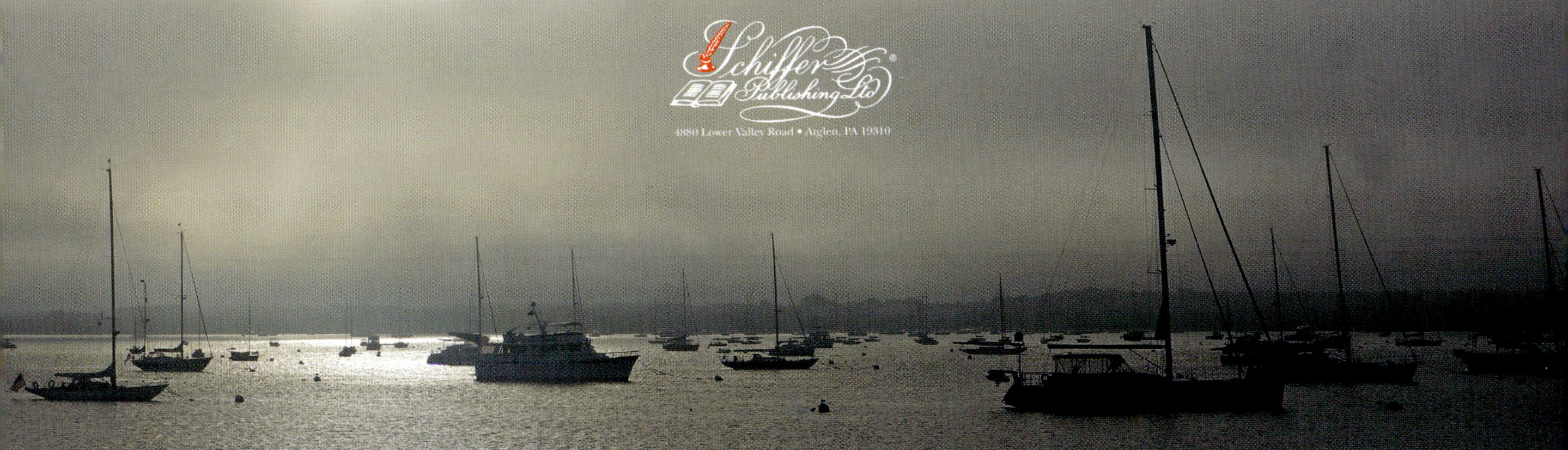

Nantucket Vistas

Arthur P. Richmond

Schiffer Publishing Ltd
4880 Lower Valley Road • Atglen, PA 19310

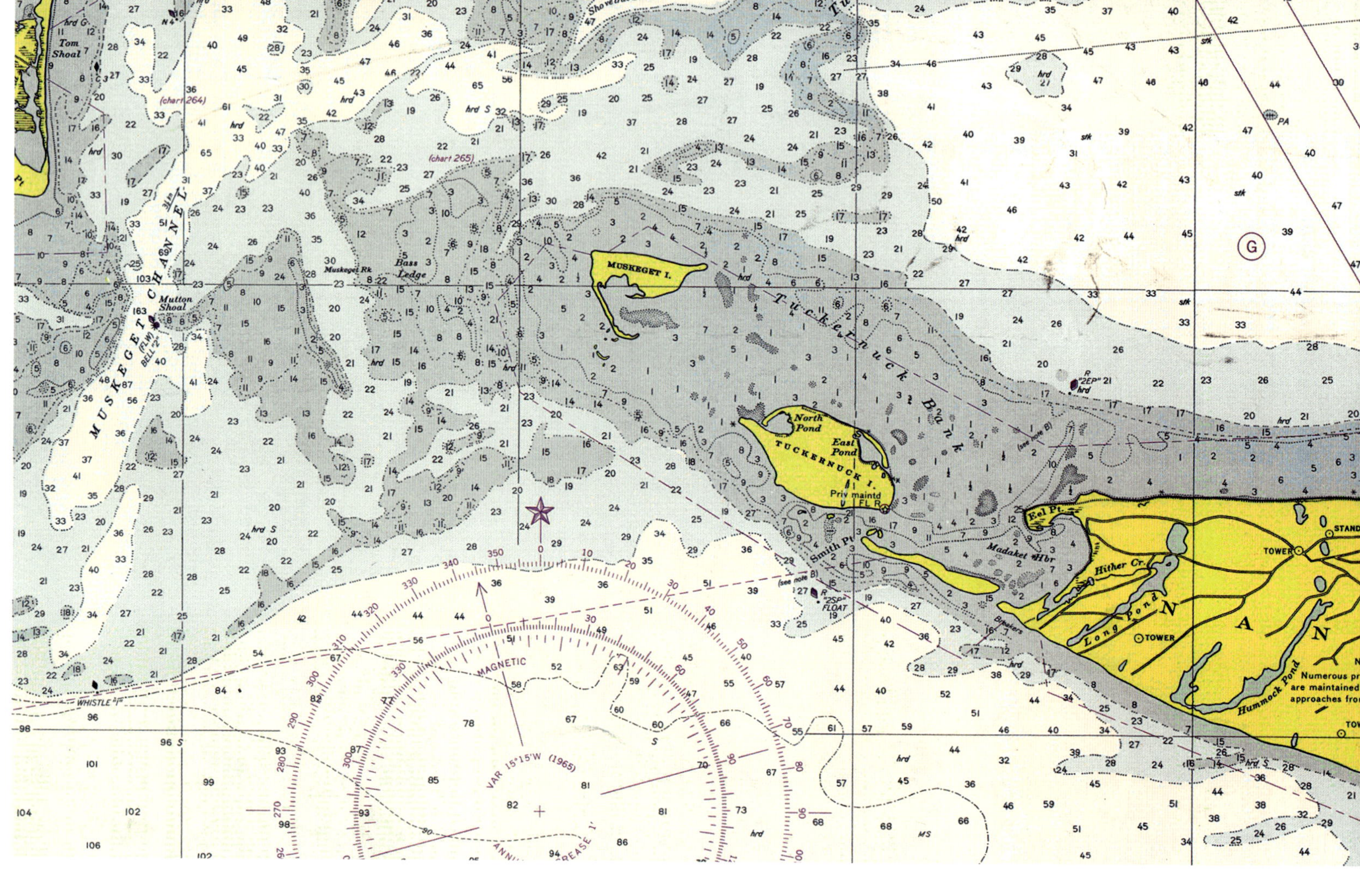

Tom Shoal
(chart 264)
(chart 265)
MUSKEGET CHANNEL
Muskeget Rk
Bass Ledge
Mutton Shoal
BELL "2"
MUSKEGET I.
Tuckernuck Bank
North Pond
East Pond
TUCKERNUCK I.
Priv maintd
FL R
Eel Pt.
Smith Pt.
Madaket Hbr
Hither Cr.
Long Pond
TOWER
TOWER
STANDPIPE
TOWER
Hummock Pond
NANTUCKET
Shovelful Shoal
Breakers
MAGNETIC
VAR 15°15'W (1965)
WHISTLE
ANNUAL DECREASE 1'
Numerous priva
are maintained in
approaches from J
G

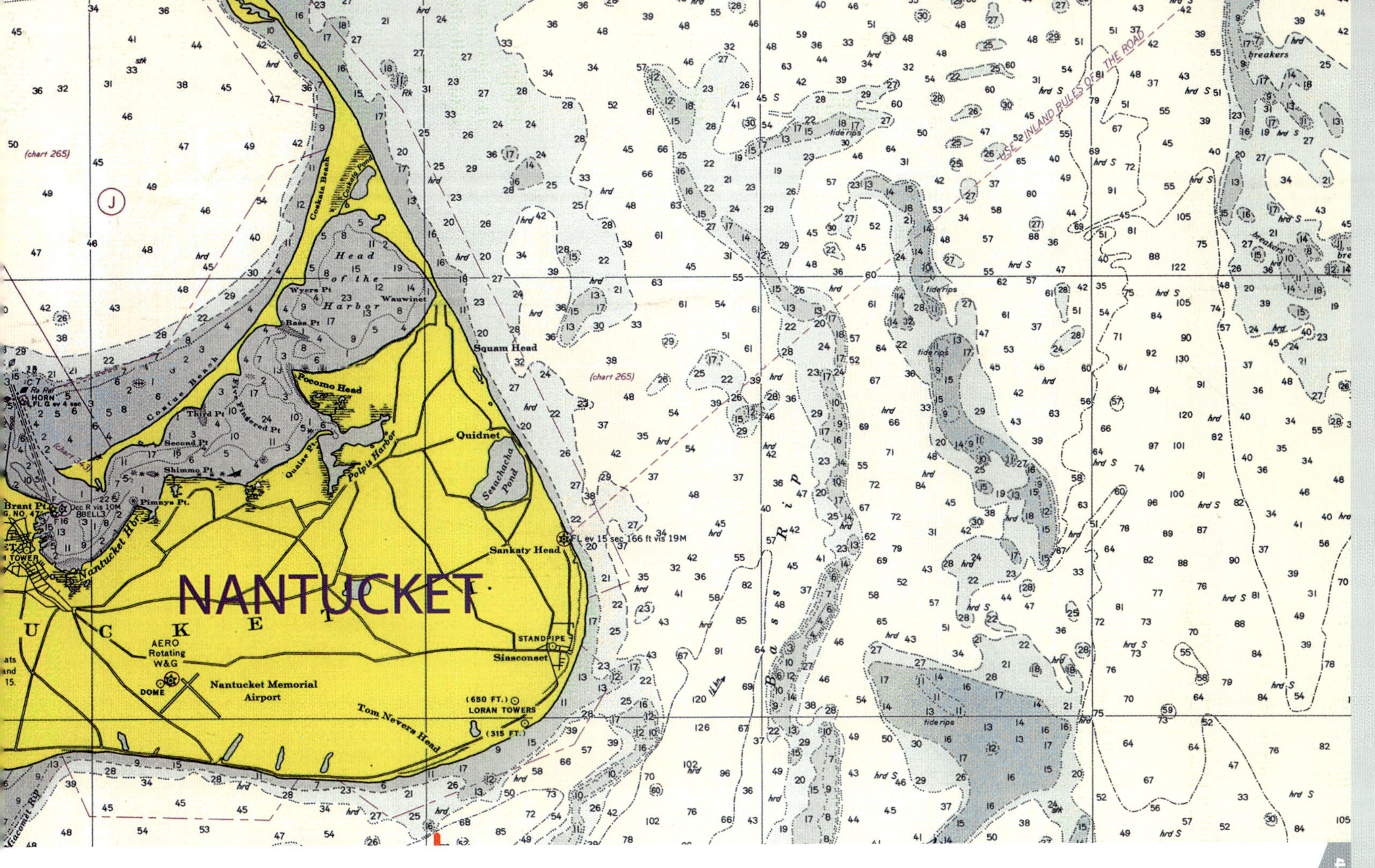

NANTUCKET
Head of the Harbor
Wyers Pt
Wauwinet
Bass Pt
Squam Head
Pocomo Head
Coskata Beach
Coskata Pond
Third Pt
Five Fingered Pt
Second Pt
Quaise Pt
Polpis Harbor
Quidnet
Sesachacha Pond
Shimmo Pt
Pimneys Pt
Brant Pt
Nantucket Harbor
Sankaty Head
STANDPIPE
Siasconset
Nantucket Memorial Airport
AERO Rotating W&G
DOME
Tom Nevers Head
LORAN TOWERS
(650 FT.)
(315 FT.)
TOWER
USE INLAND RULES OF THE ROAD
(chart 265)
J
breakers

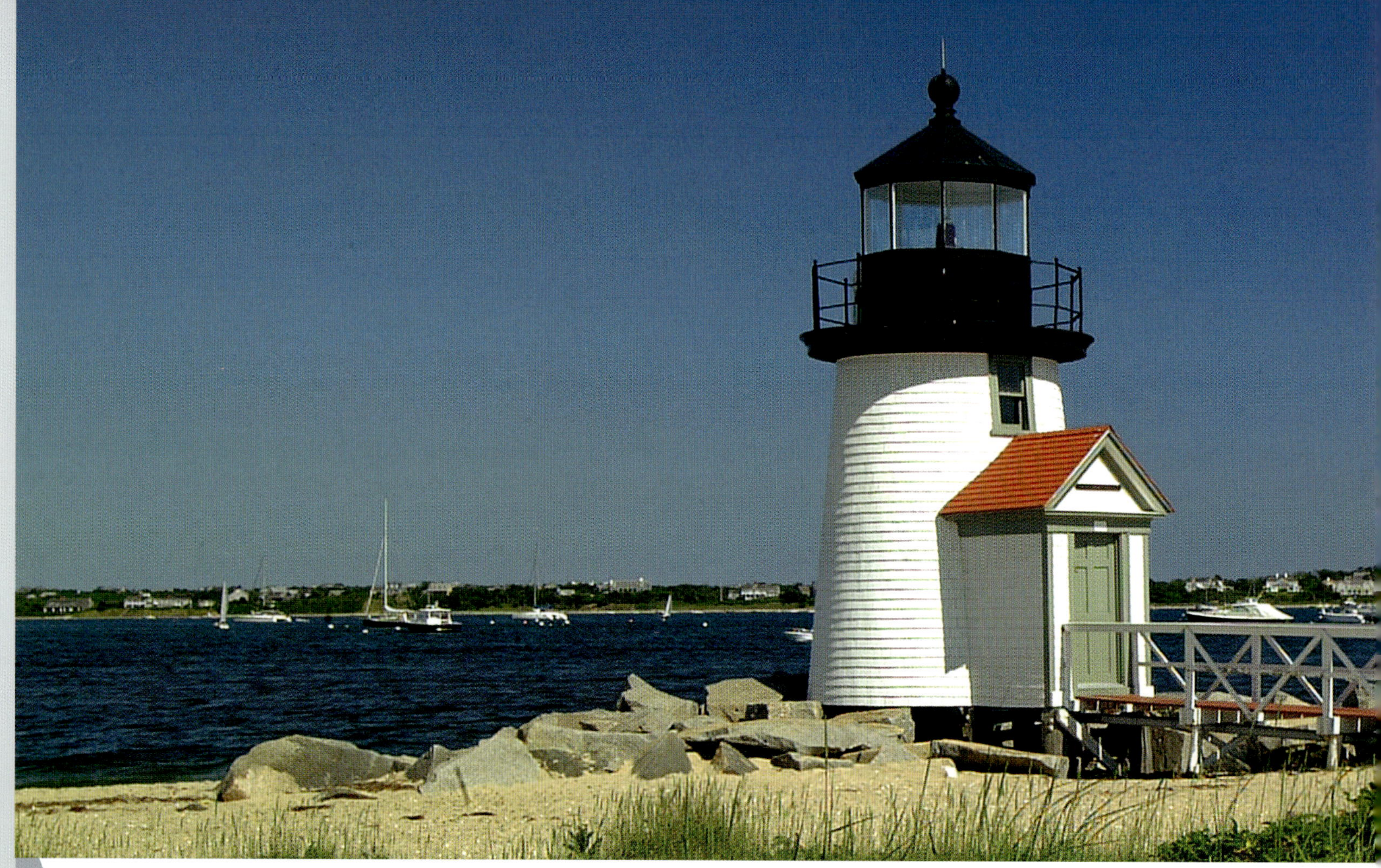

Brant Point Light, first built in 1746, welcomes visitors to Nantucket Island.

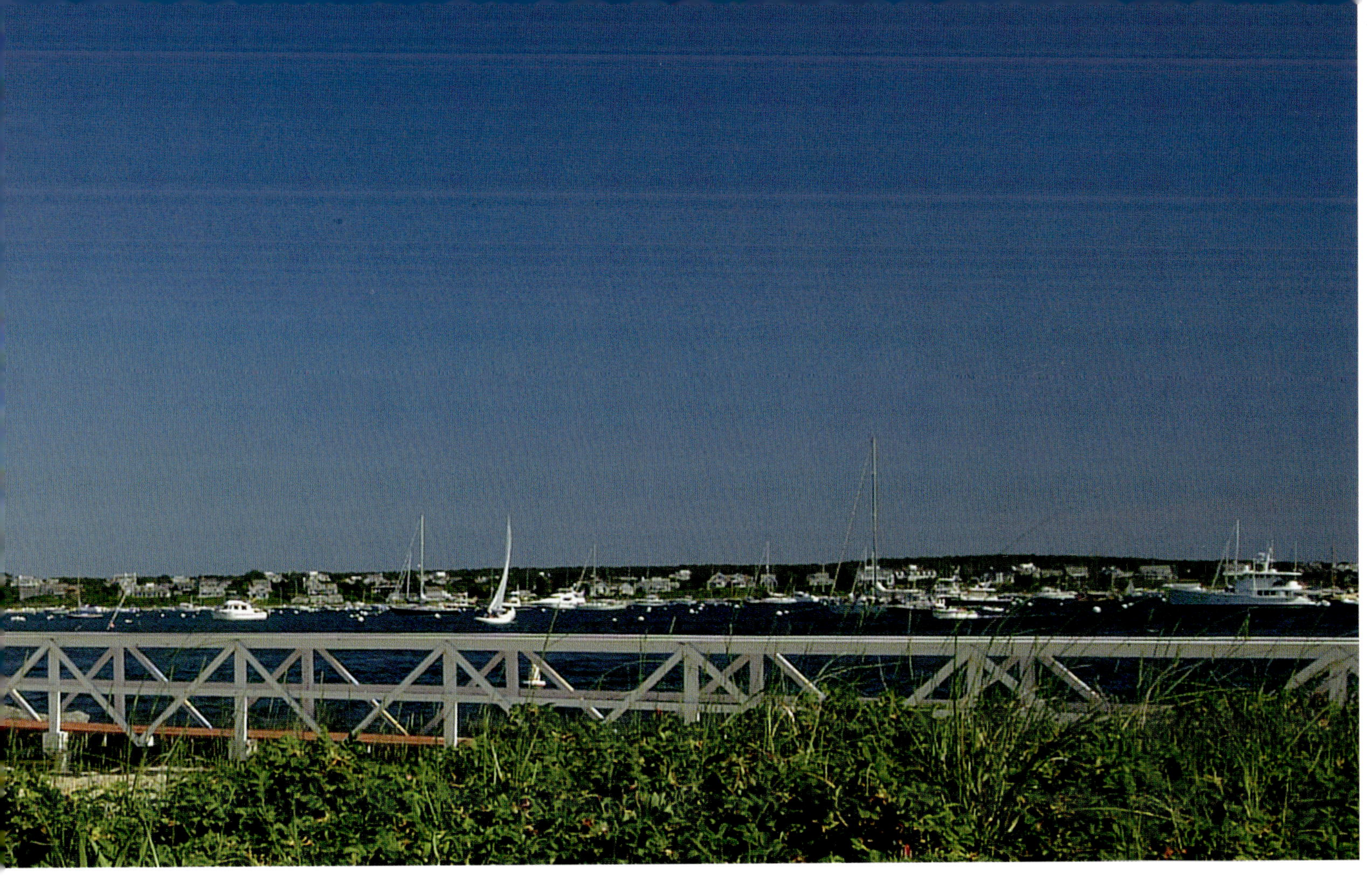

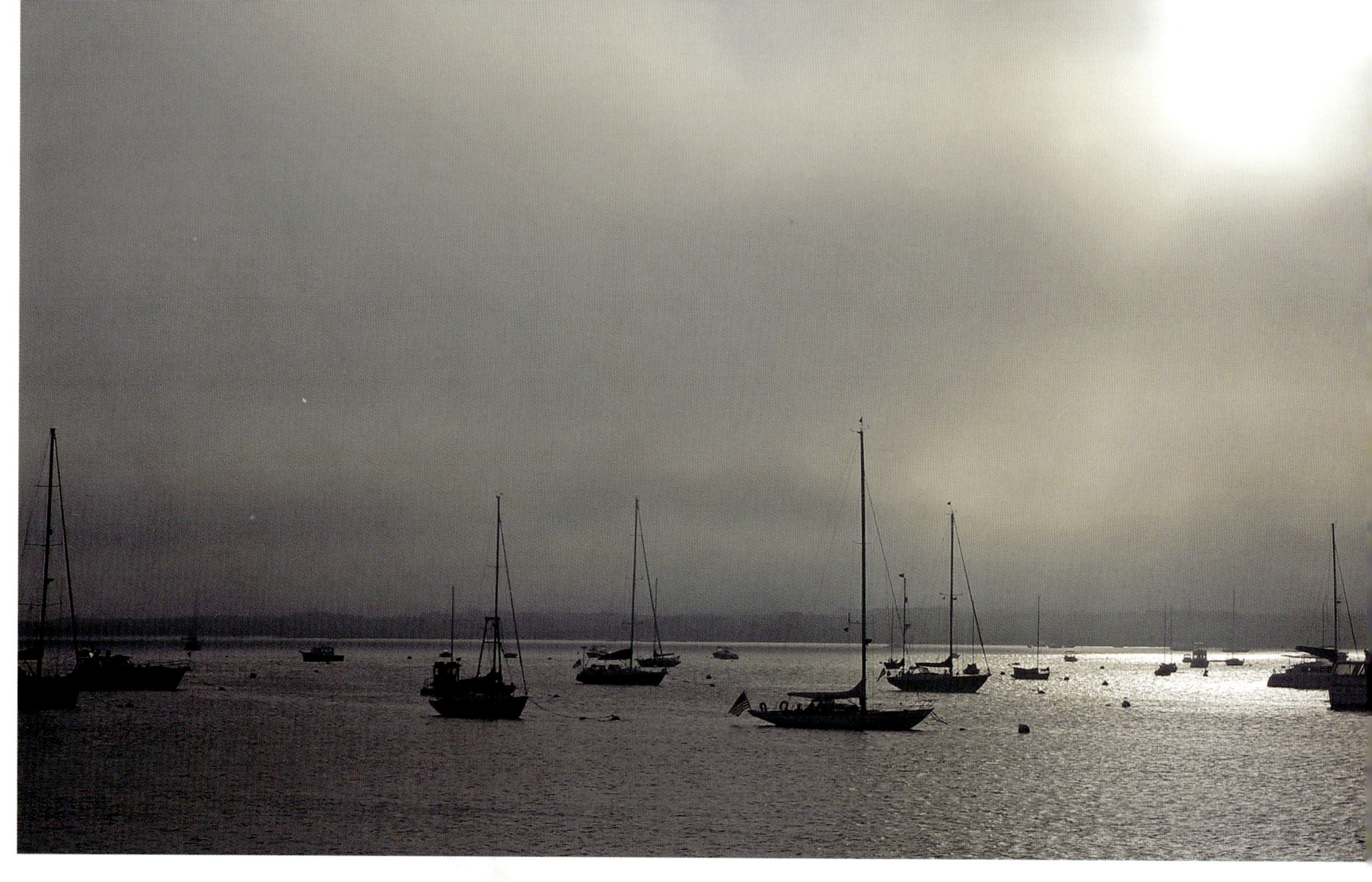

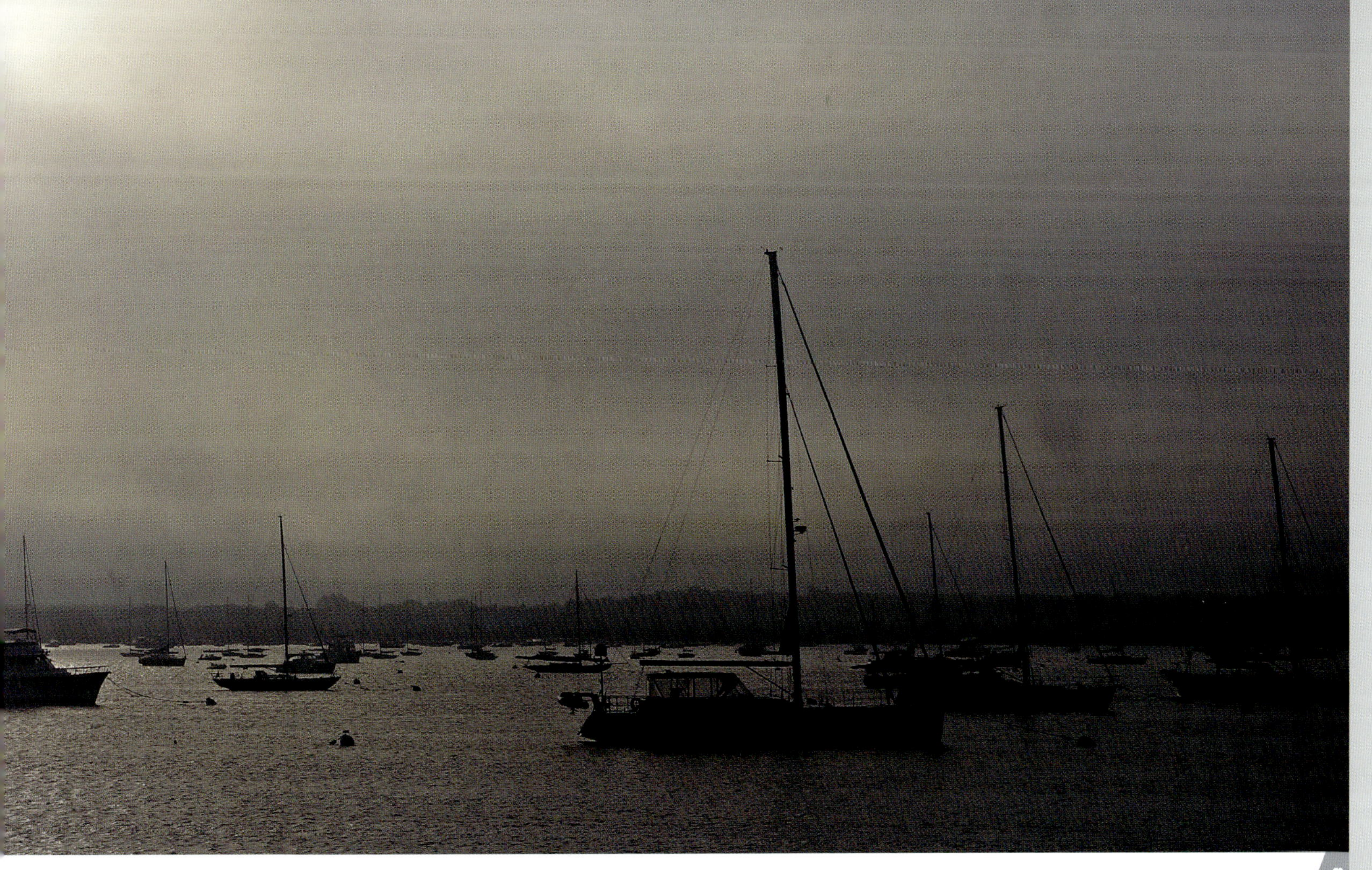

The sun tries to break through a foggy morning in the harbor.

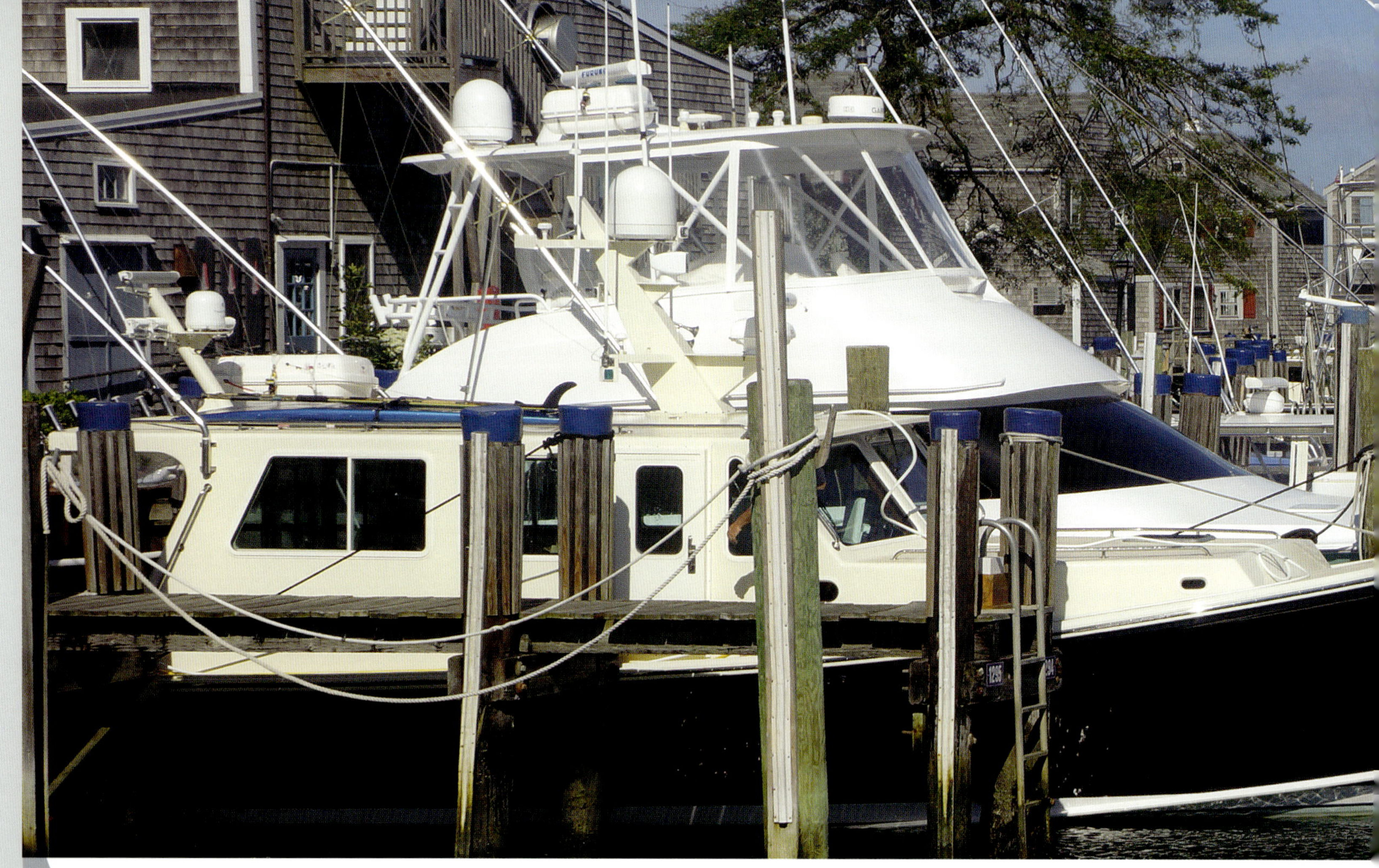

Sportfishing boats line the docks in the harbor.

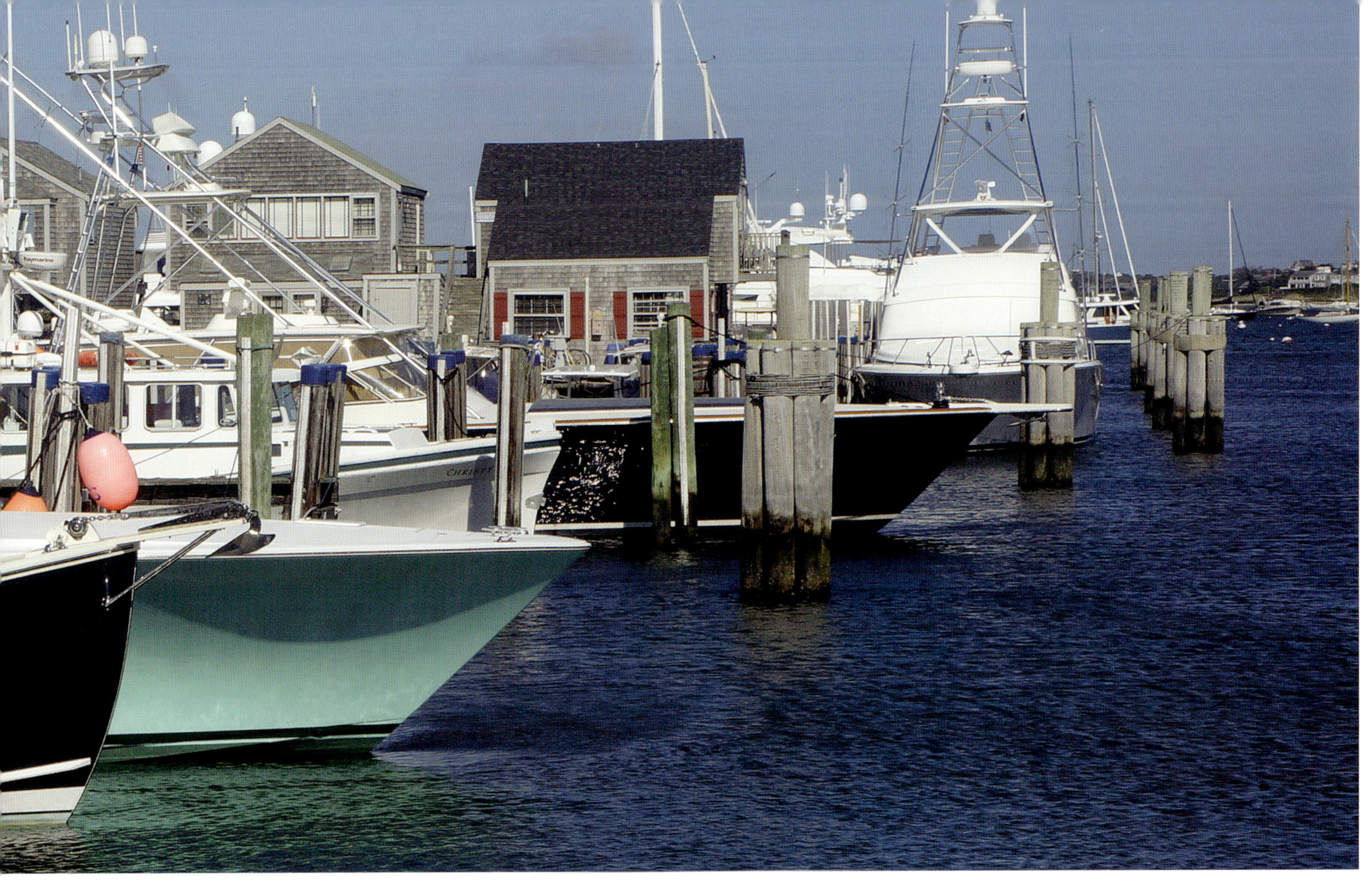

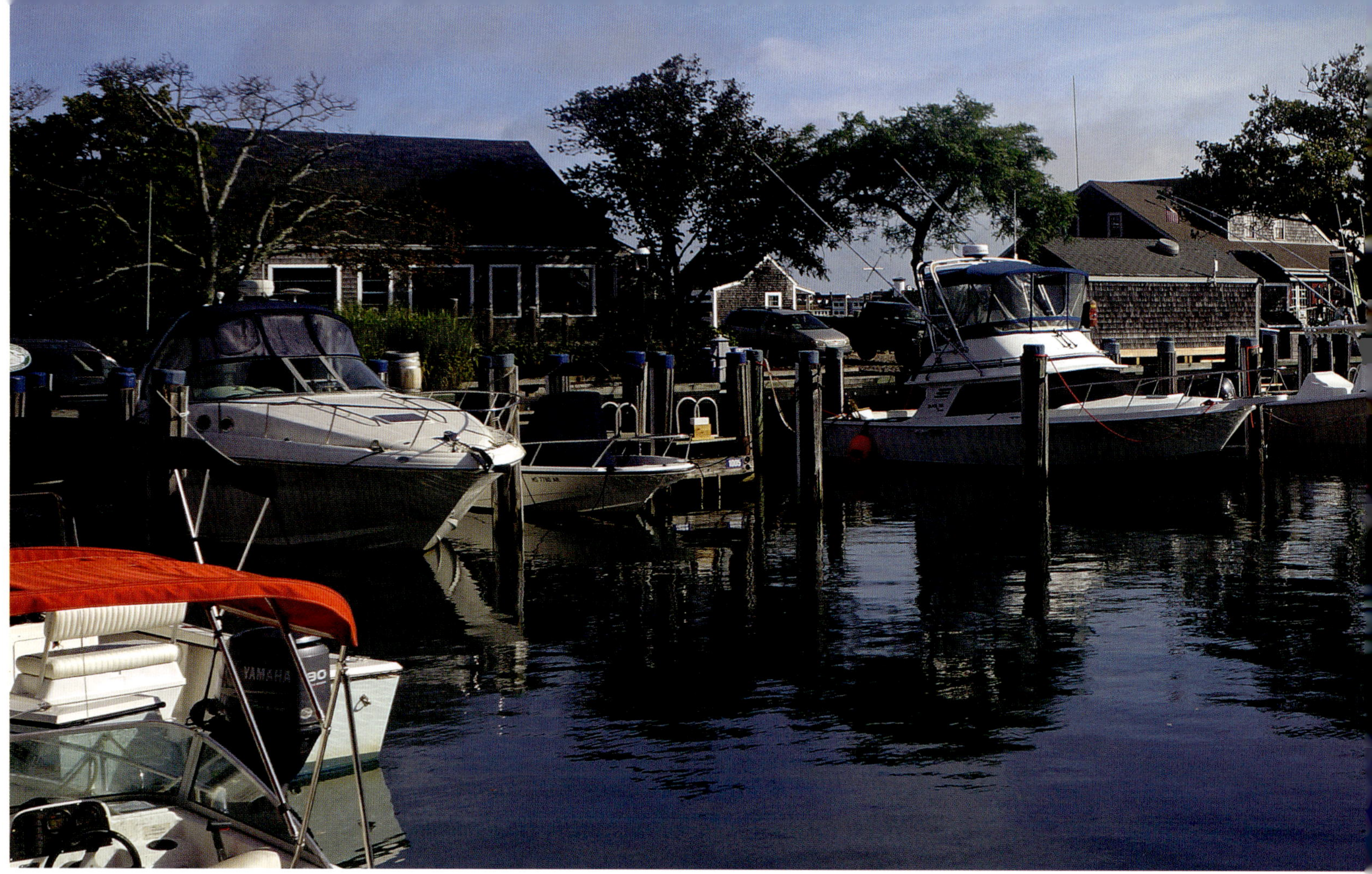

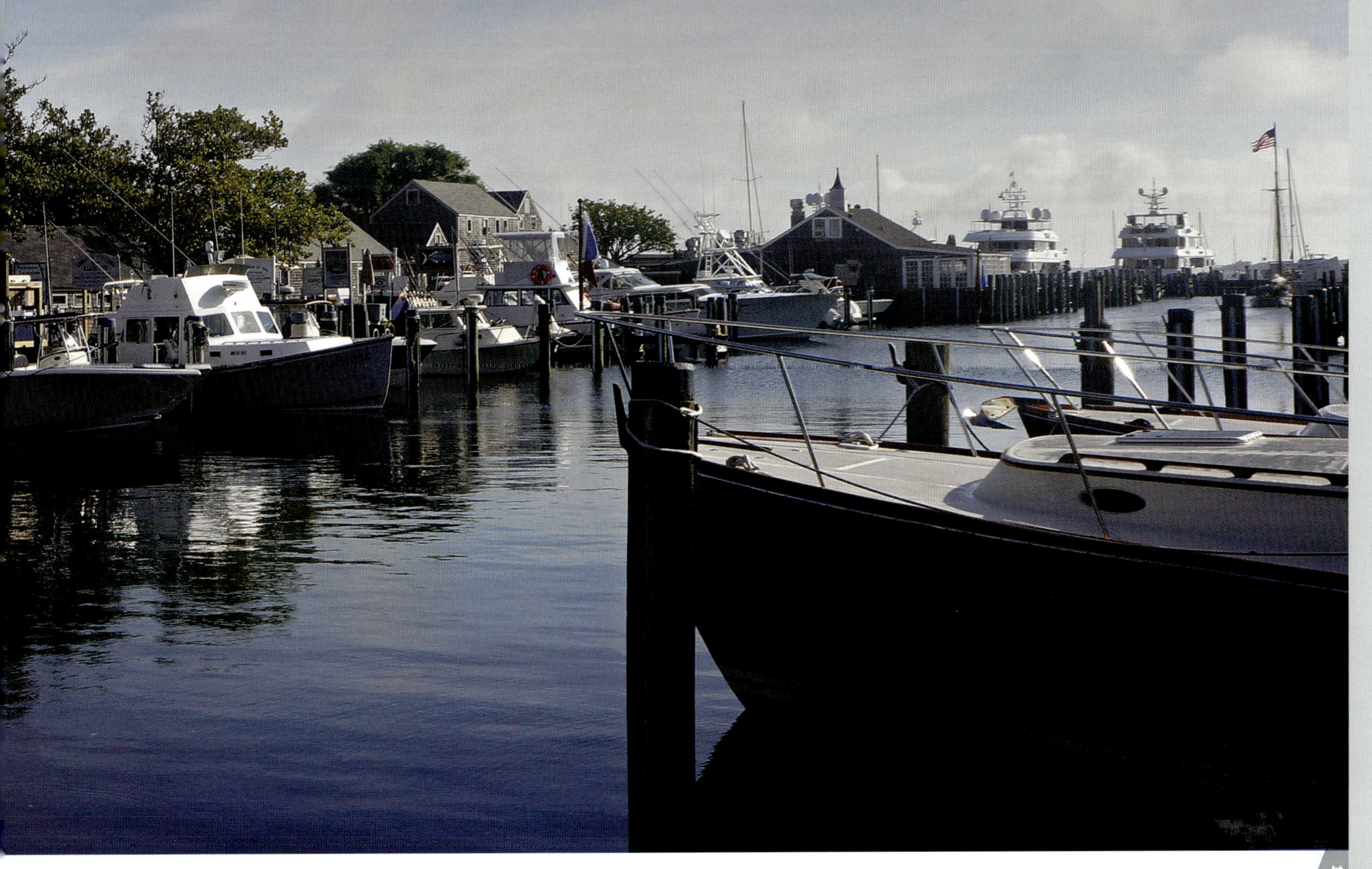

Vessels of all sizes and styles are found at the docks.

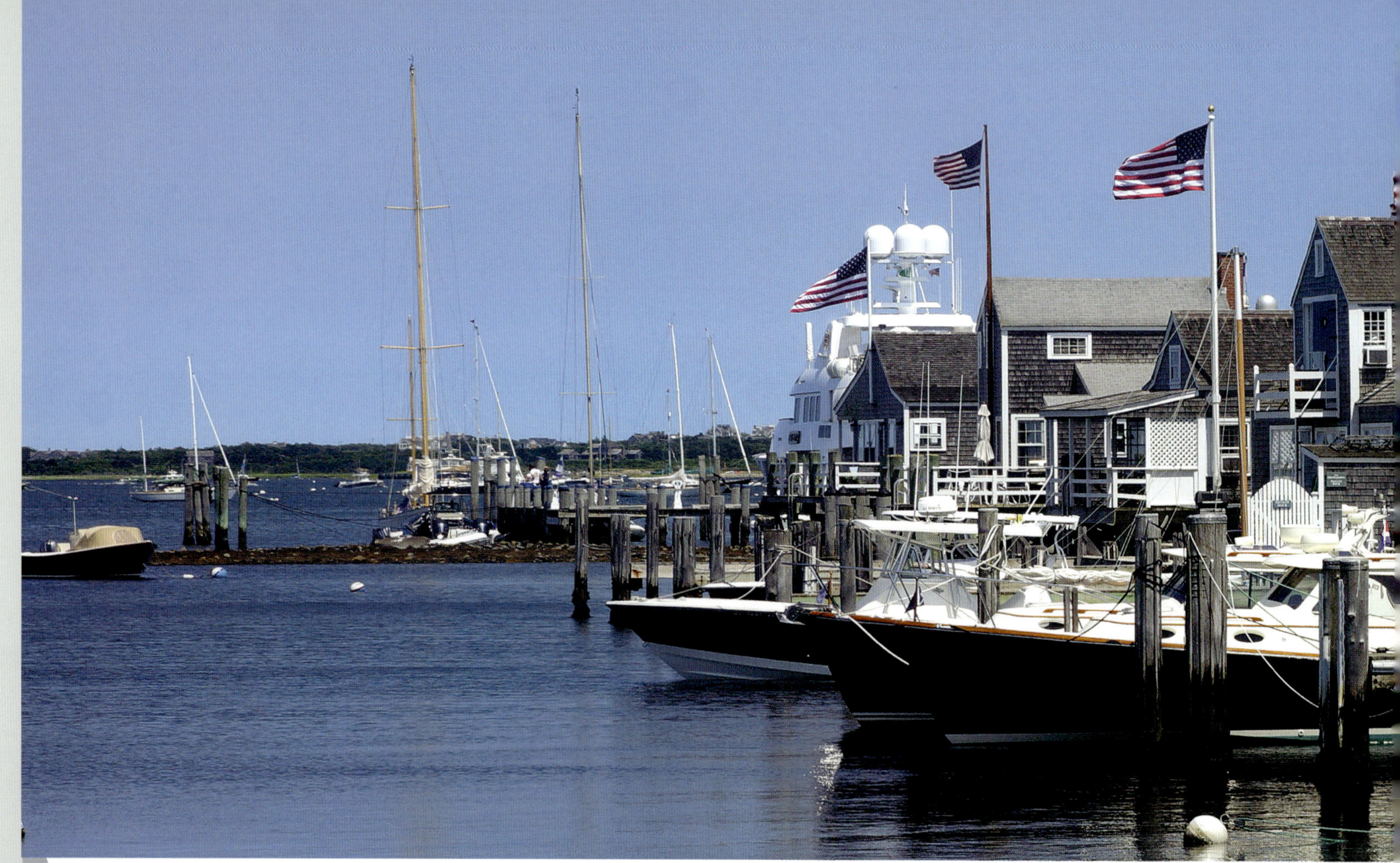

Flags fly over the slips in the harbor.

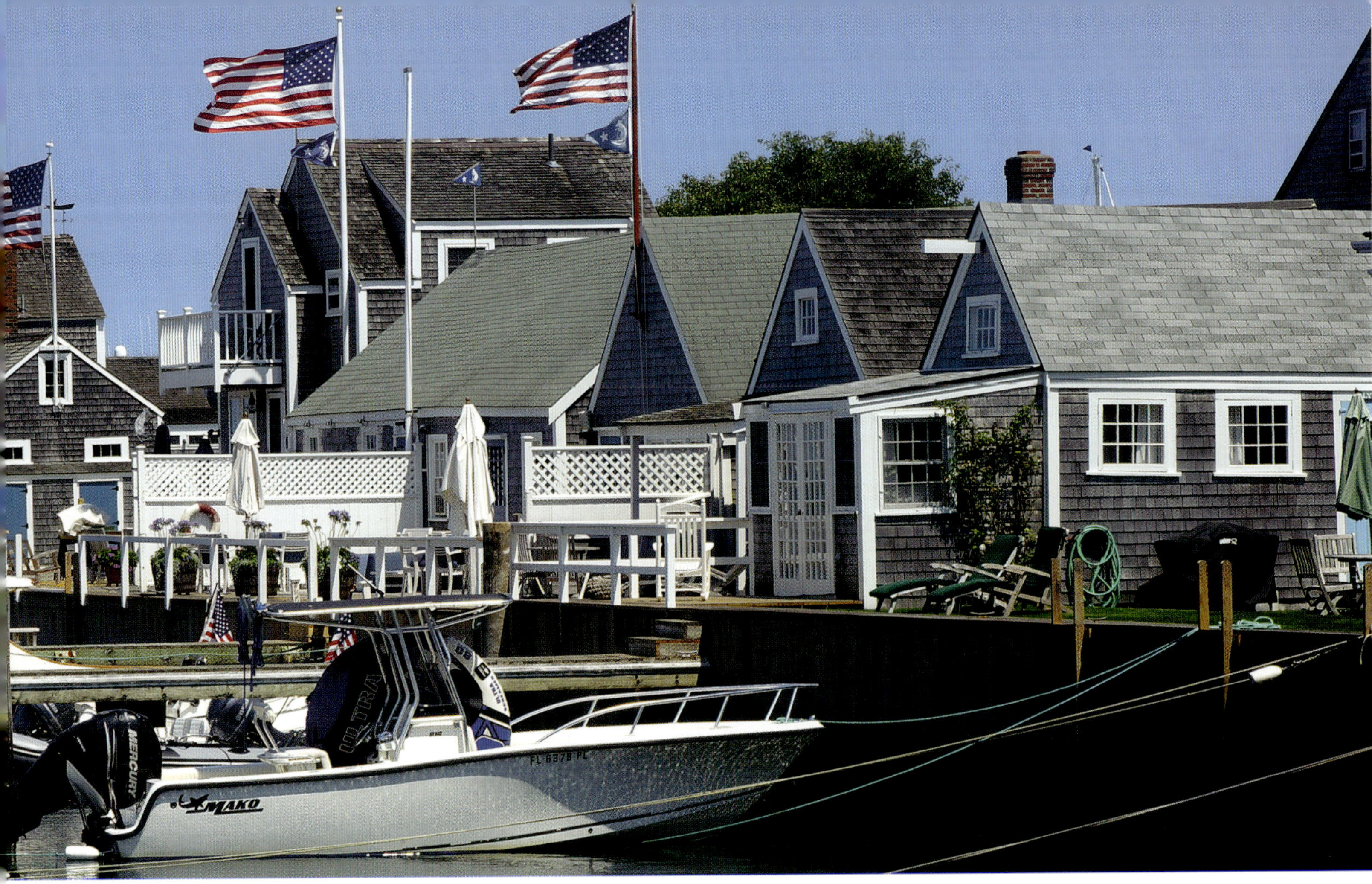

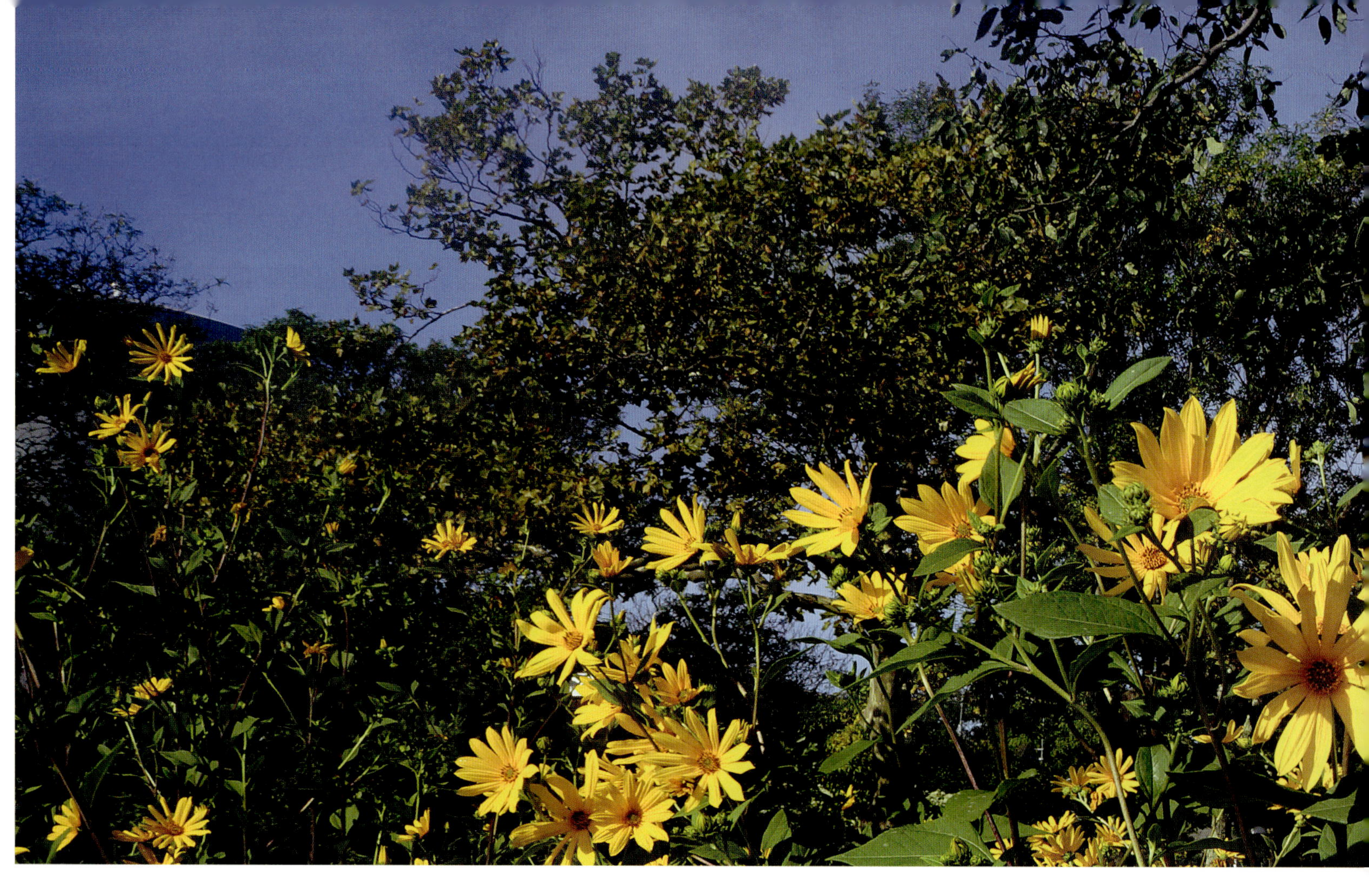

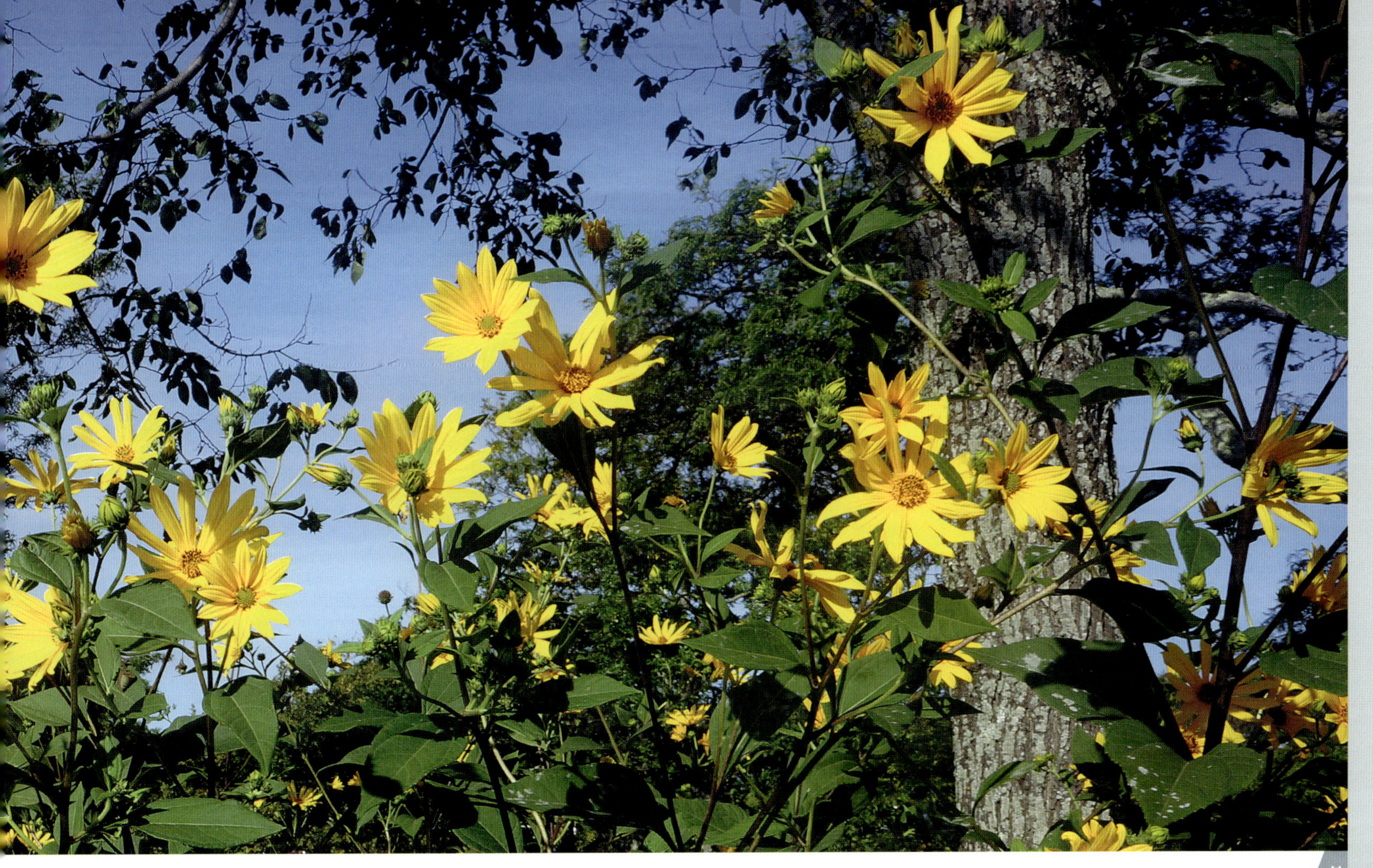

Bright flowers bloom throughout the island.

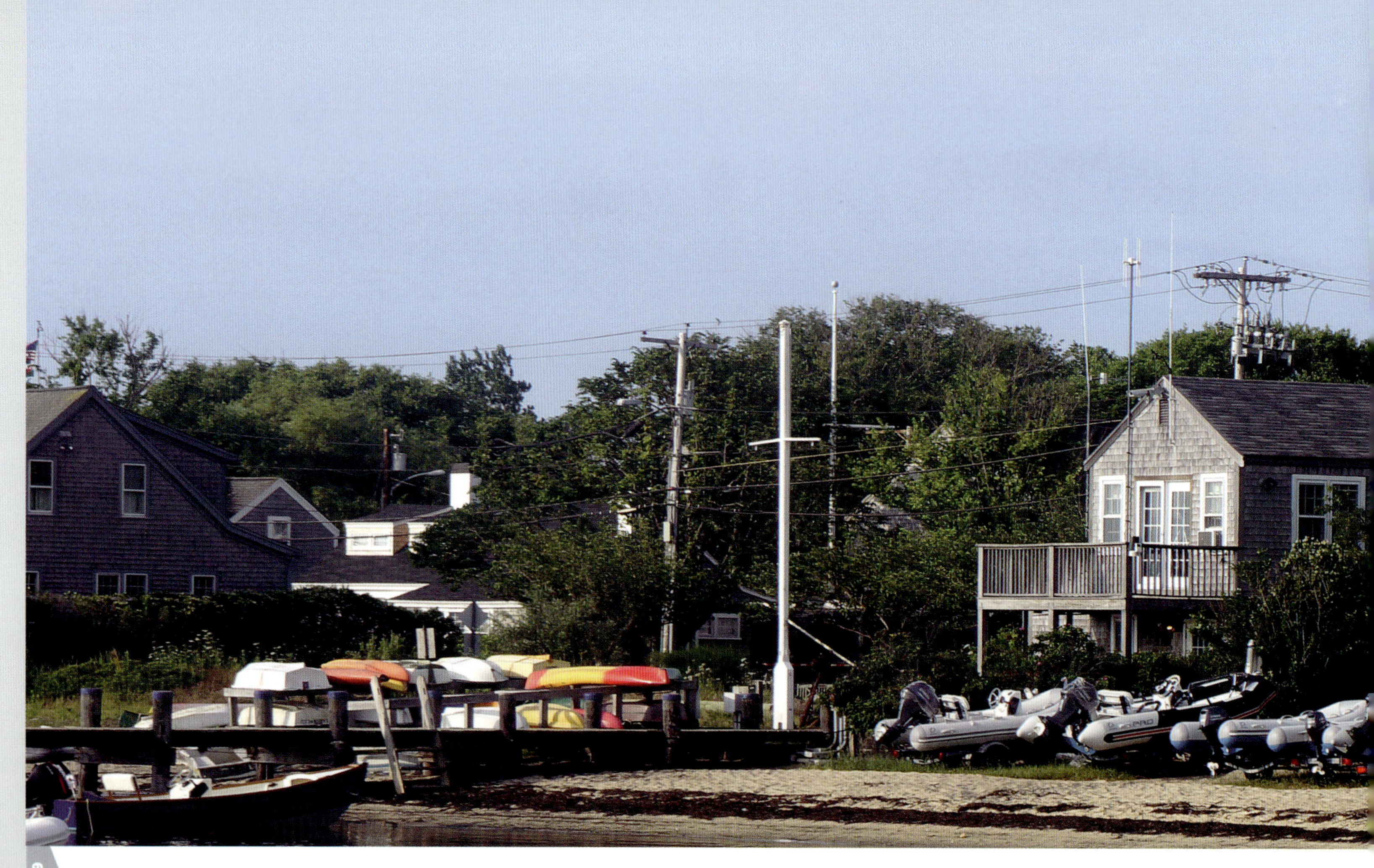

A variety of watercraft rests along the shore of the harbor.

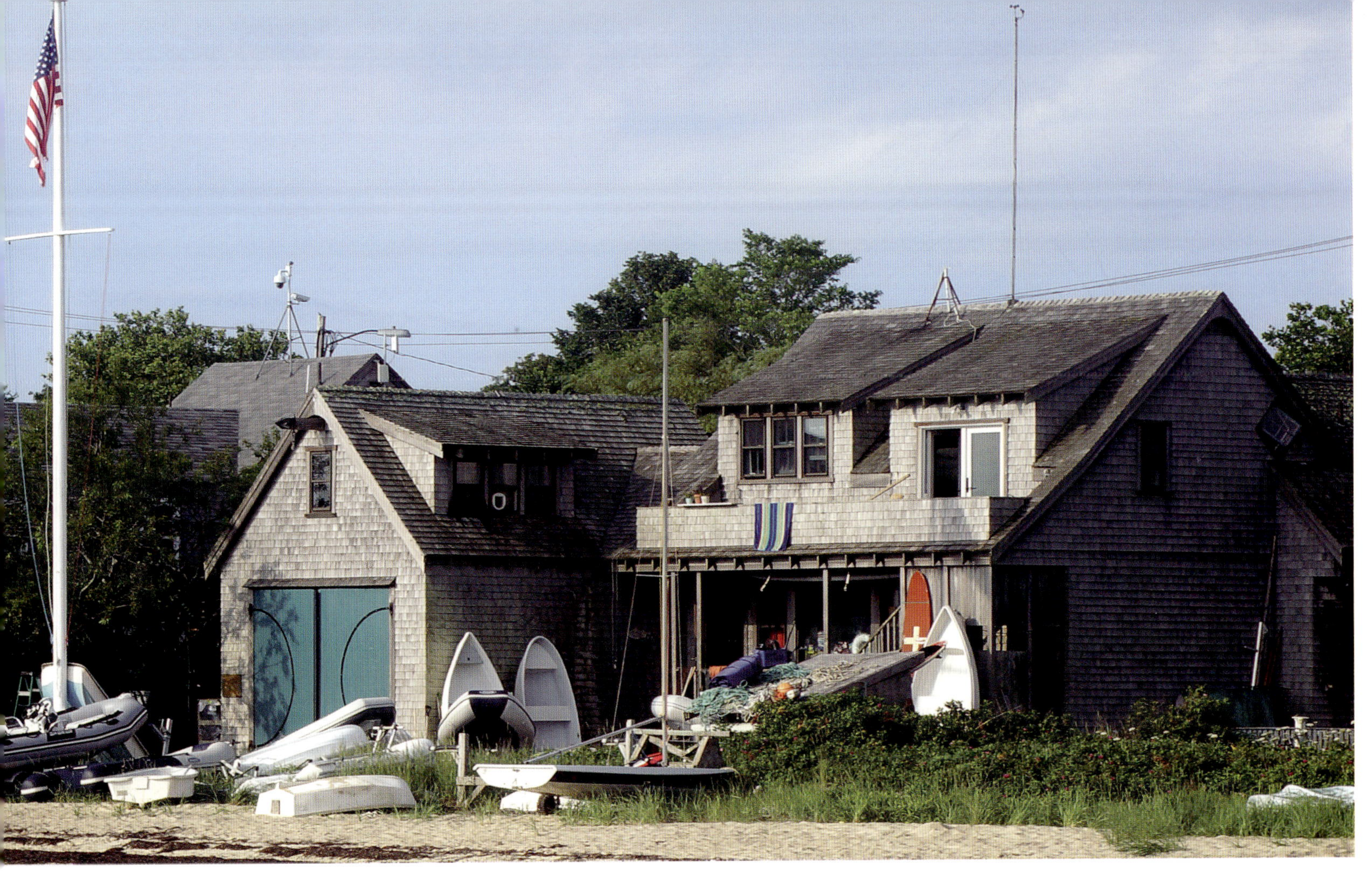

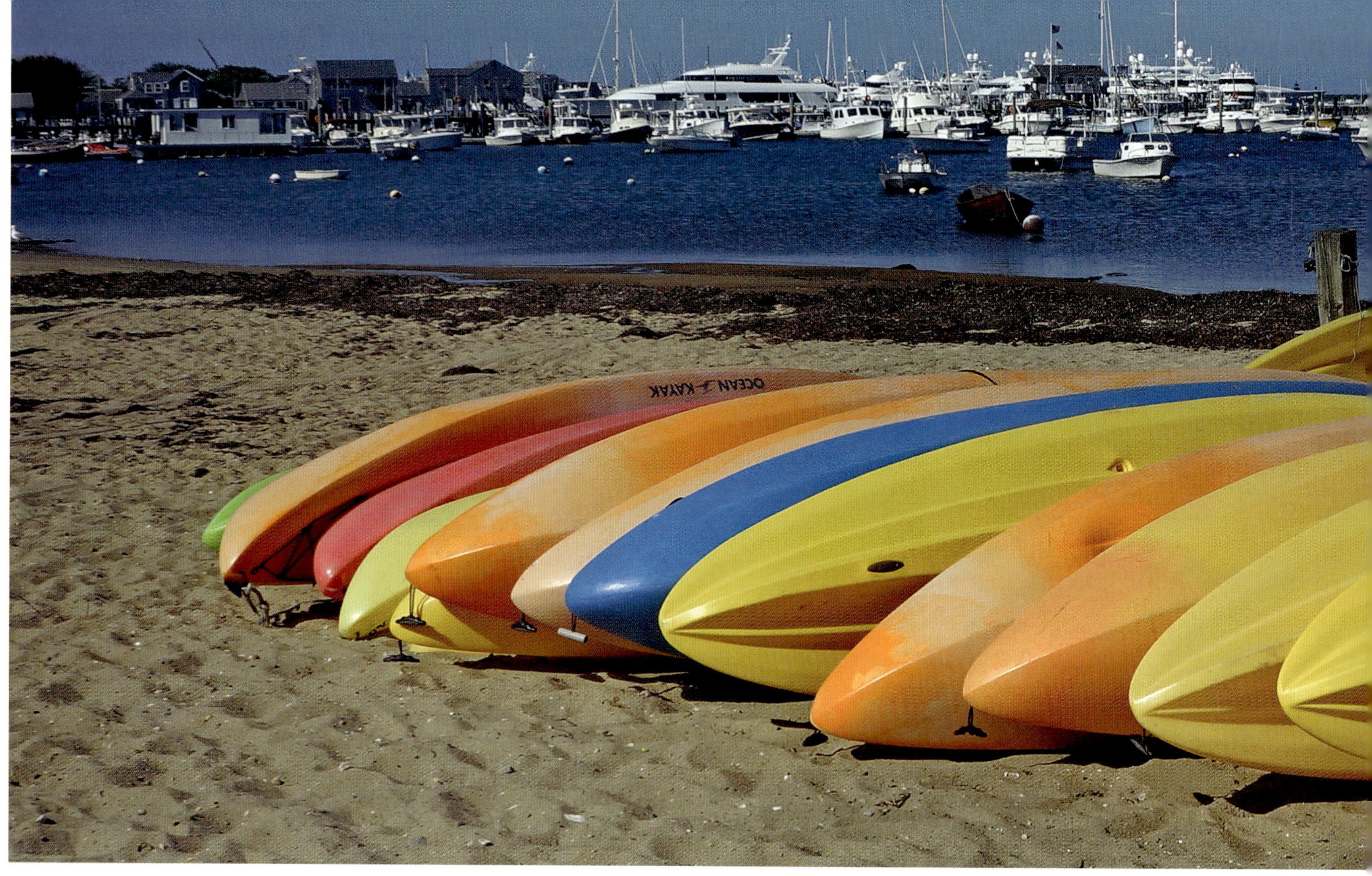

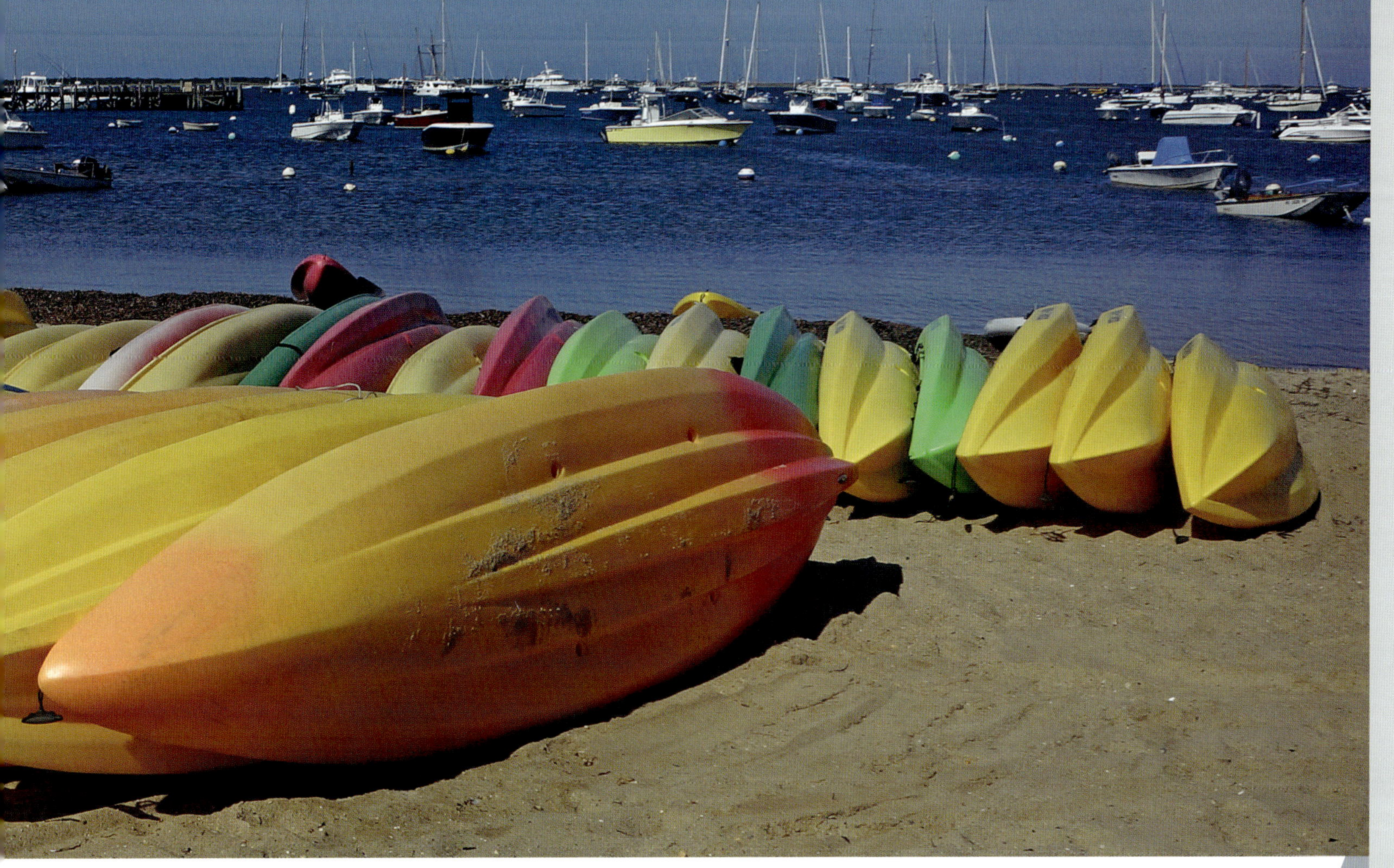

Rental kayaks line the beach, with the harbor in the background.

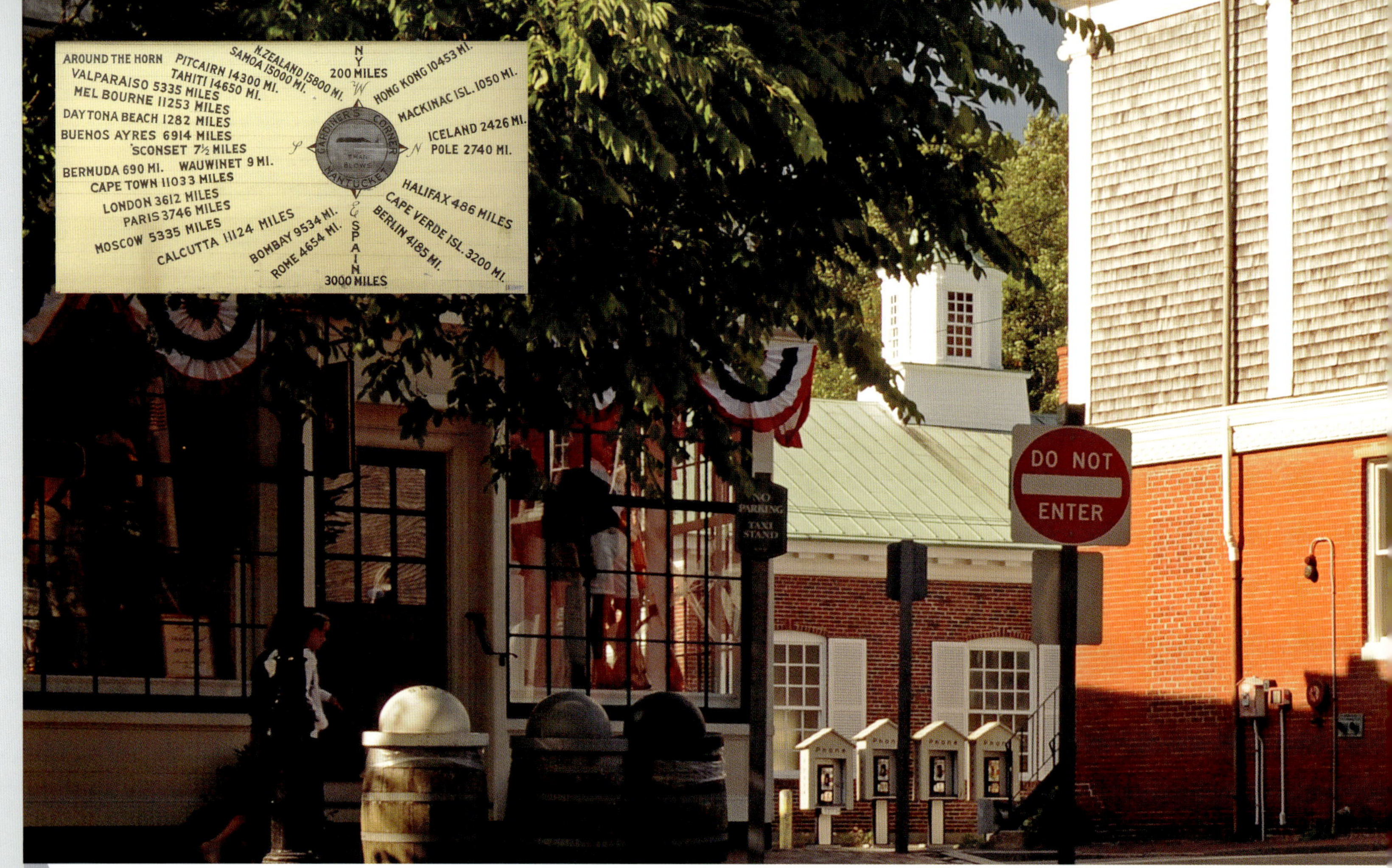

A sign off of Main Street shows the distance to other world locations from Nantucket.
On Main Street, the former watering trough is now a decorative planter.

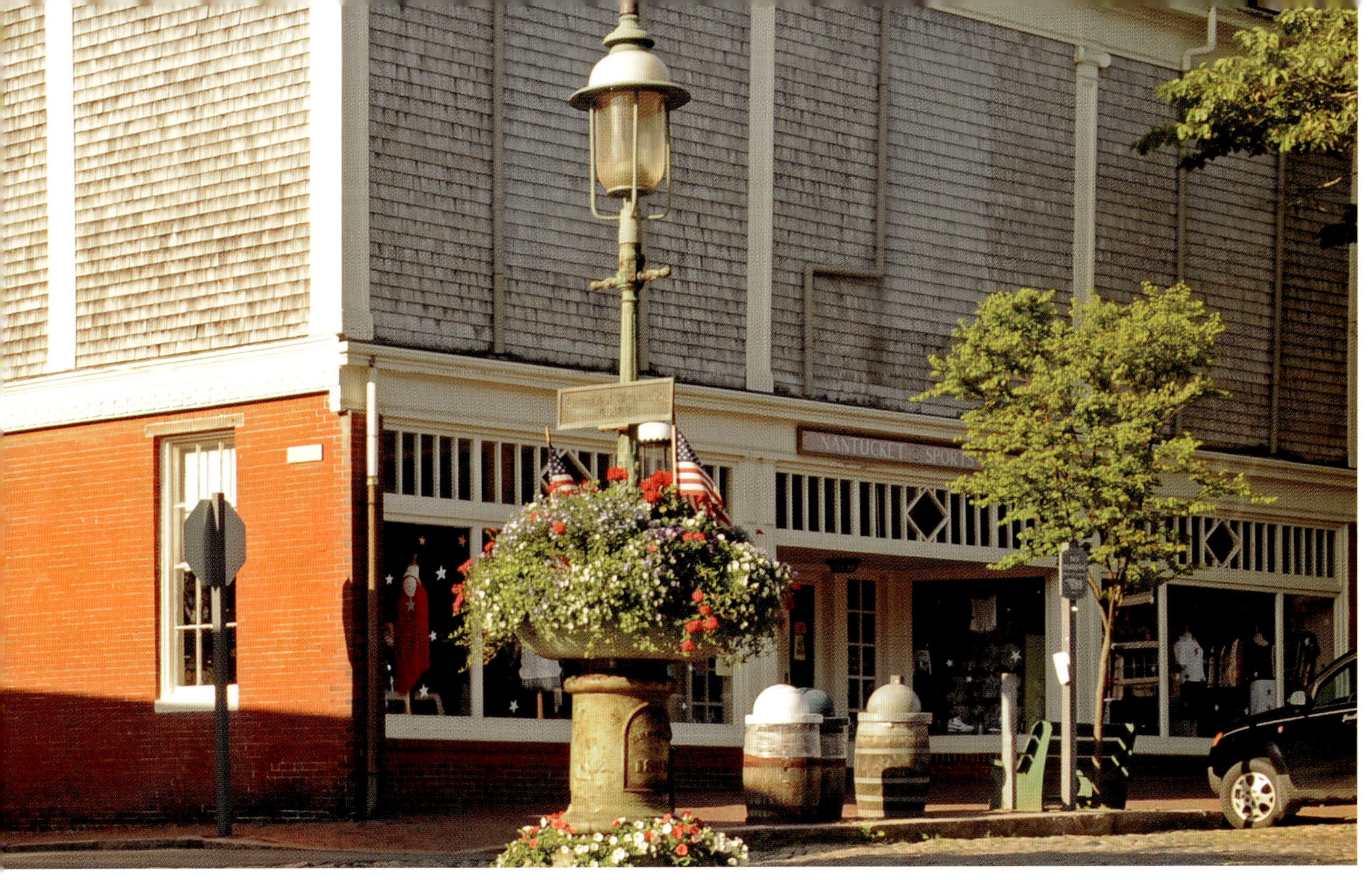

NANTUCKET SPORTS

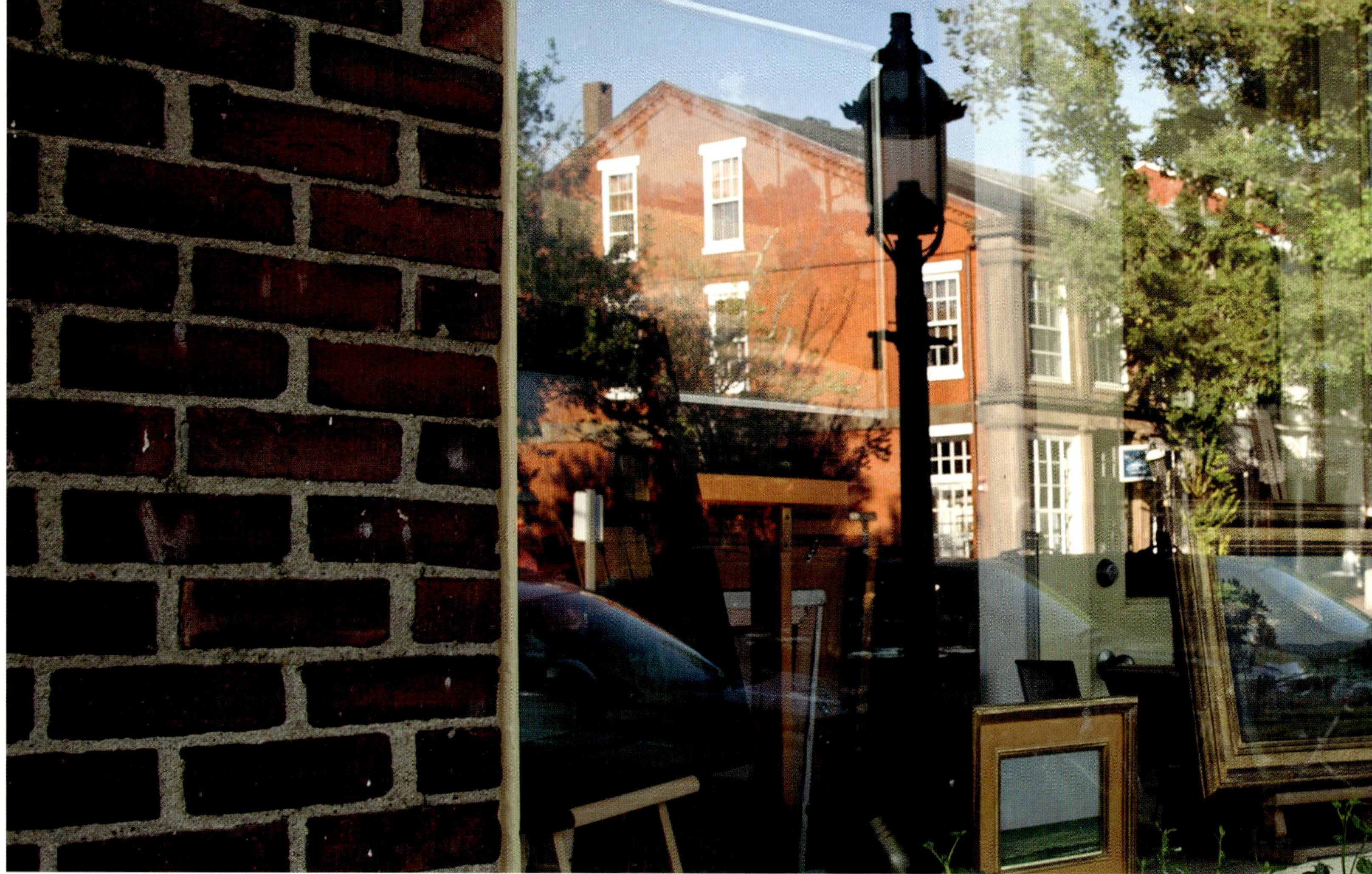

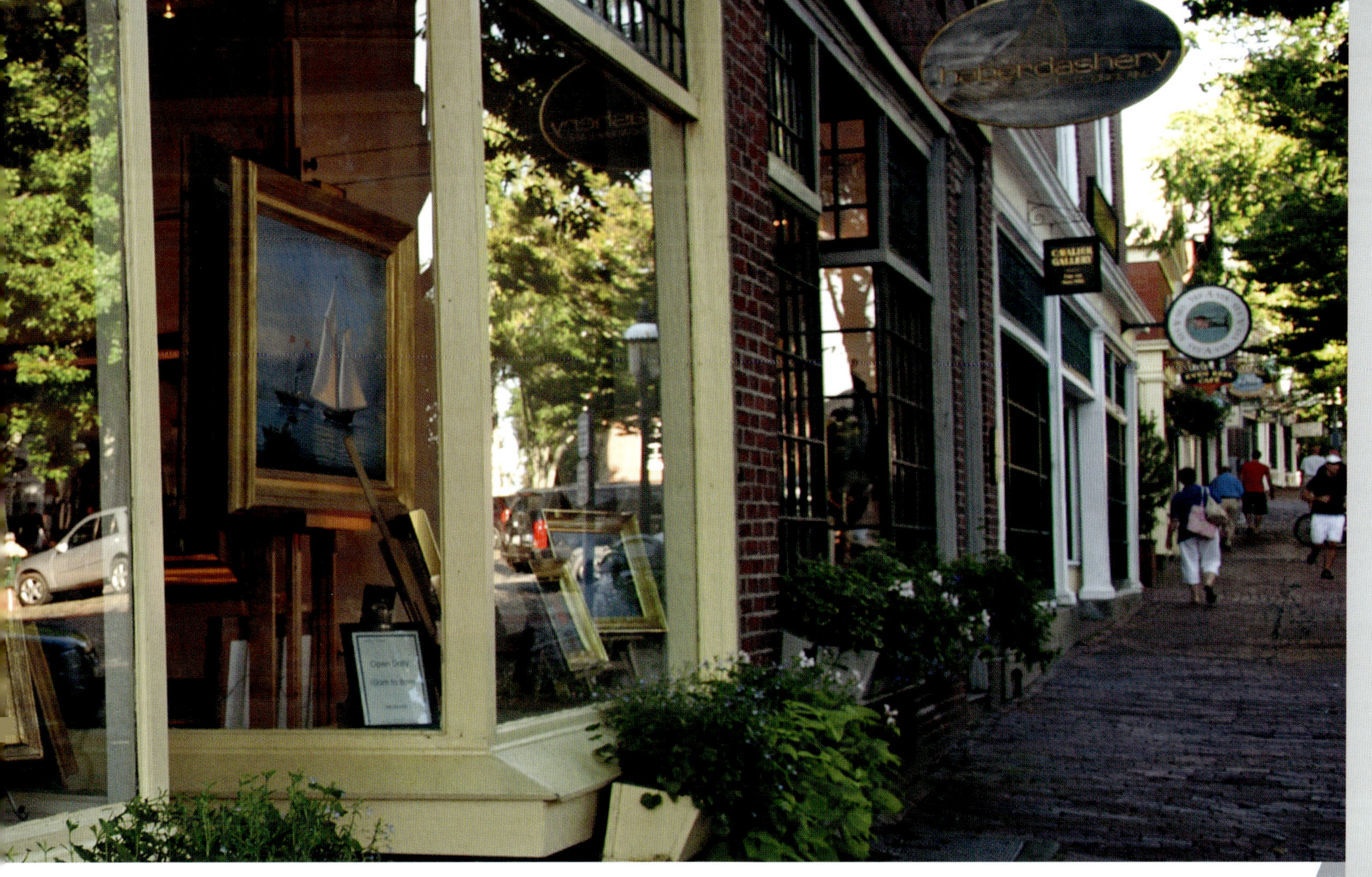

Looking up Main Street with its many shops and galleries.

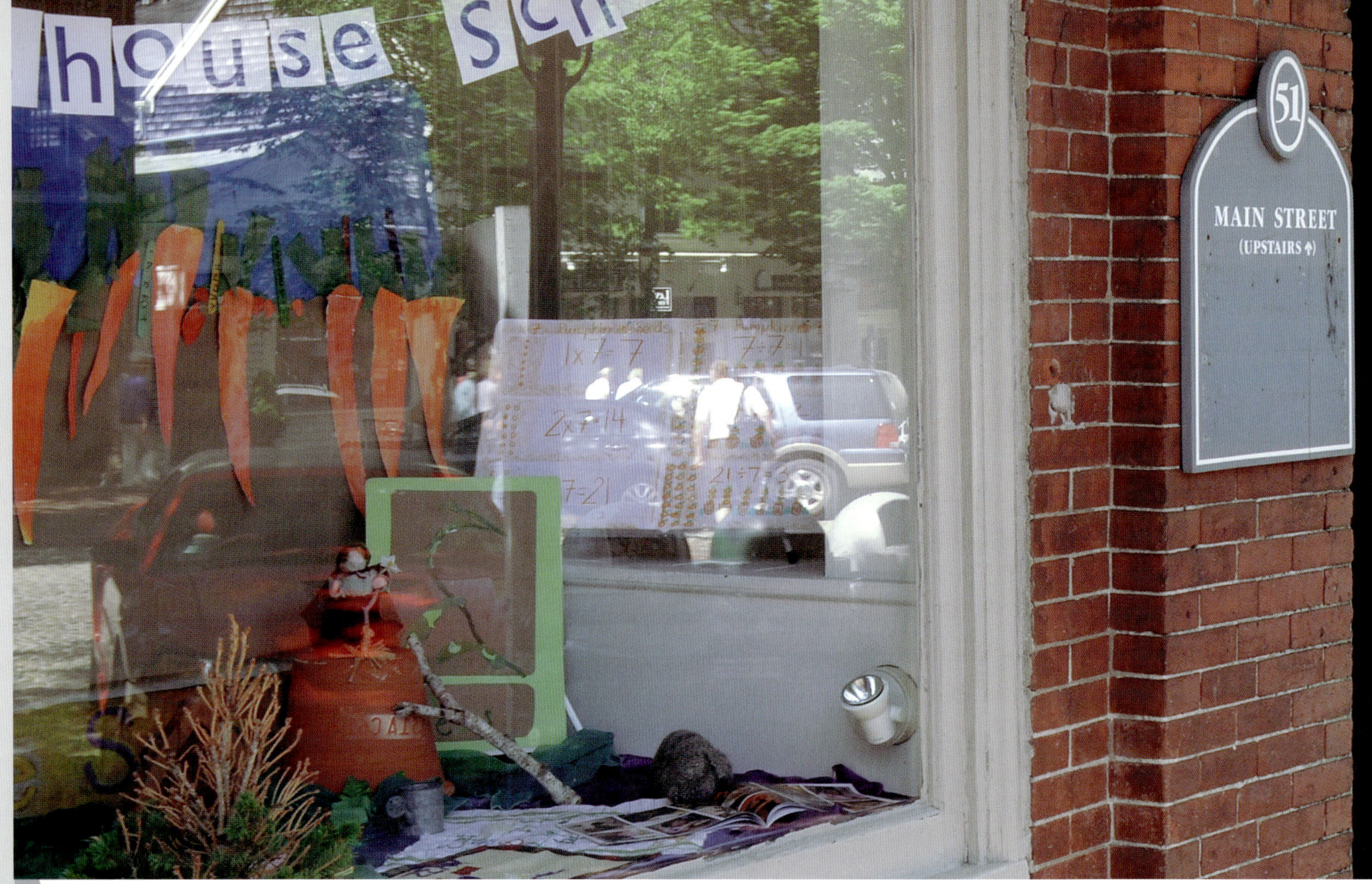

More shops along Main Street.

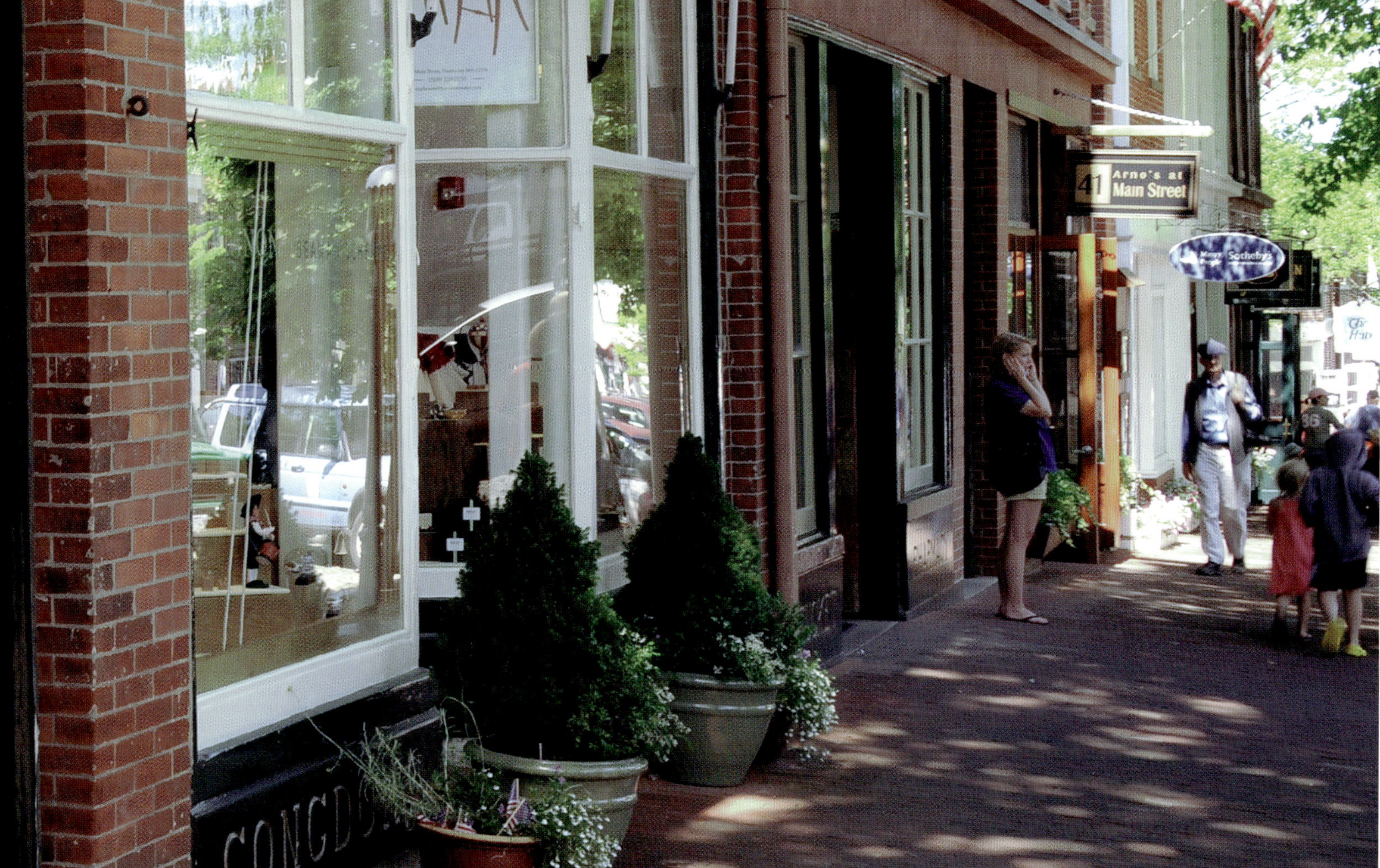
41
Arne's at
Main Street
Sotheby's
CONGDON

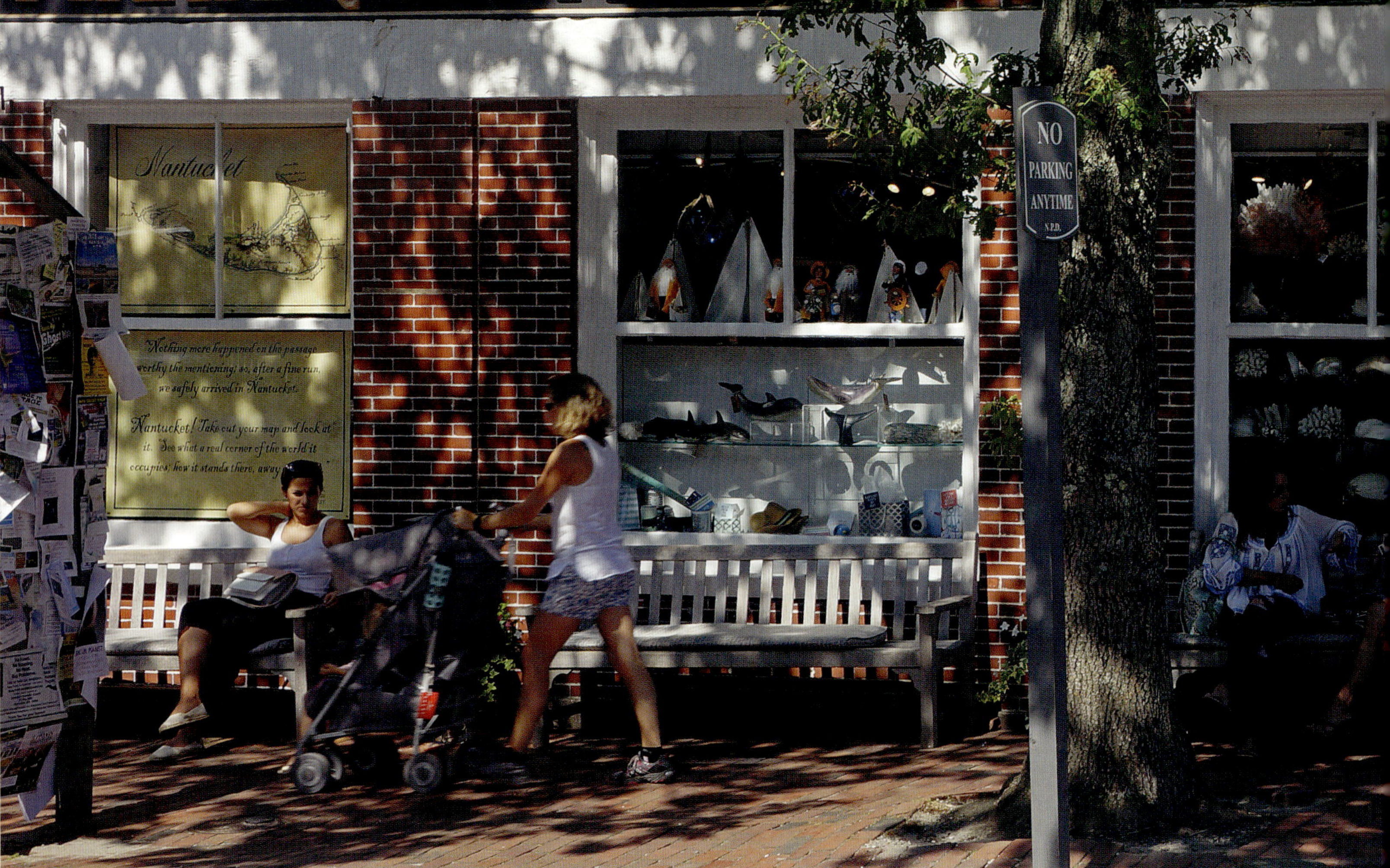
Nantucket
Nothing more happened on the passage worthy the mentioning; so, after a fine run, we safely arrived in Nantucket.
Nantucket! Take out your map and look at it. See what a real corner of the world it occupies; how it stands there, away
NO PARKING ANYTIME N.P.D.

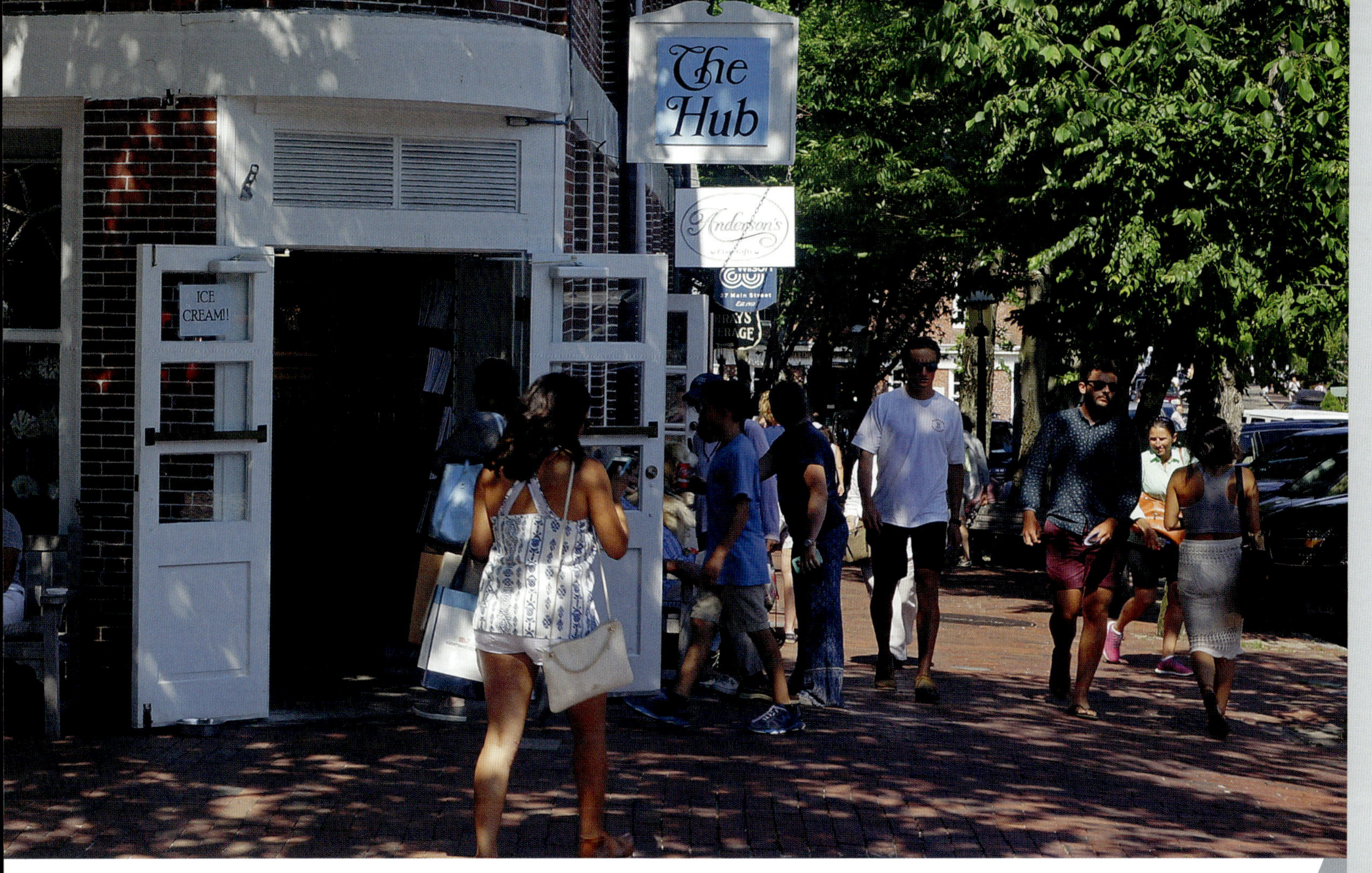

The Hub is a popular spot to get the morning news.

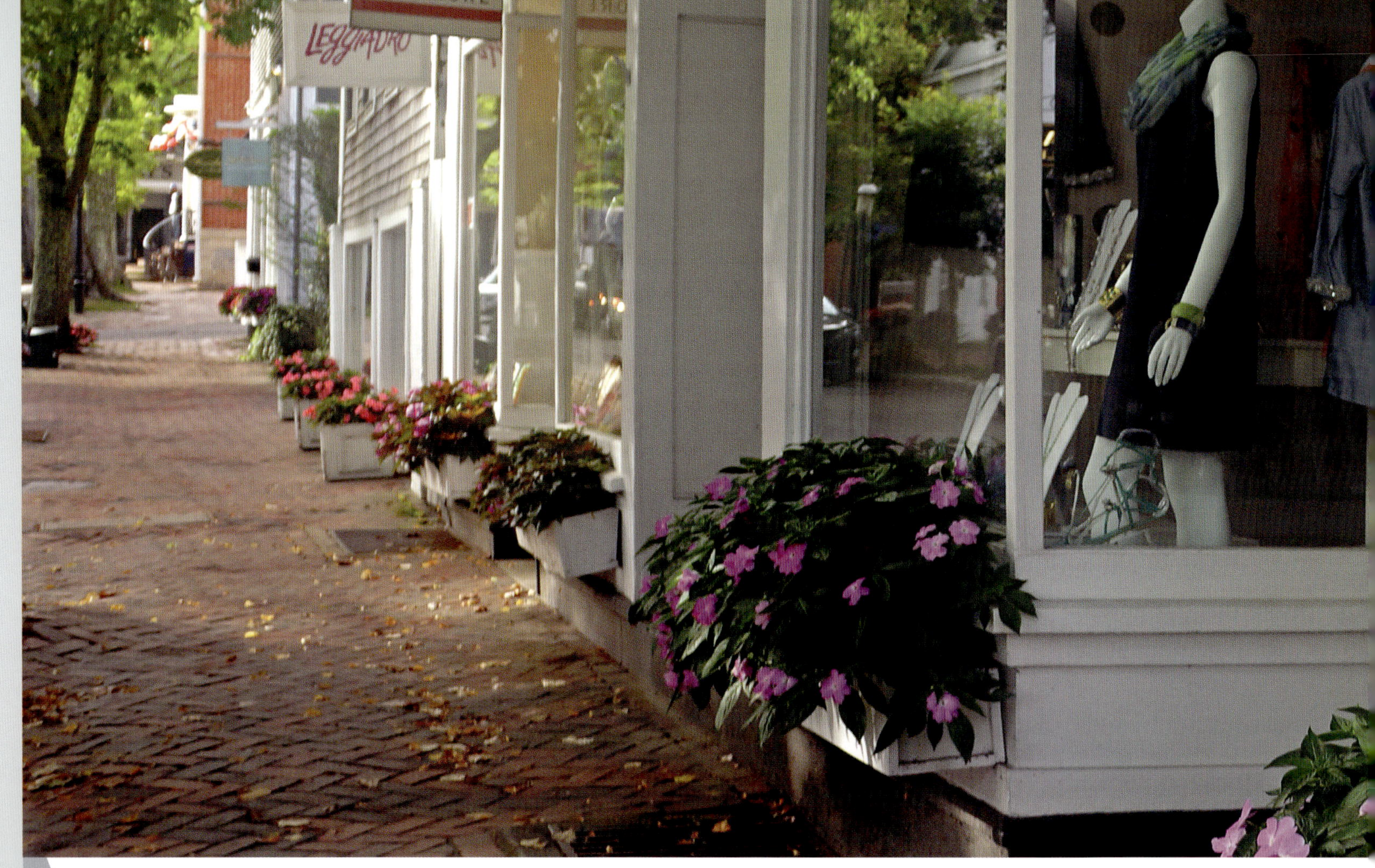

Centre Street also features popular and varied shops.

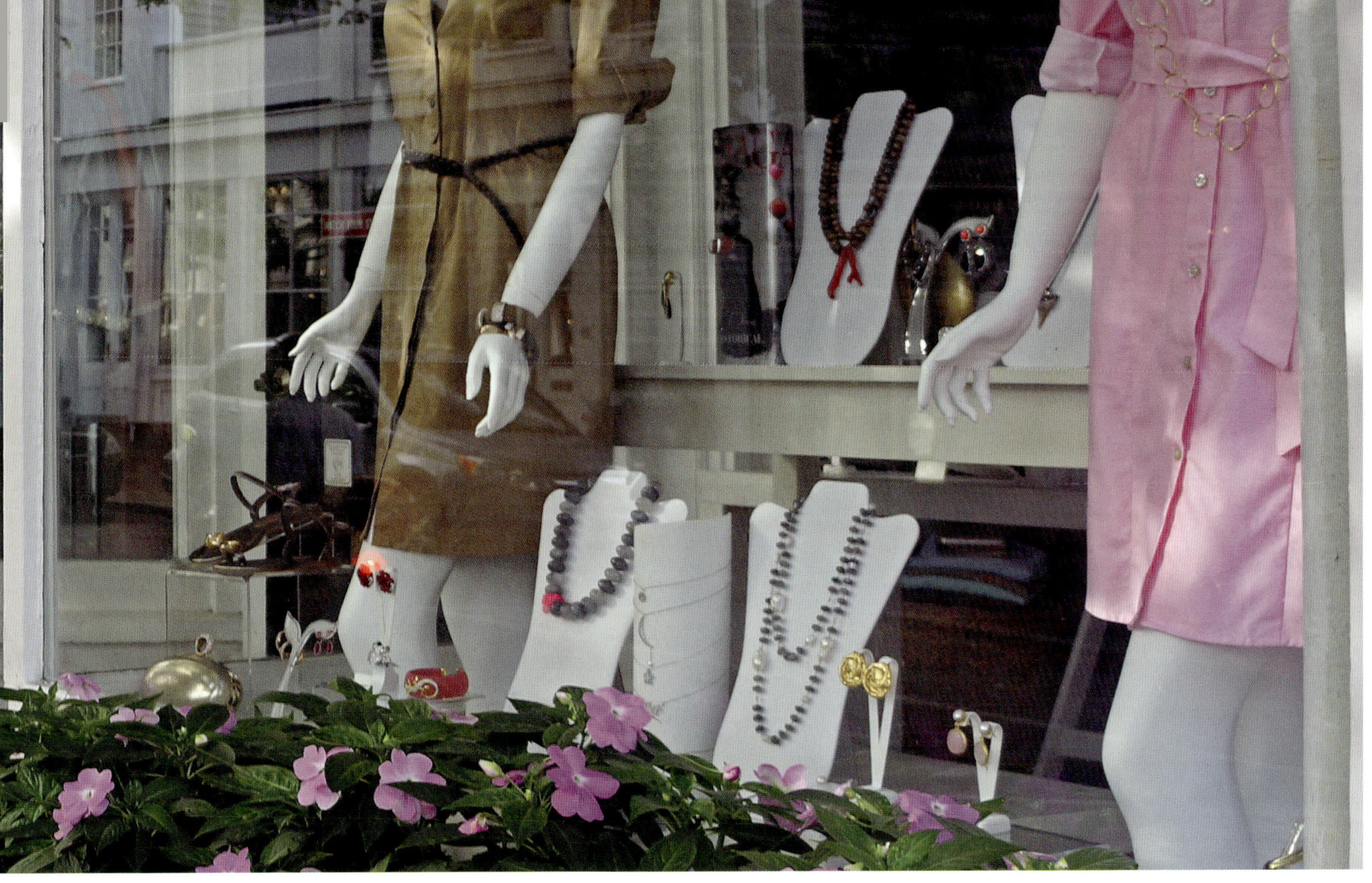

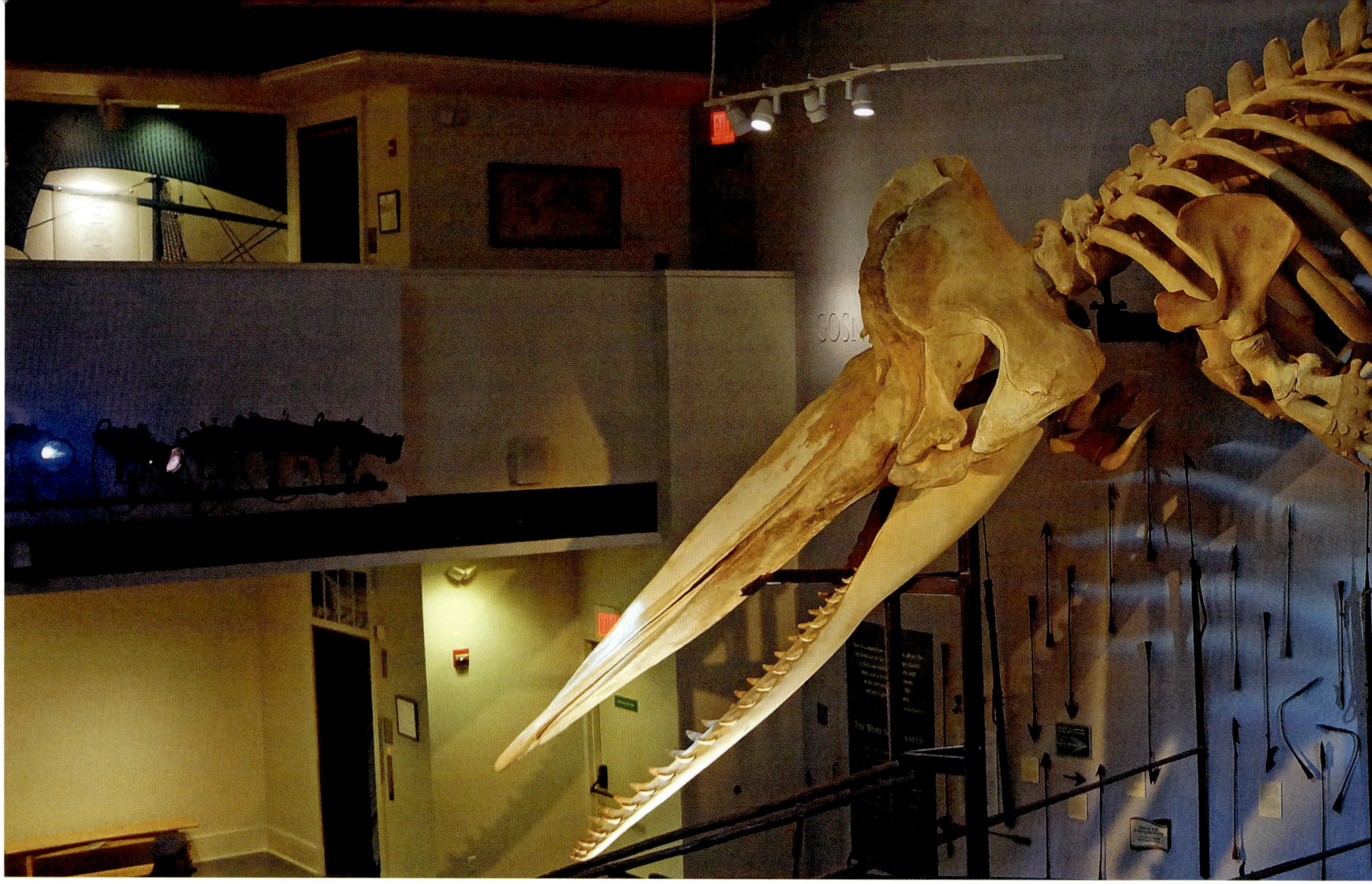

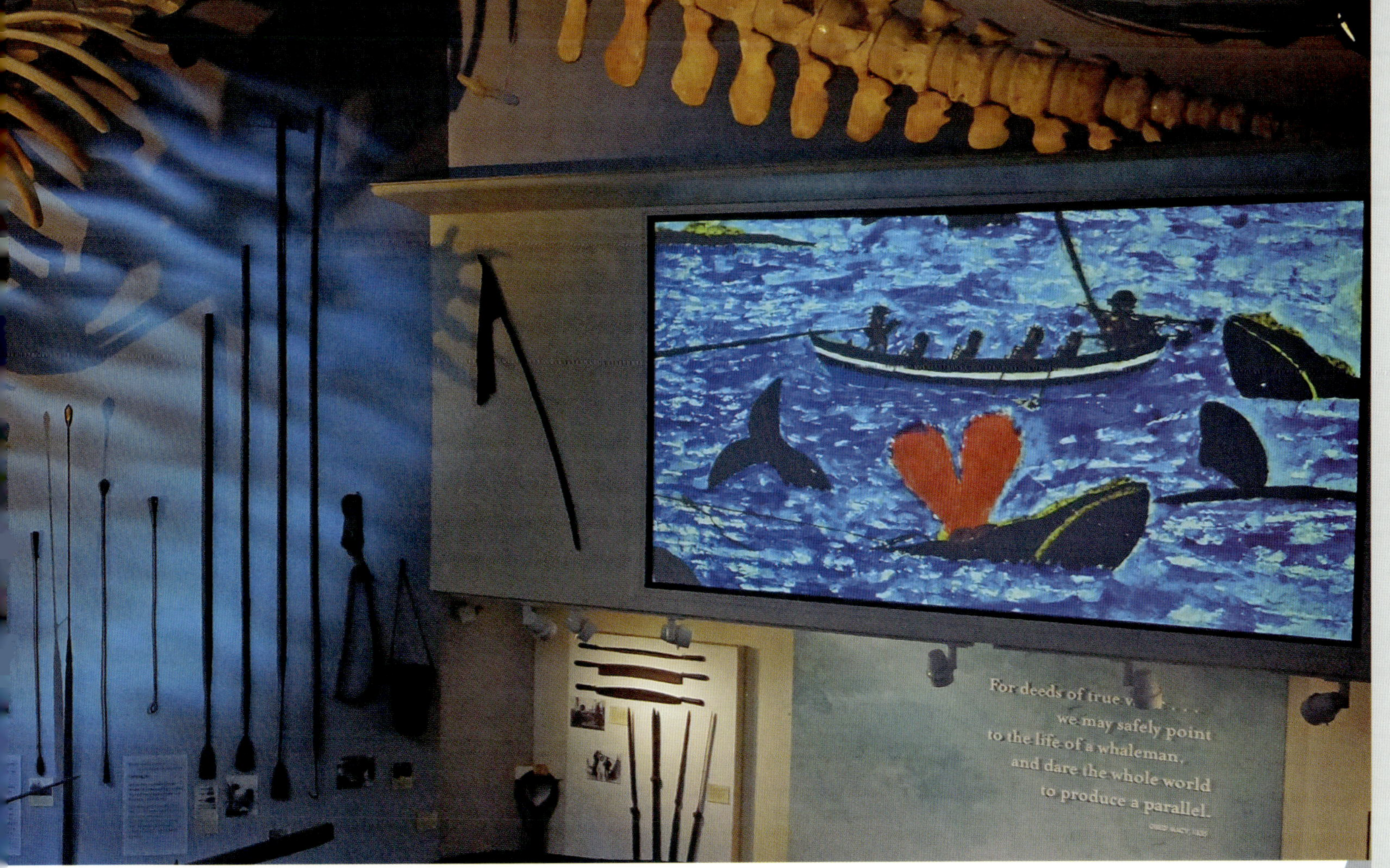

The skeleton of the sperm whale dominates the exhibits at the Whaling Museum.

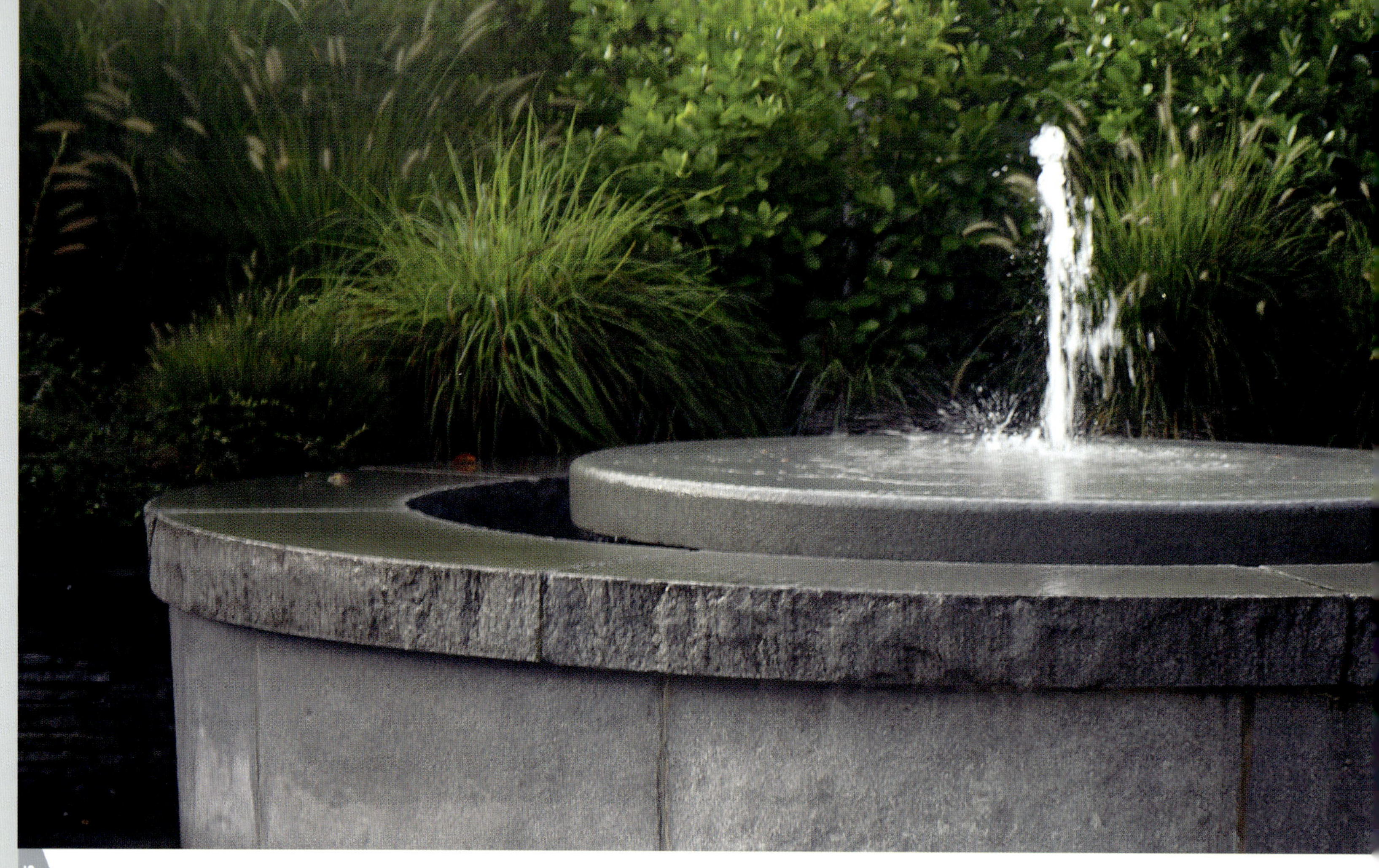

At the corner of Main and Fair streets, a small park with a fountain provides a welcome respite.

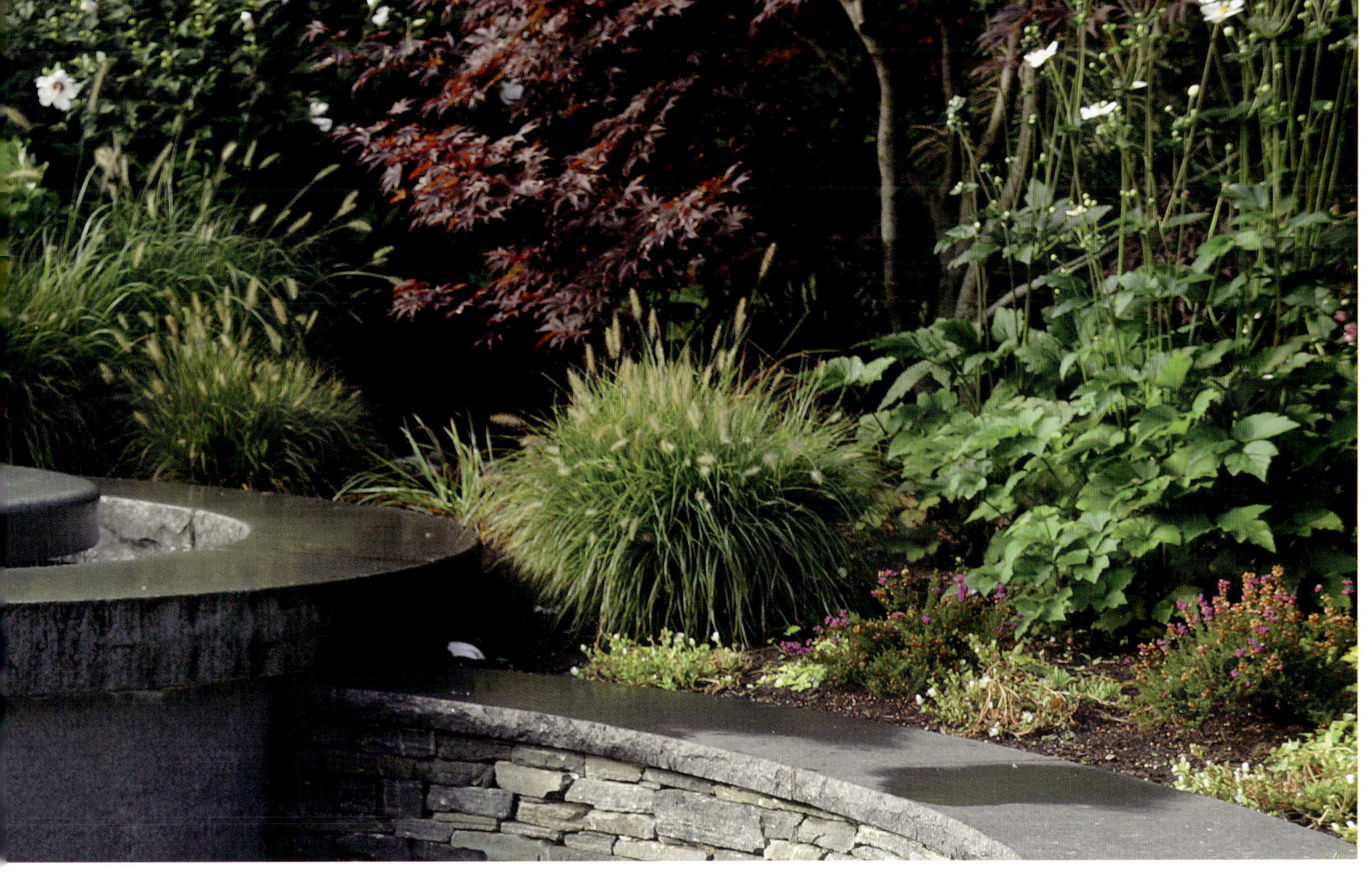

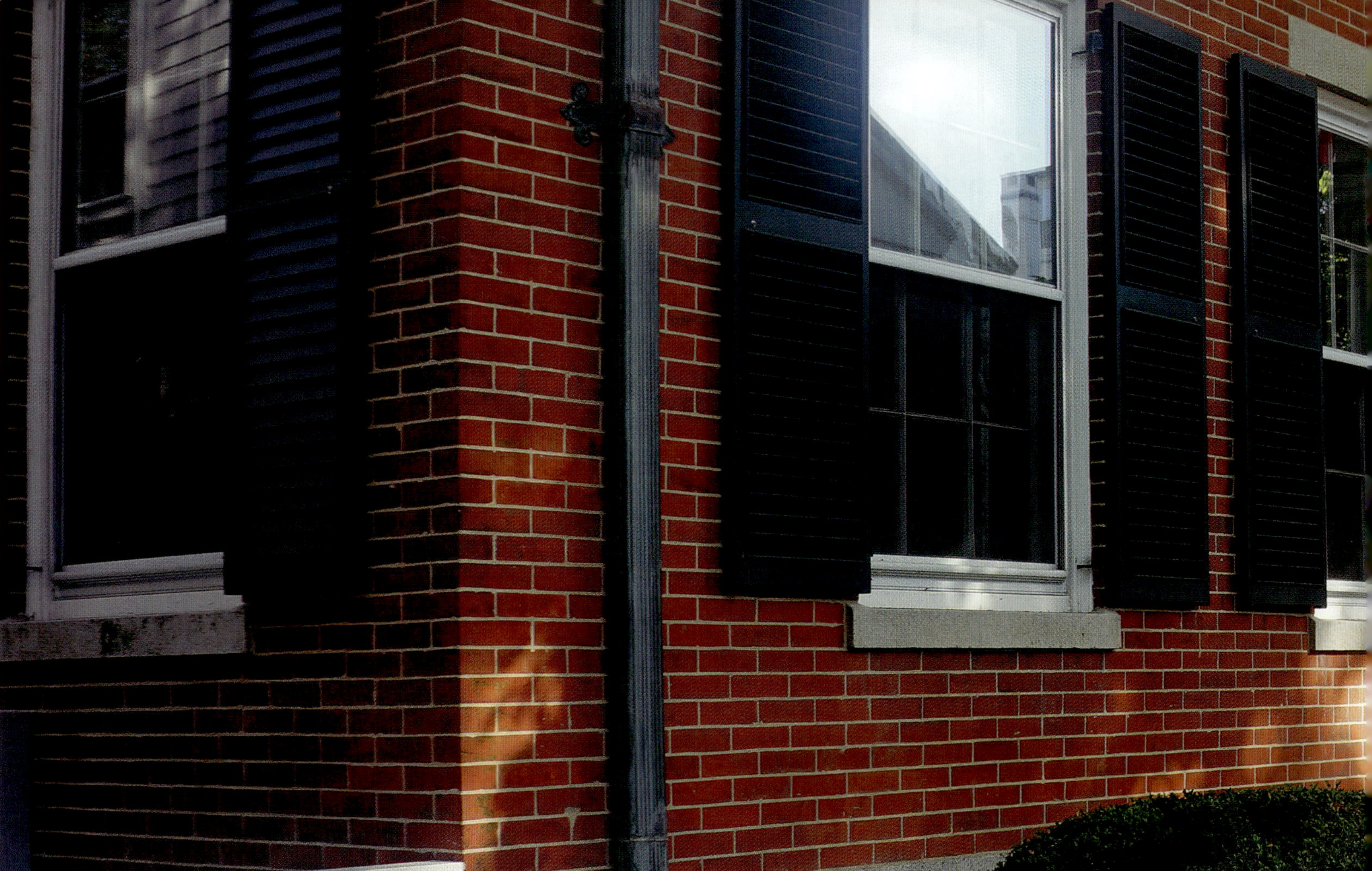

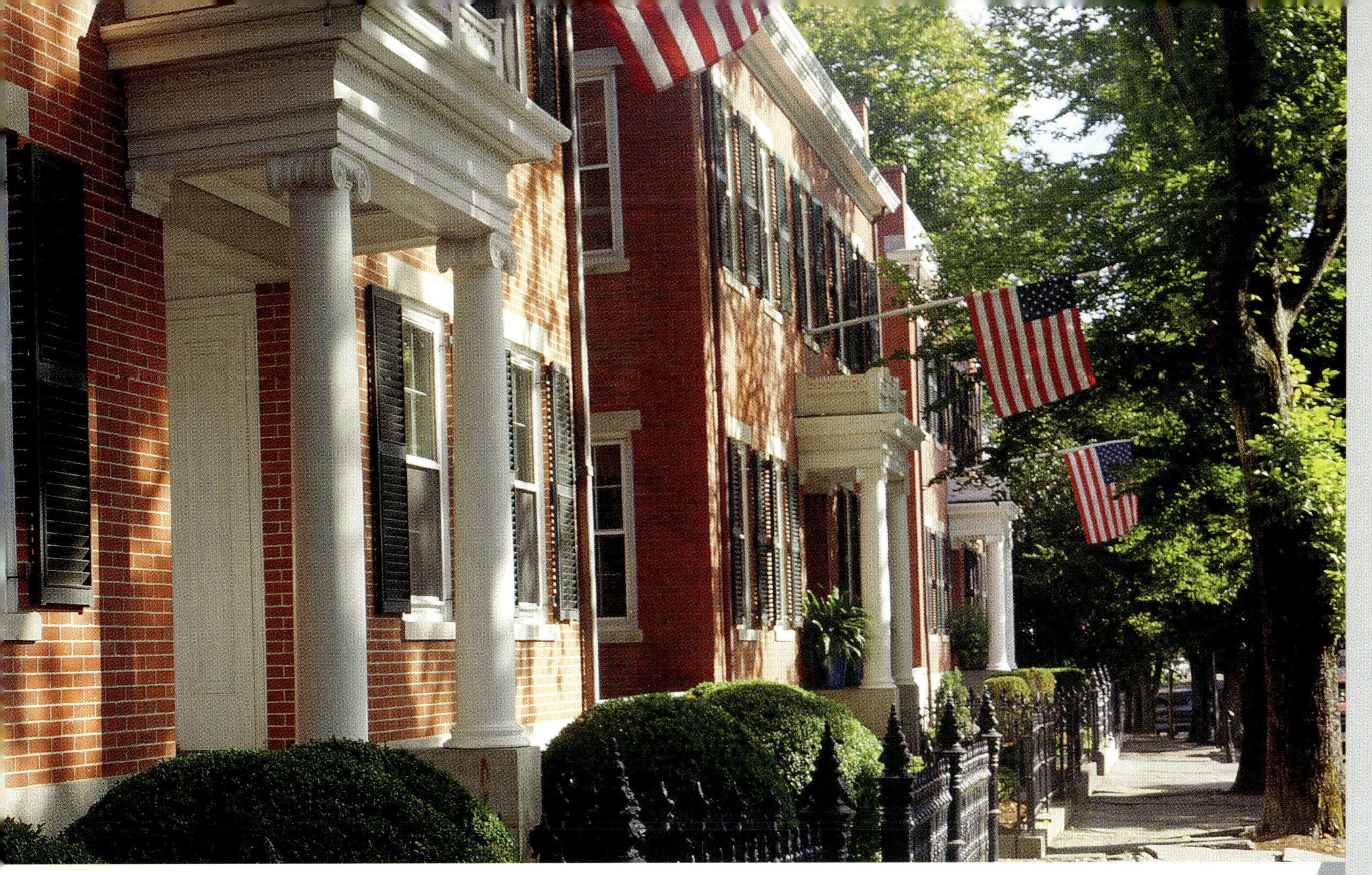

On upper Main Street, the "Three Bricks" are classic residences.
They were built in the late 1830s by whaling merchant Joseph Starbuck for his three sons.

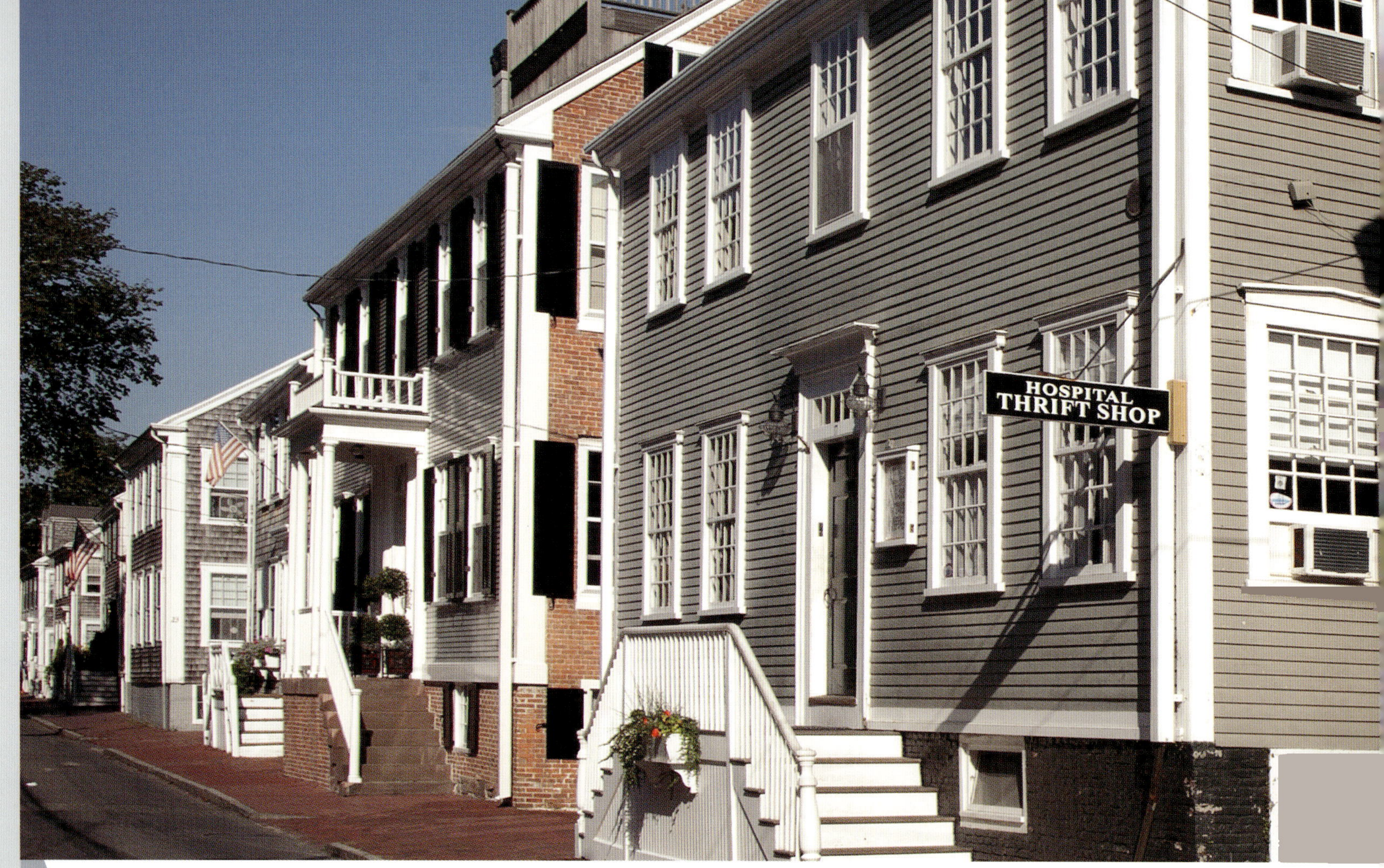

Some of the houses on India Street date back more than two centuries.

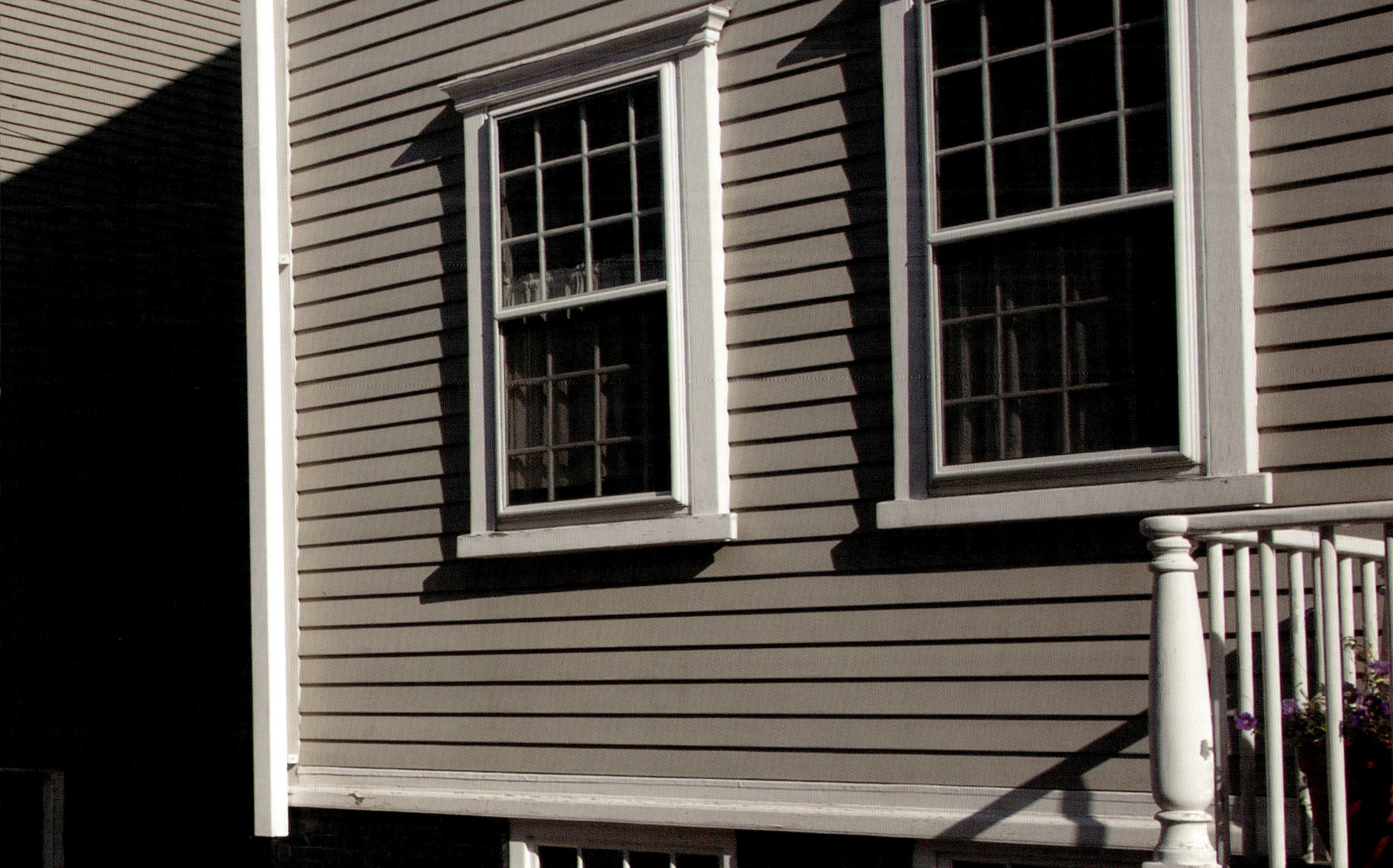

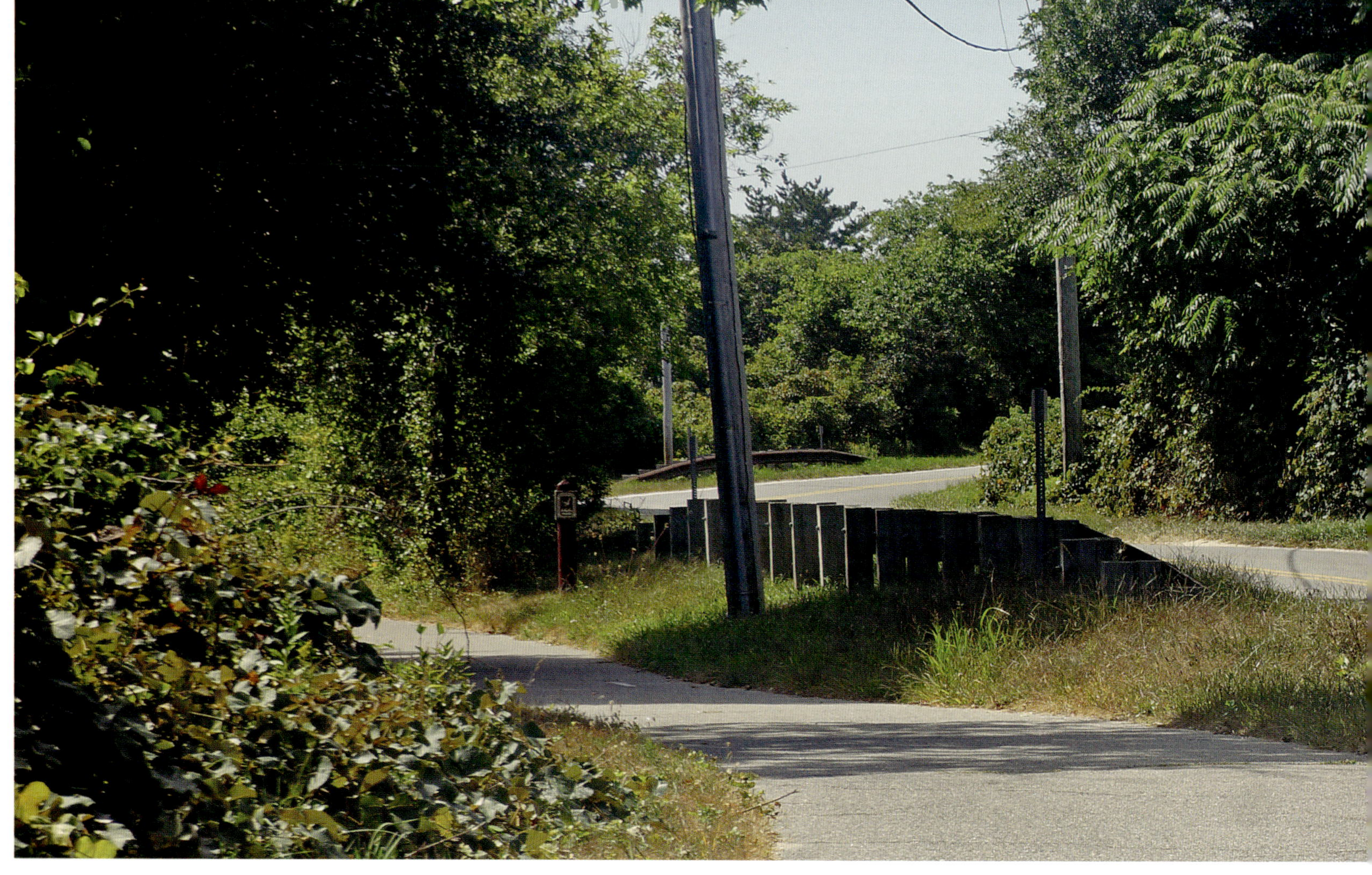

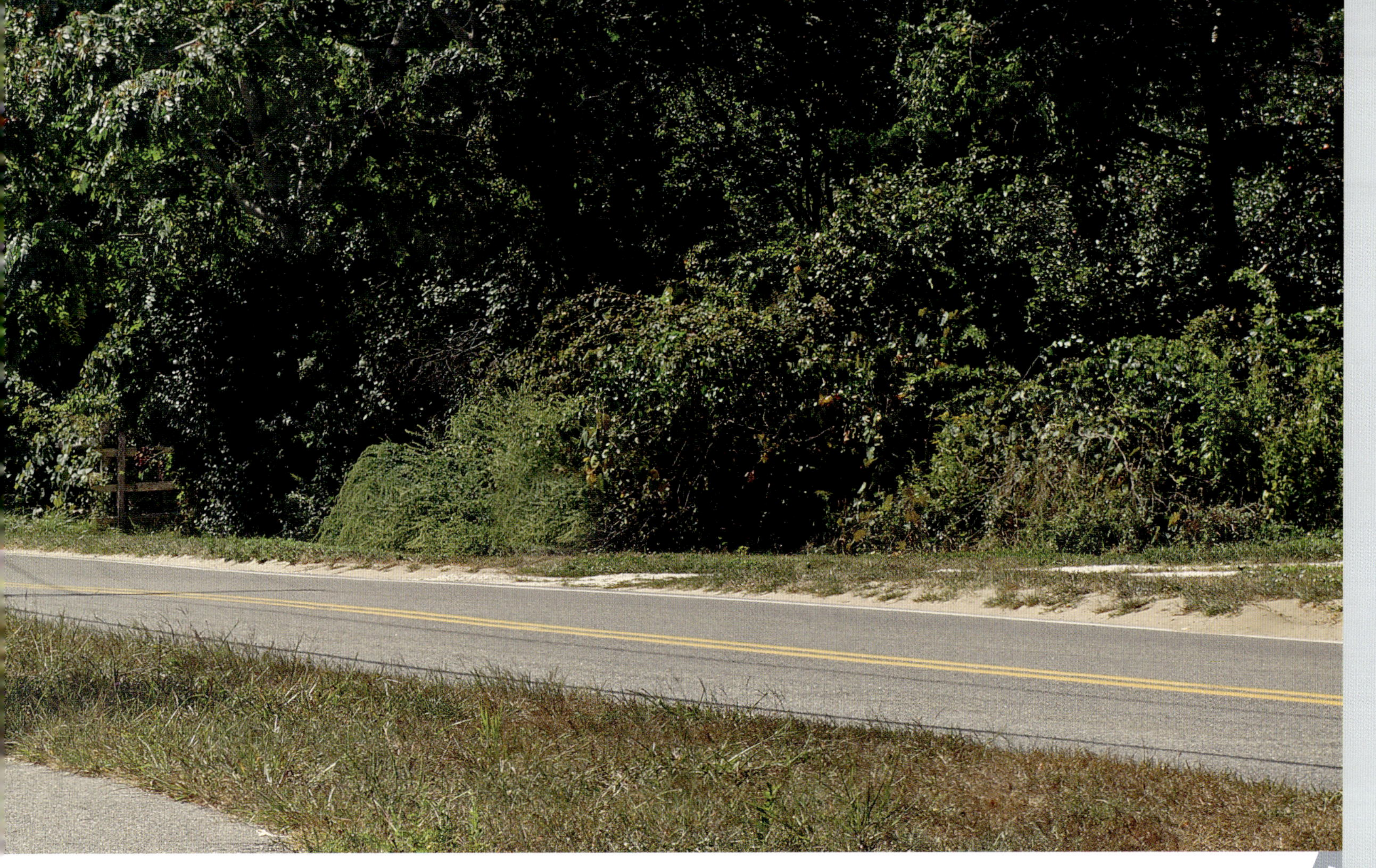

Outside of town, the bike path follows closely along the roads.

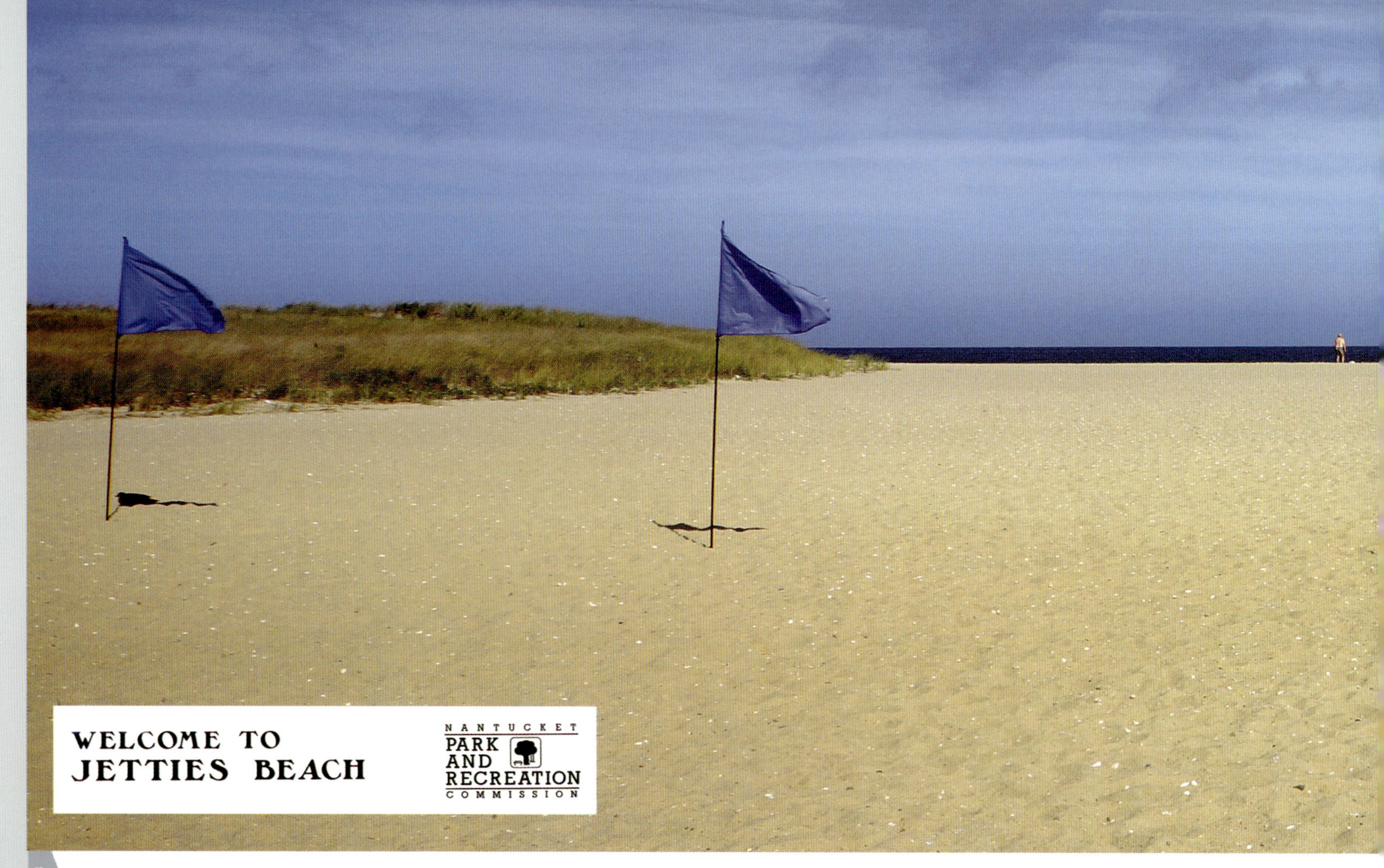

Blue flags fly in the breeze at Jetties Beach.

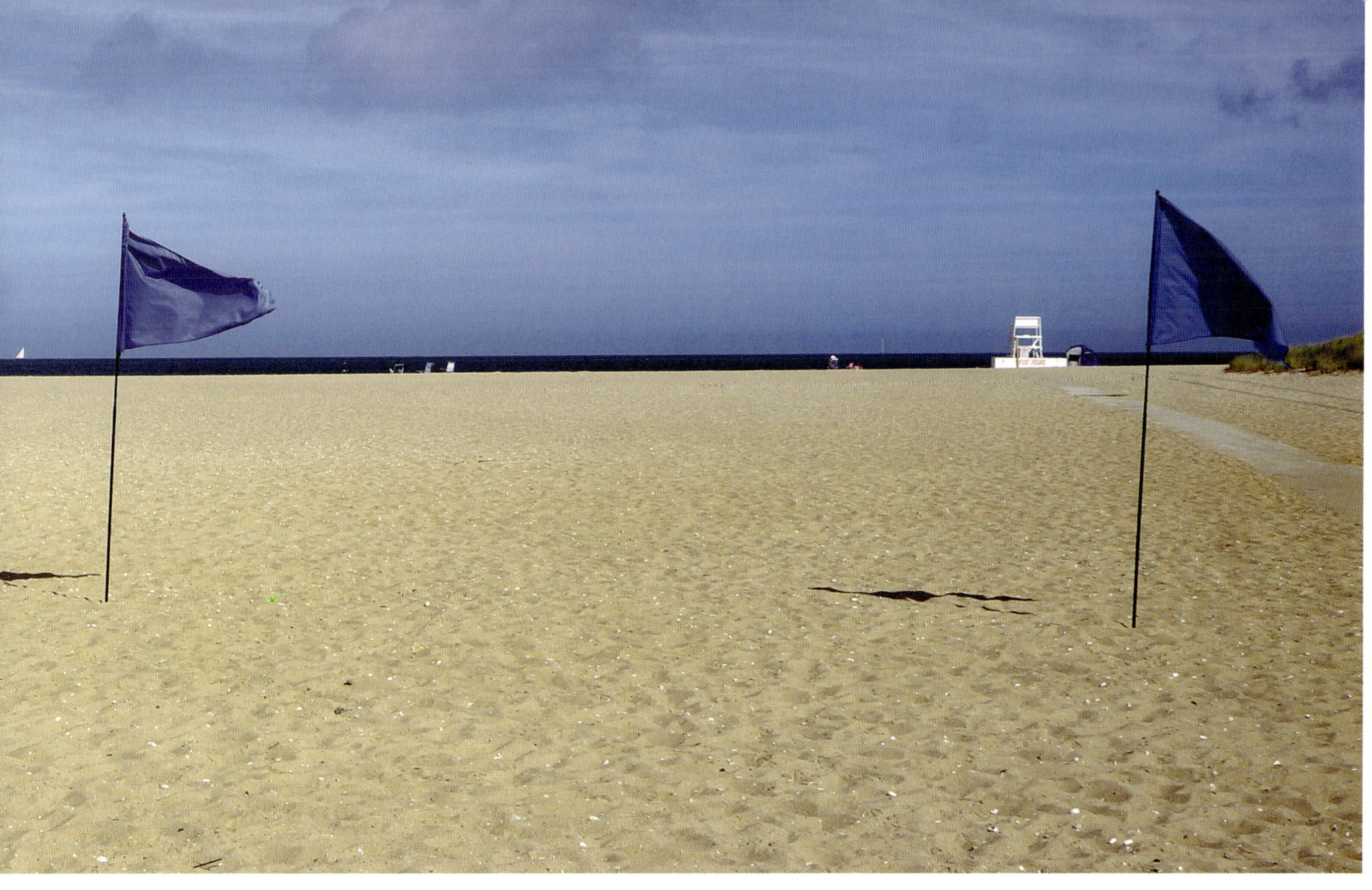

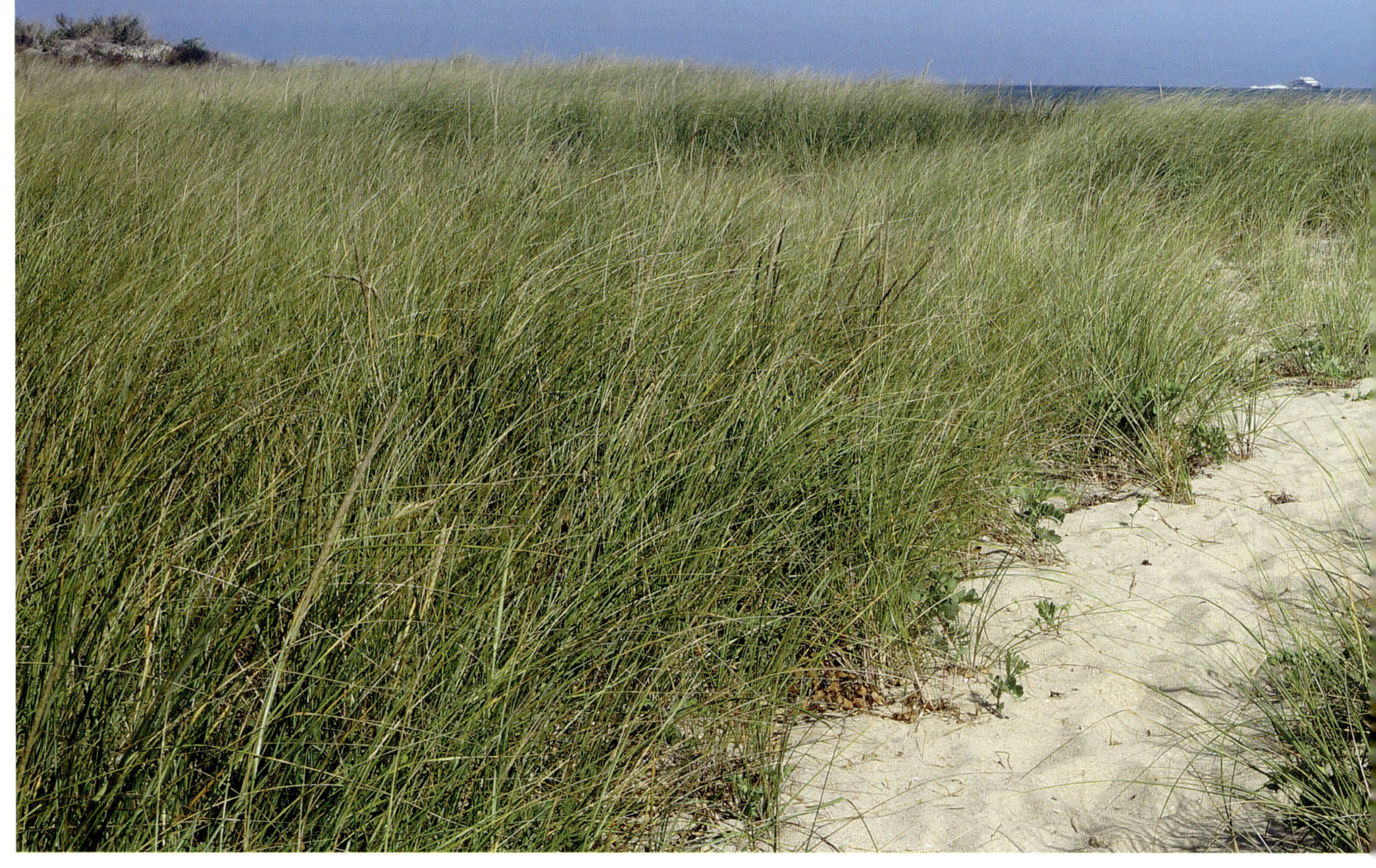

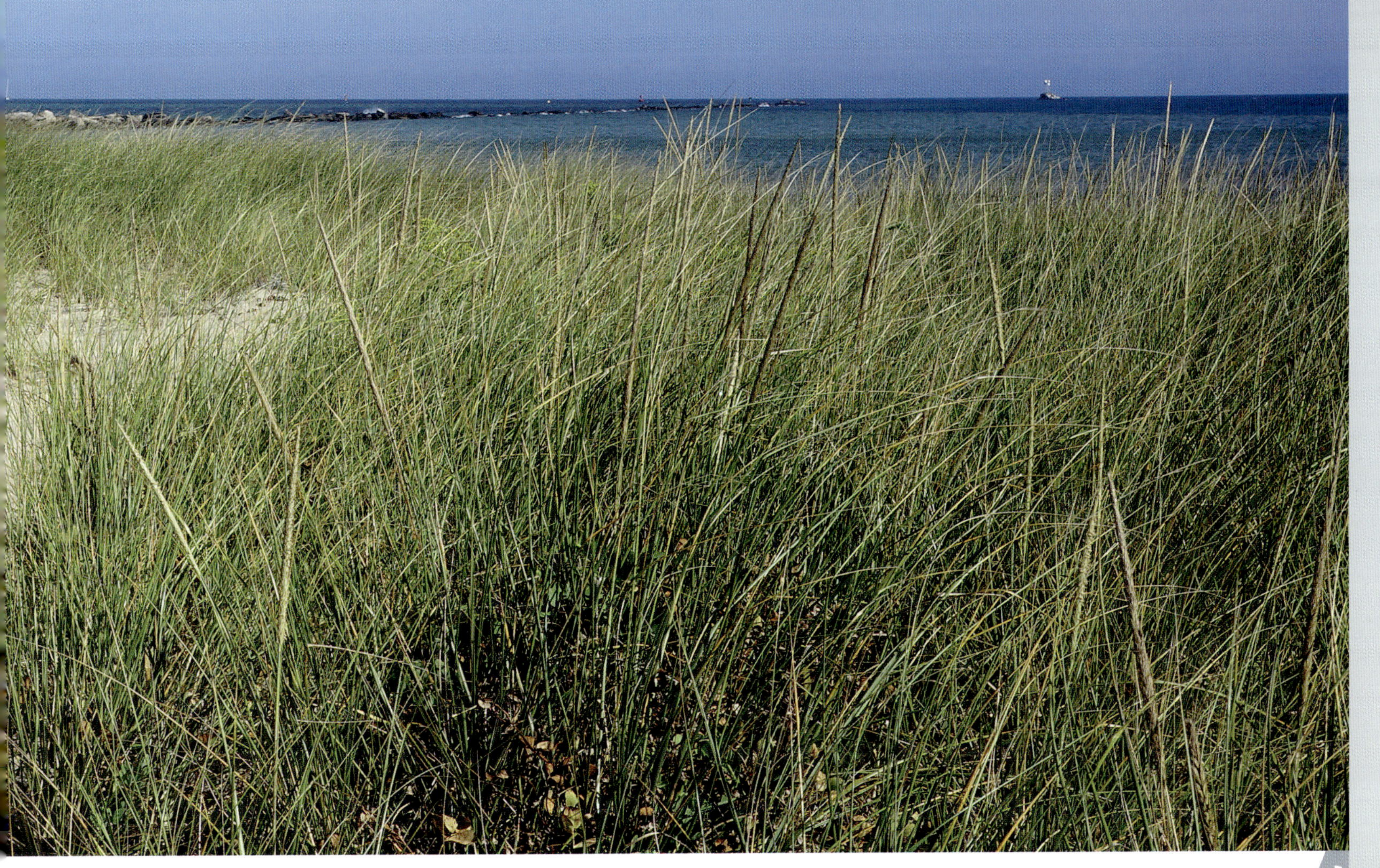

A path leads to the beach, and a jetty stretching into the water.

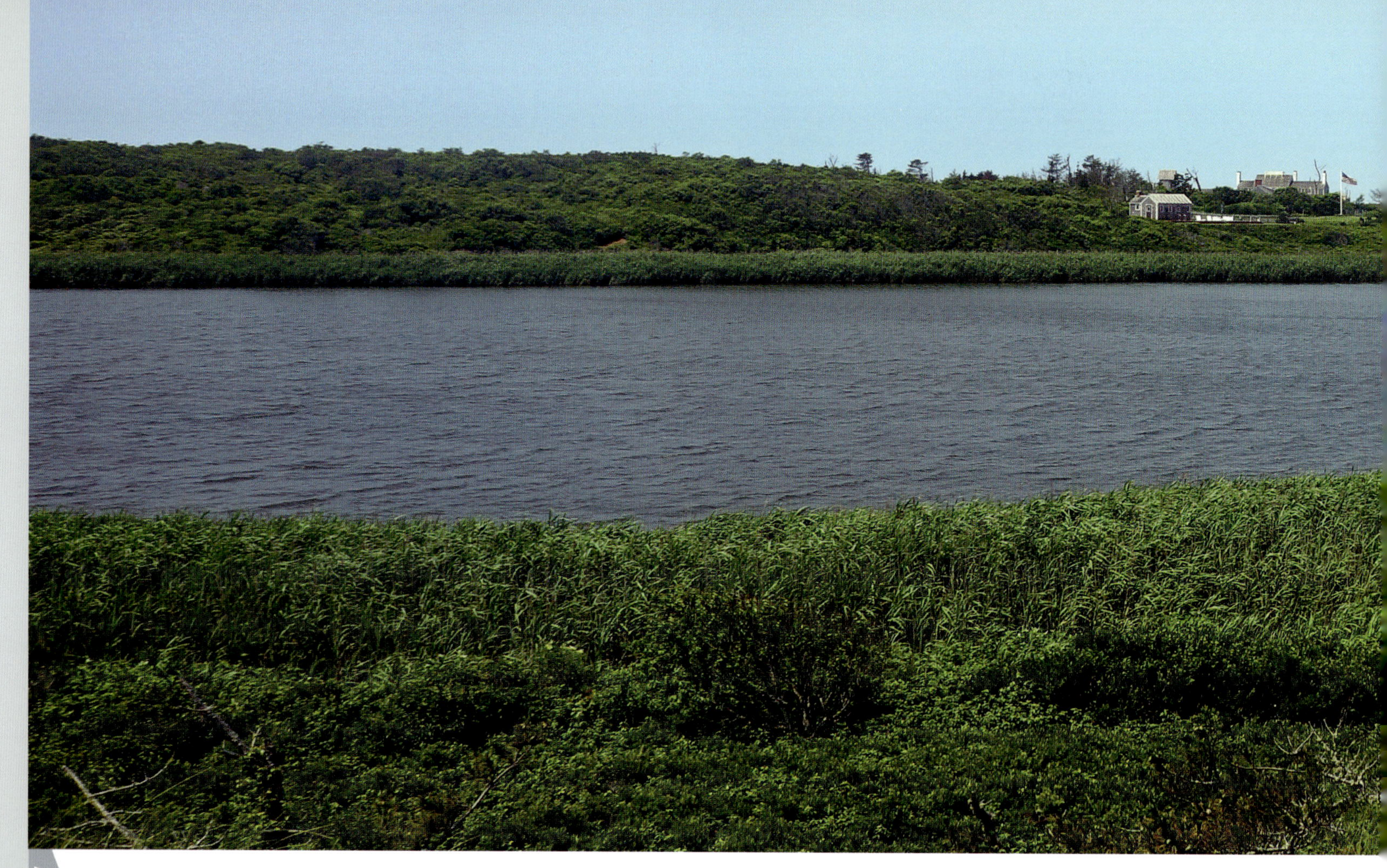

Capaum Pond was the location of the first settlement on the island.

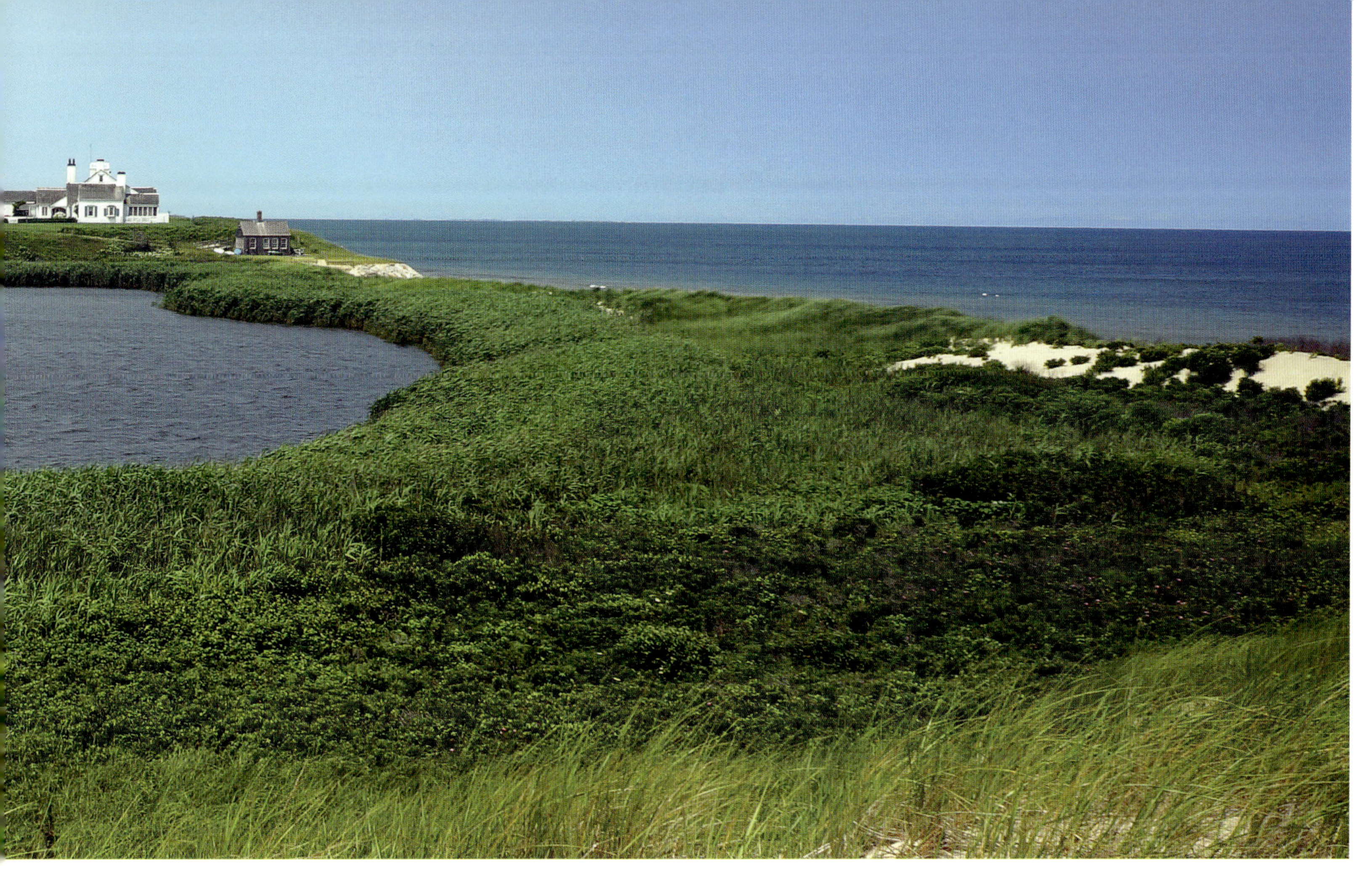

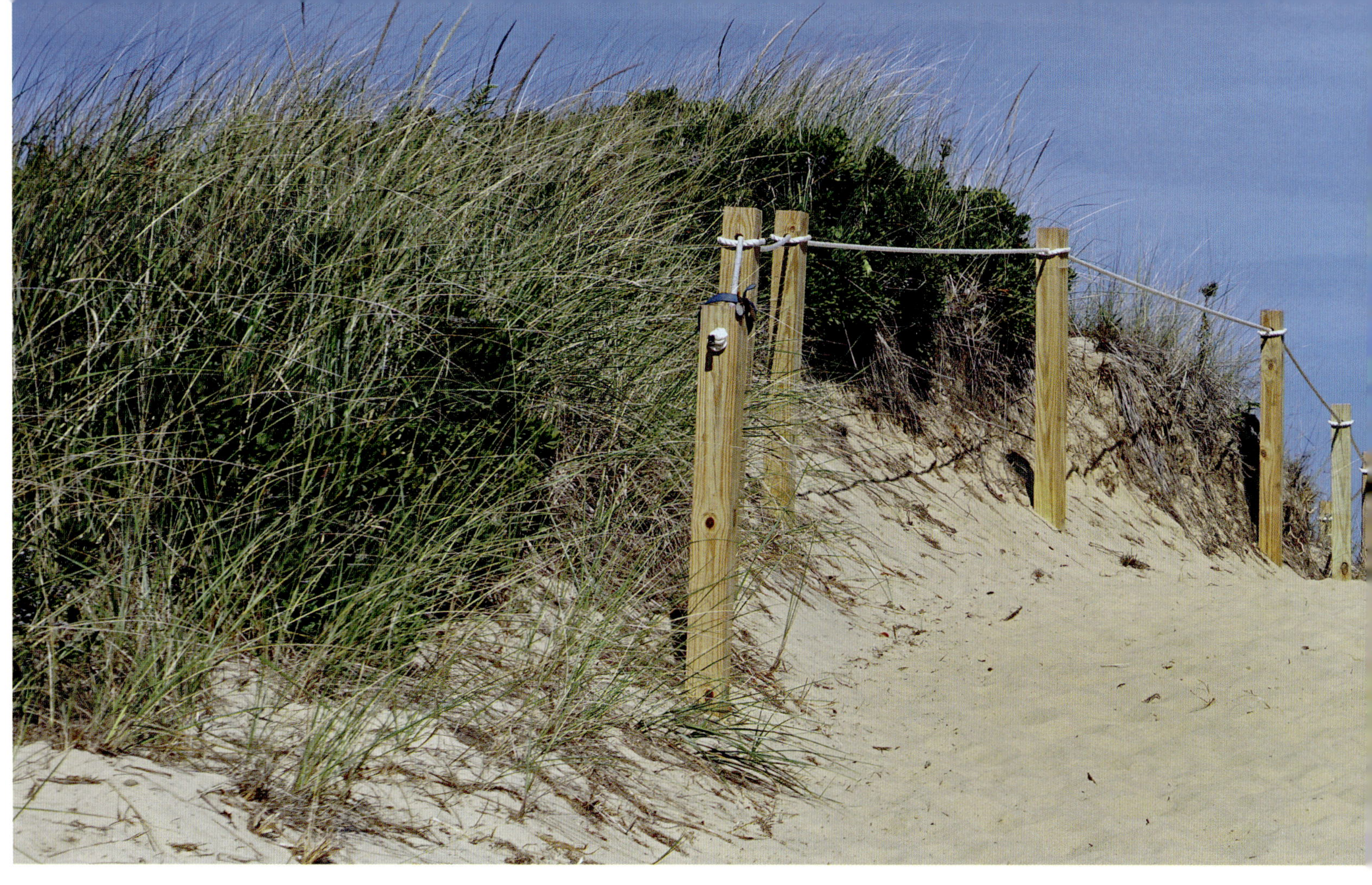

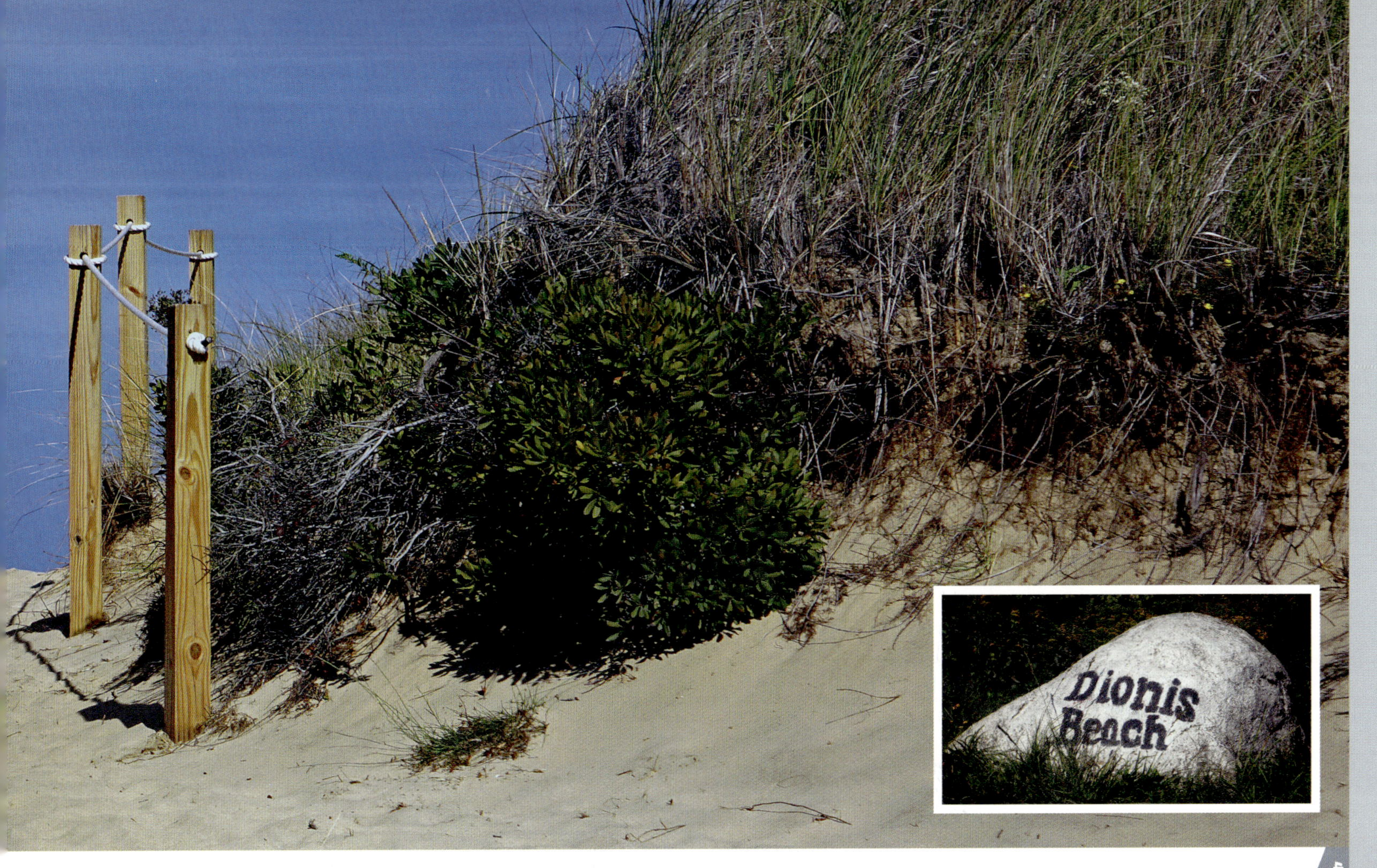

Down this sandy pathway is Dionis Beach.

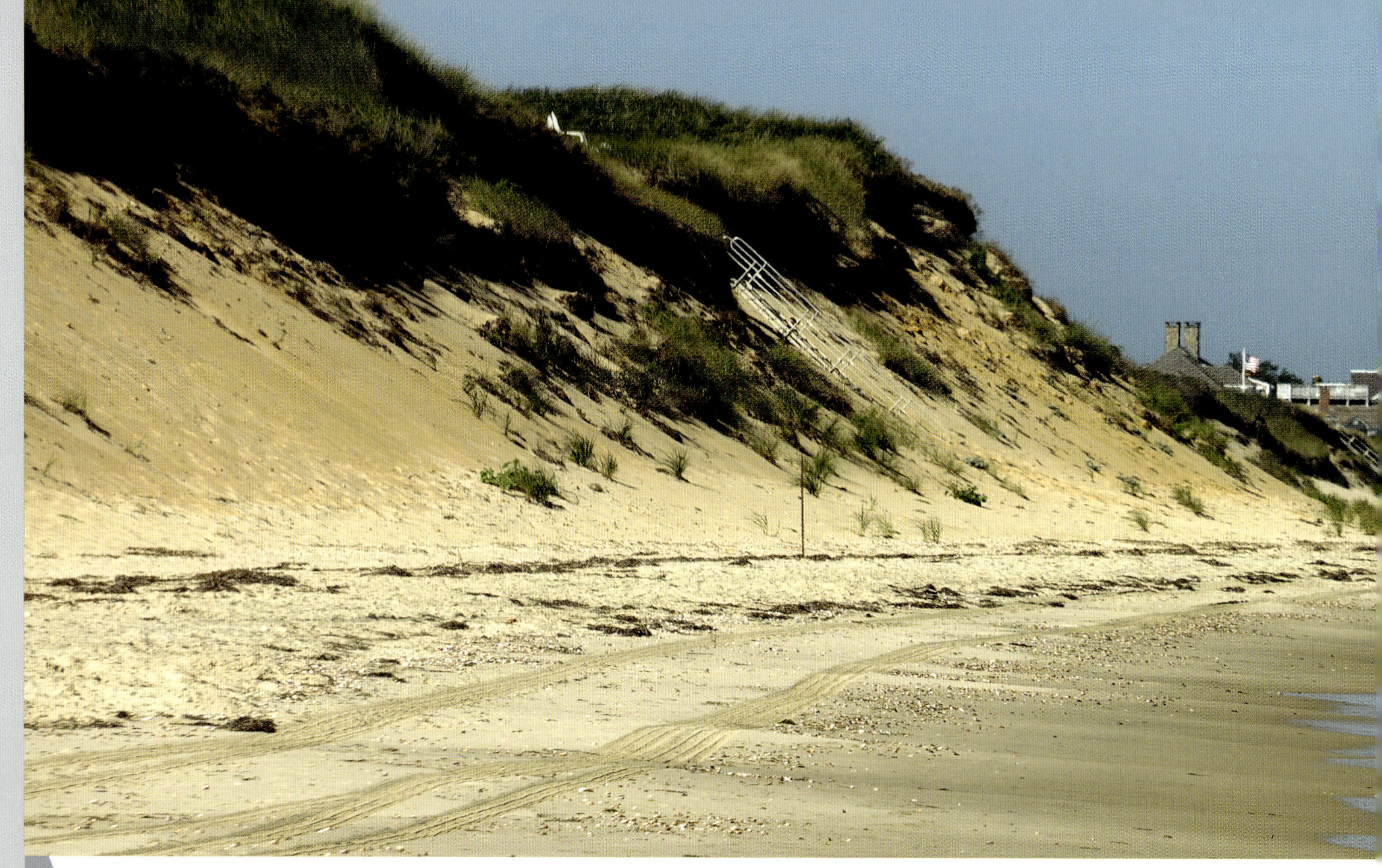

Looking west along Dionis beach.

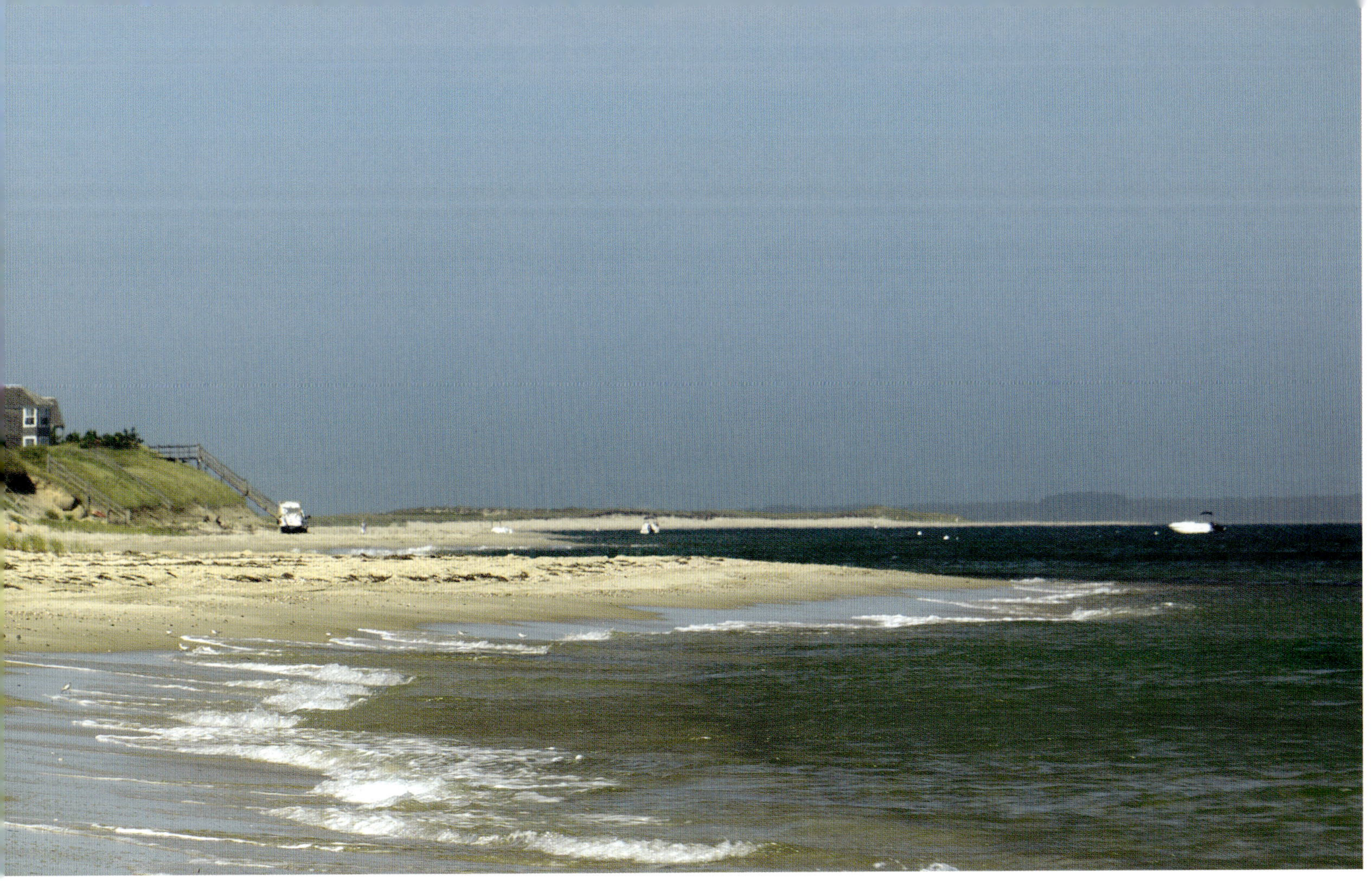

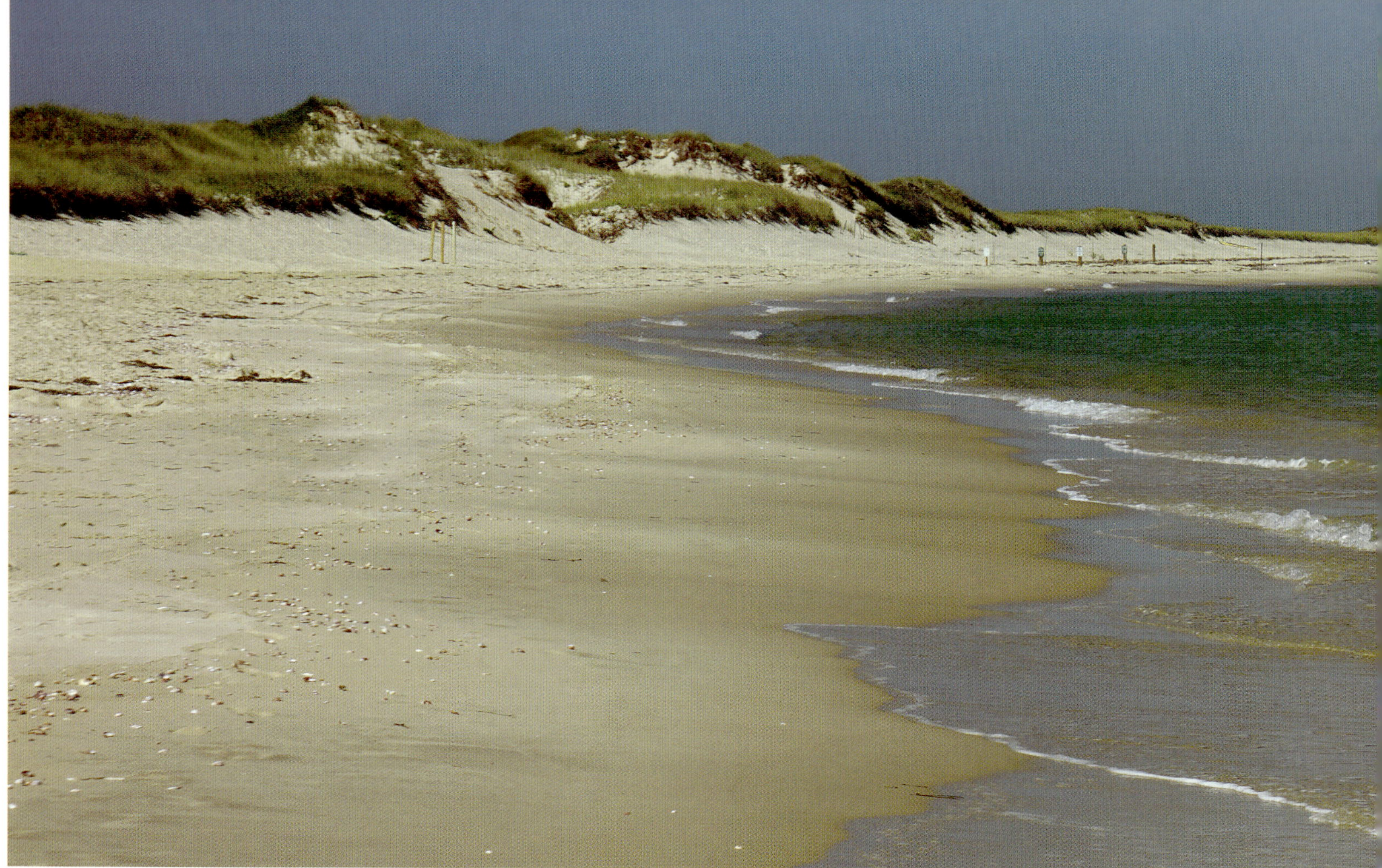

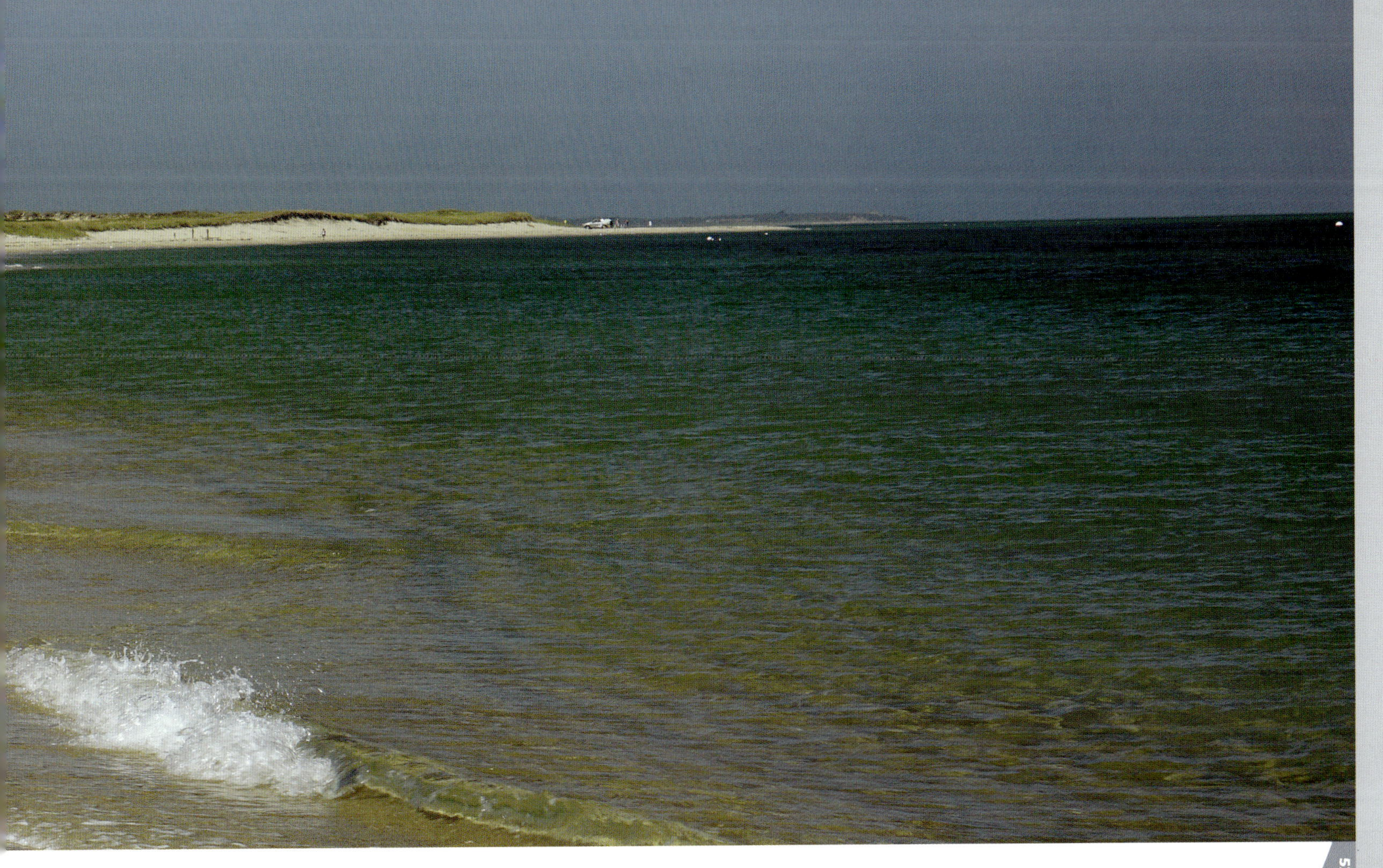

Farther along the coast is 40th Pole Beach with Eel Point in the distance.

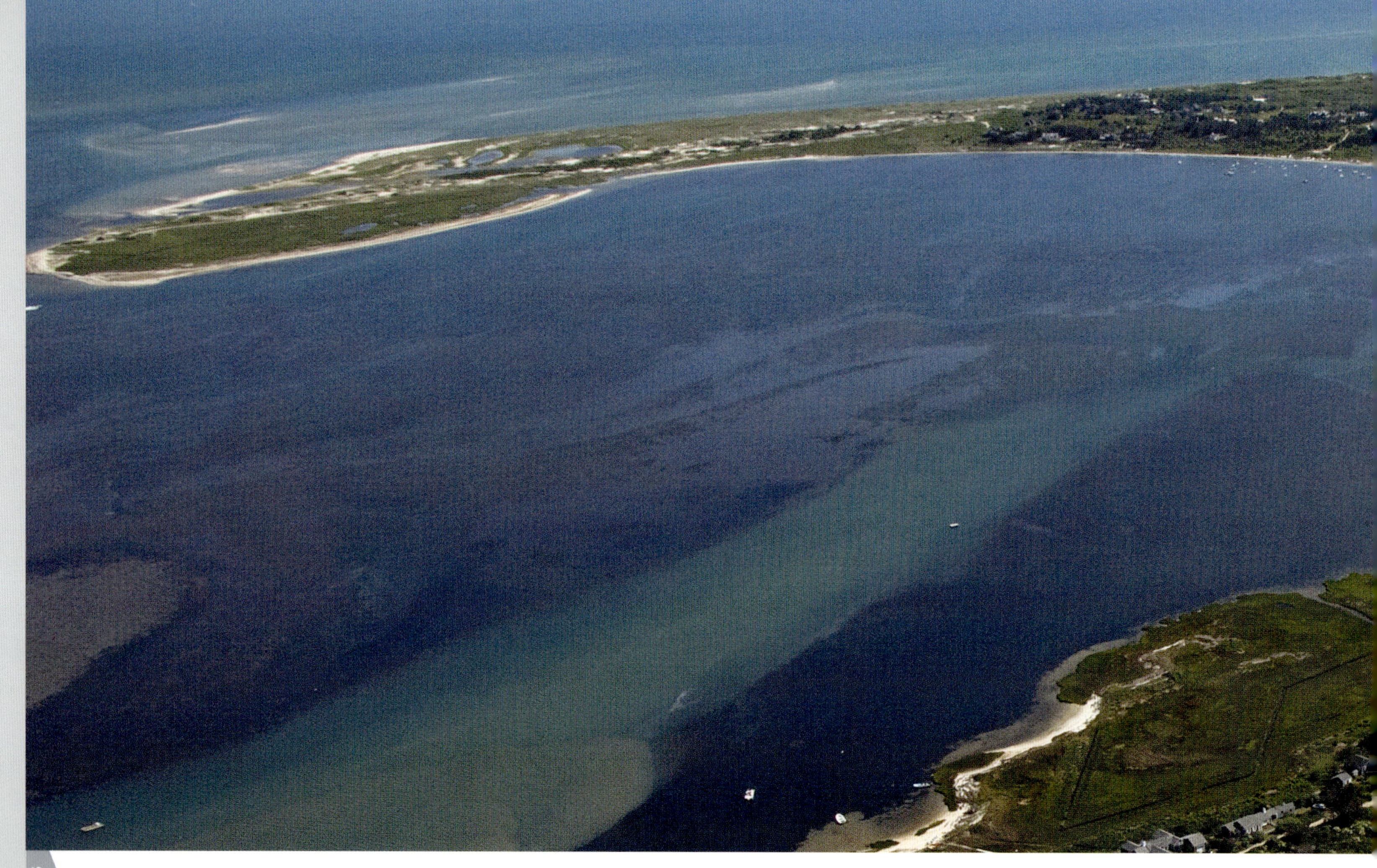

An aerial view of Madaket Harbor. Eel Point is the tip of land at the top left.

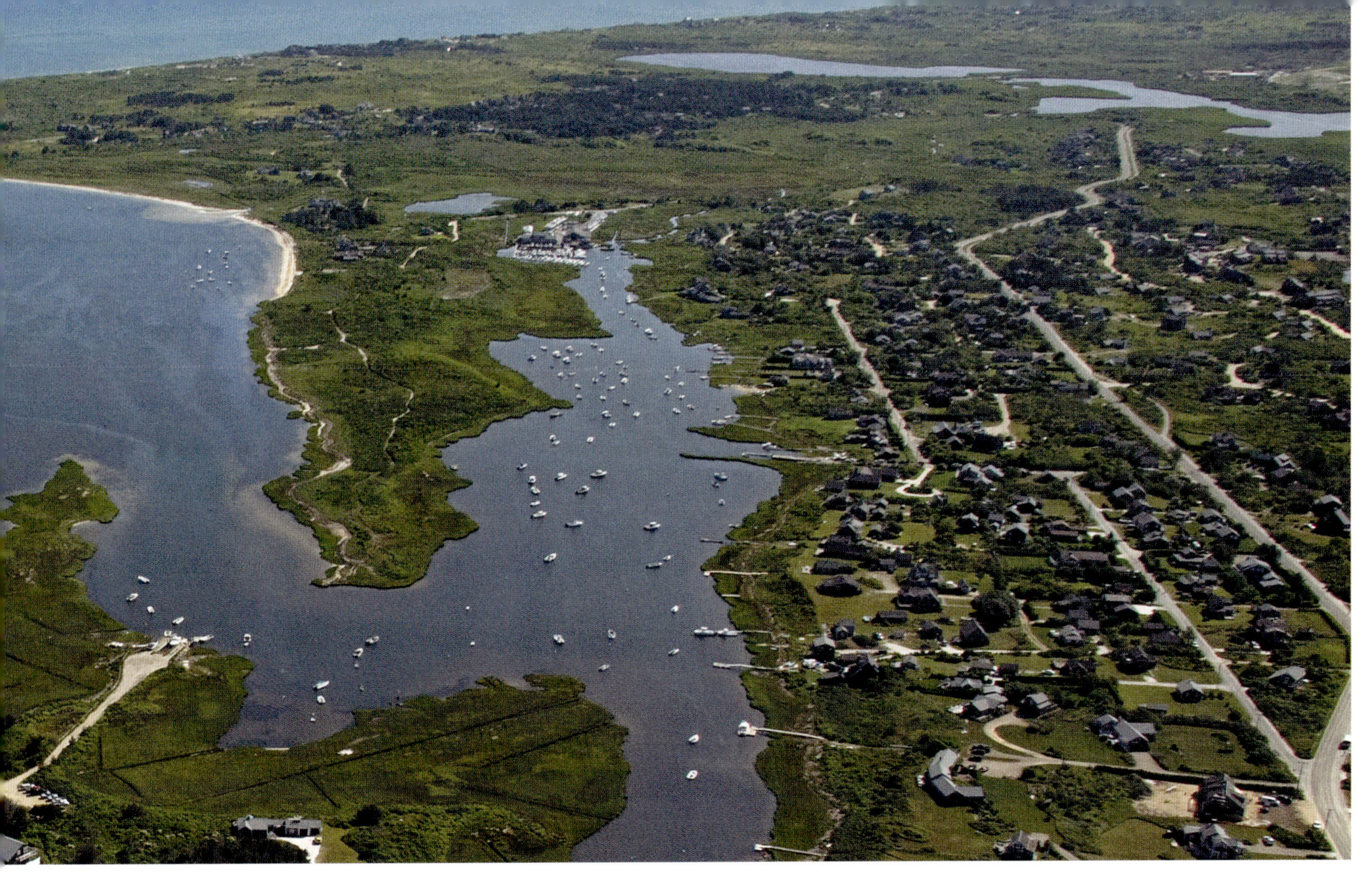

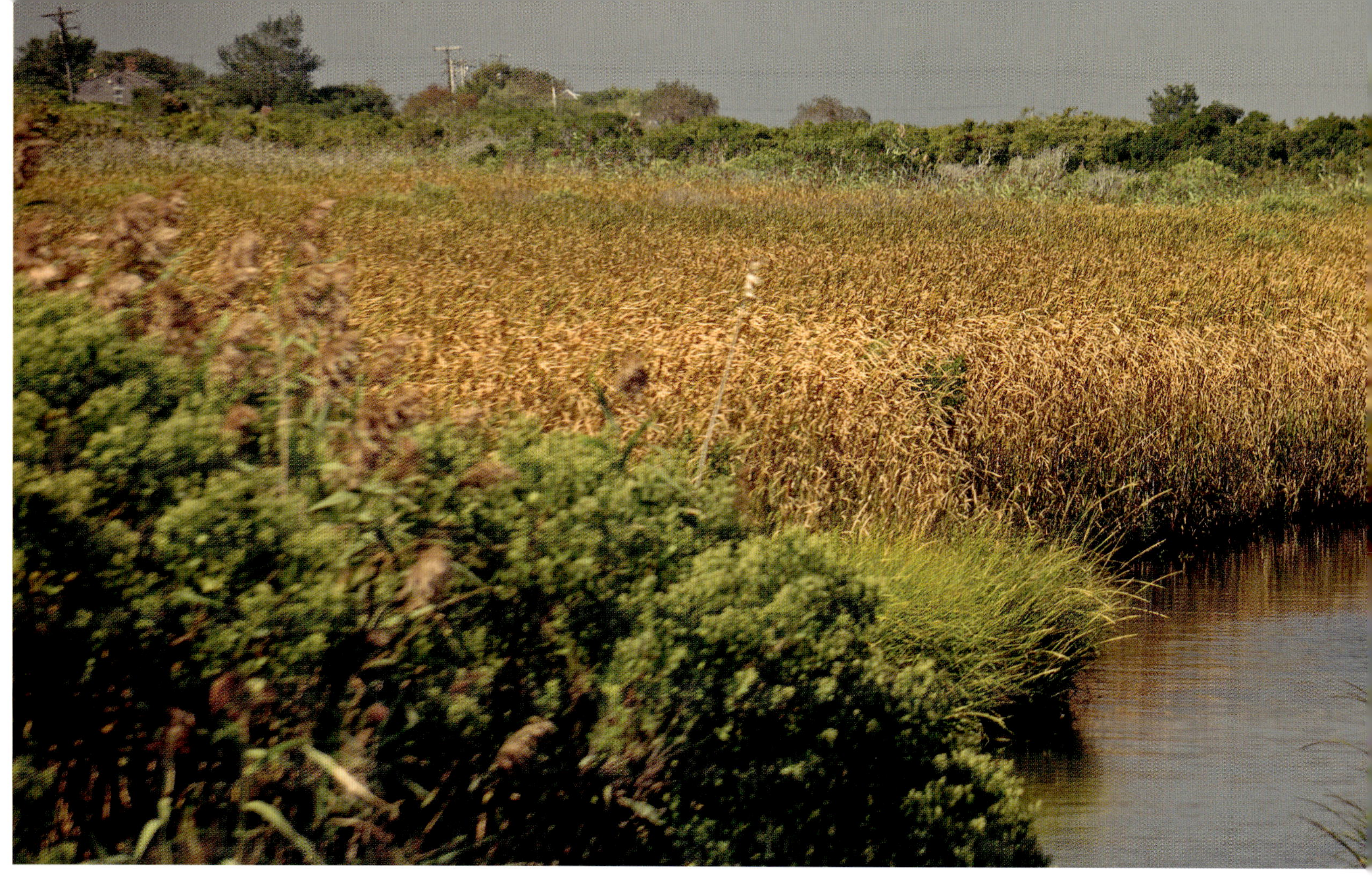

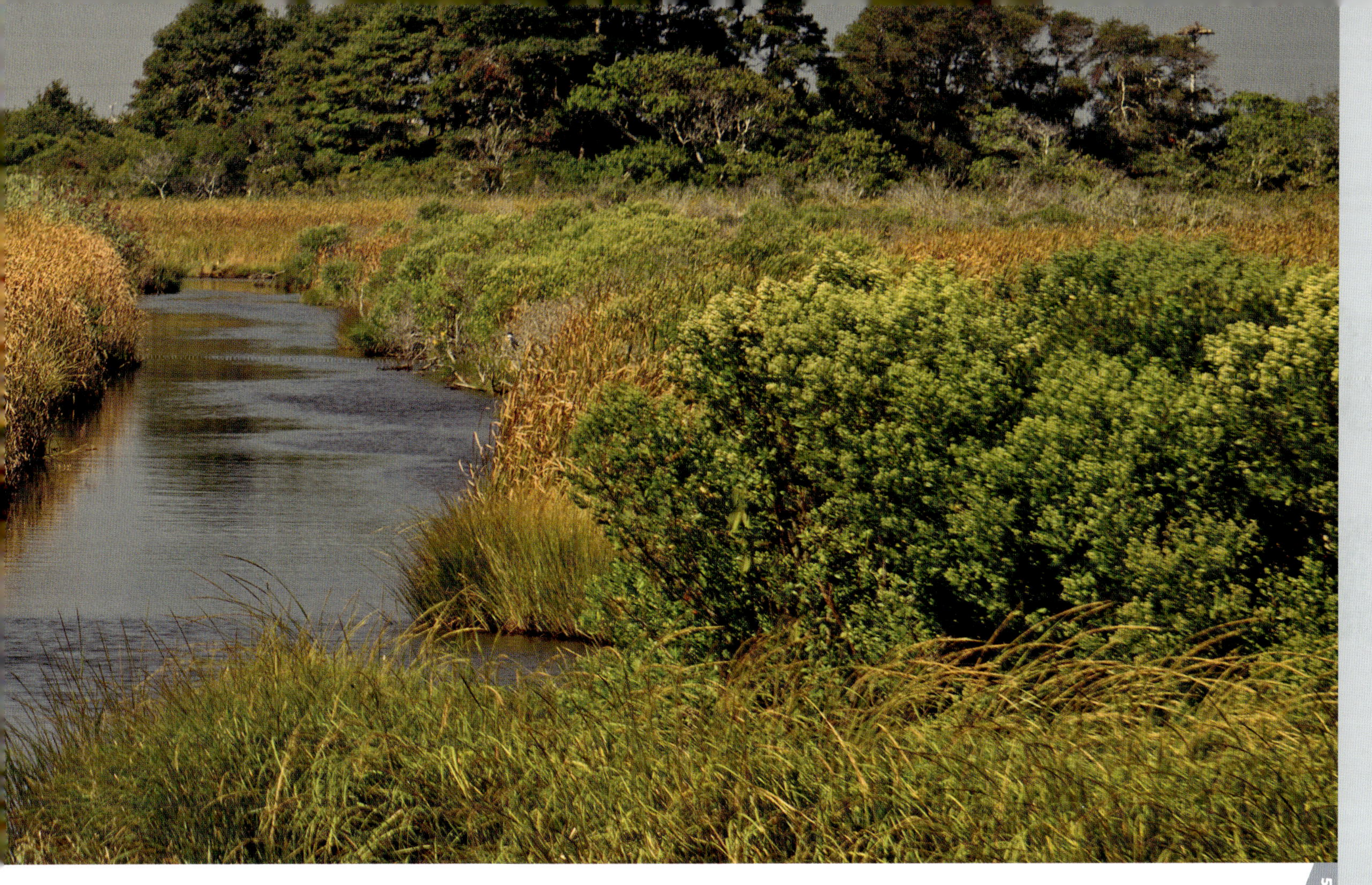

The upper section of "Madaket Ditch," built in 1665 by Native Americans and the English settlers to trap fish in weirs.

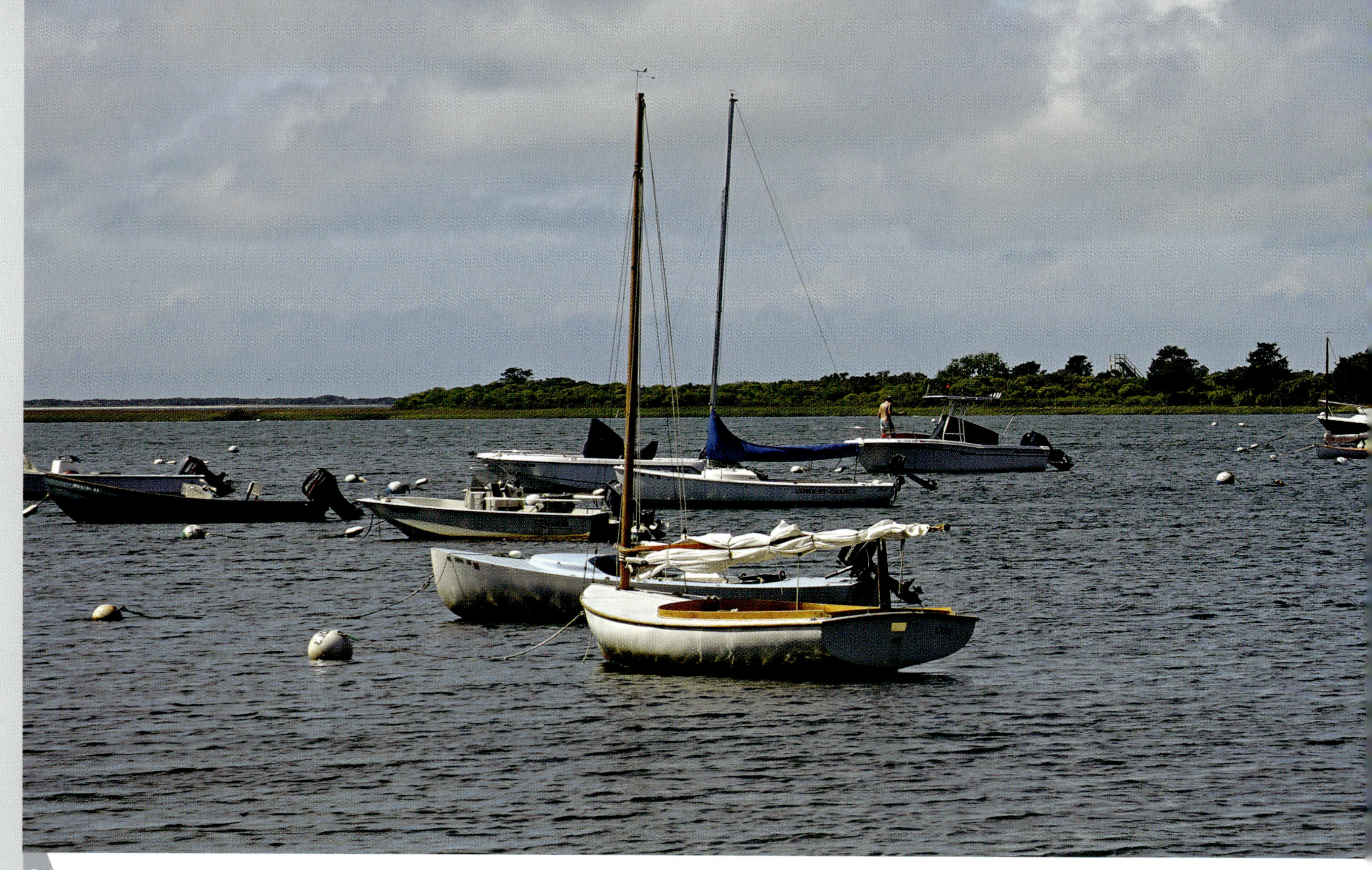

Small boats moored in Madaket Harbor.

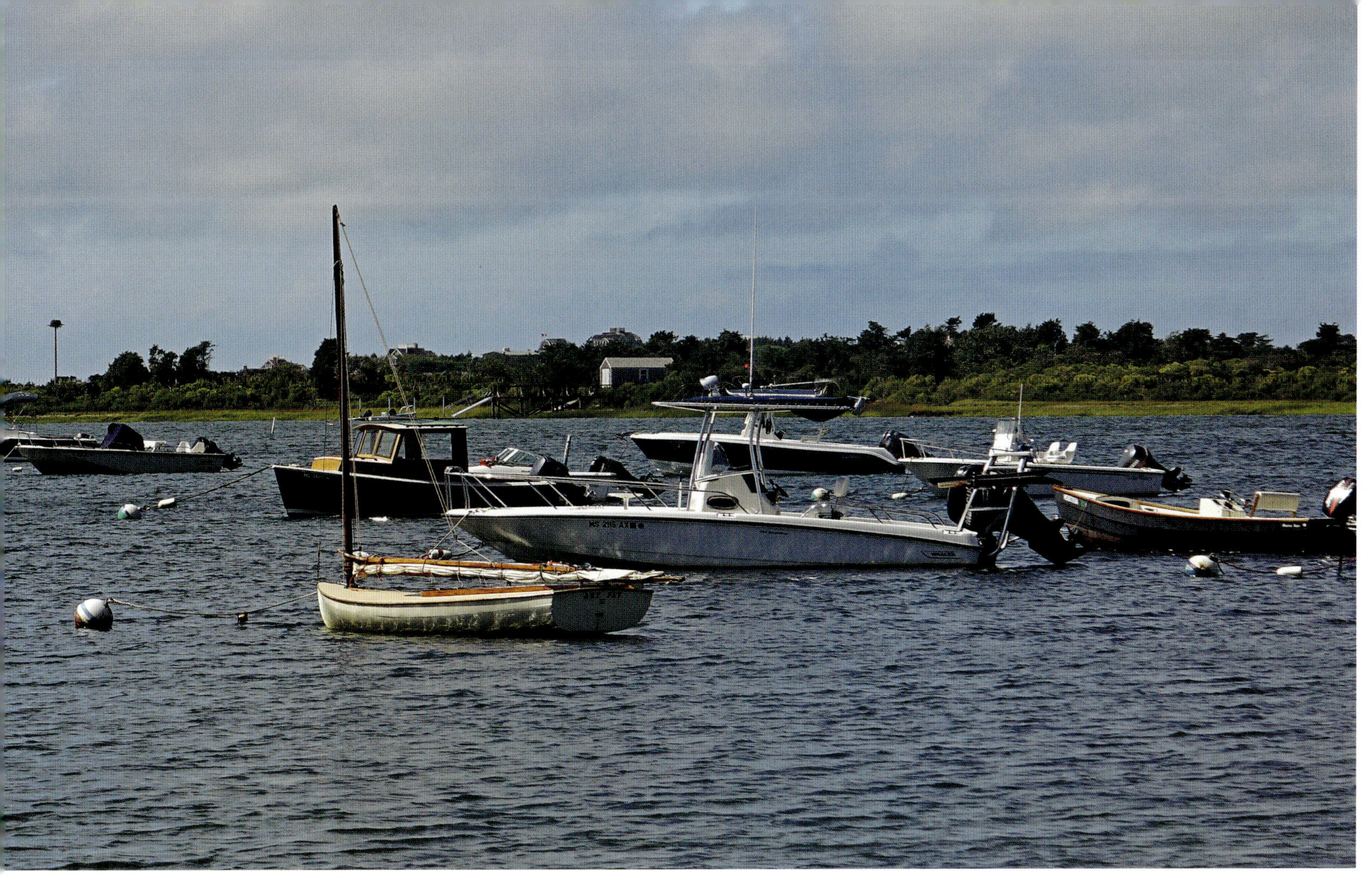

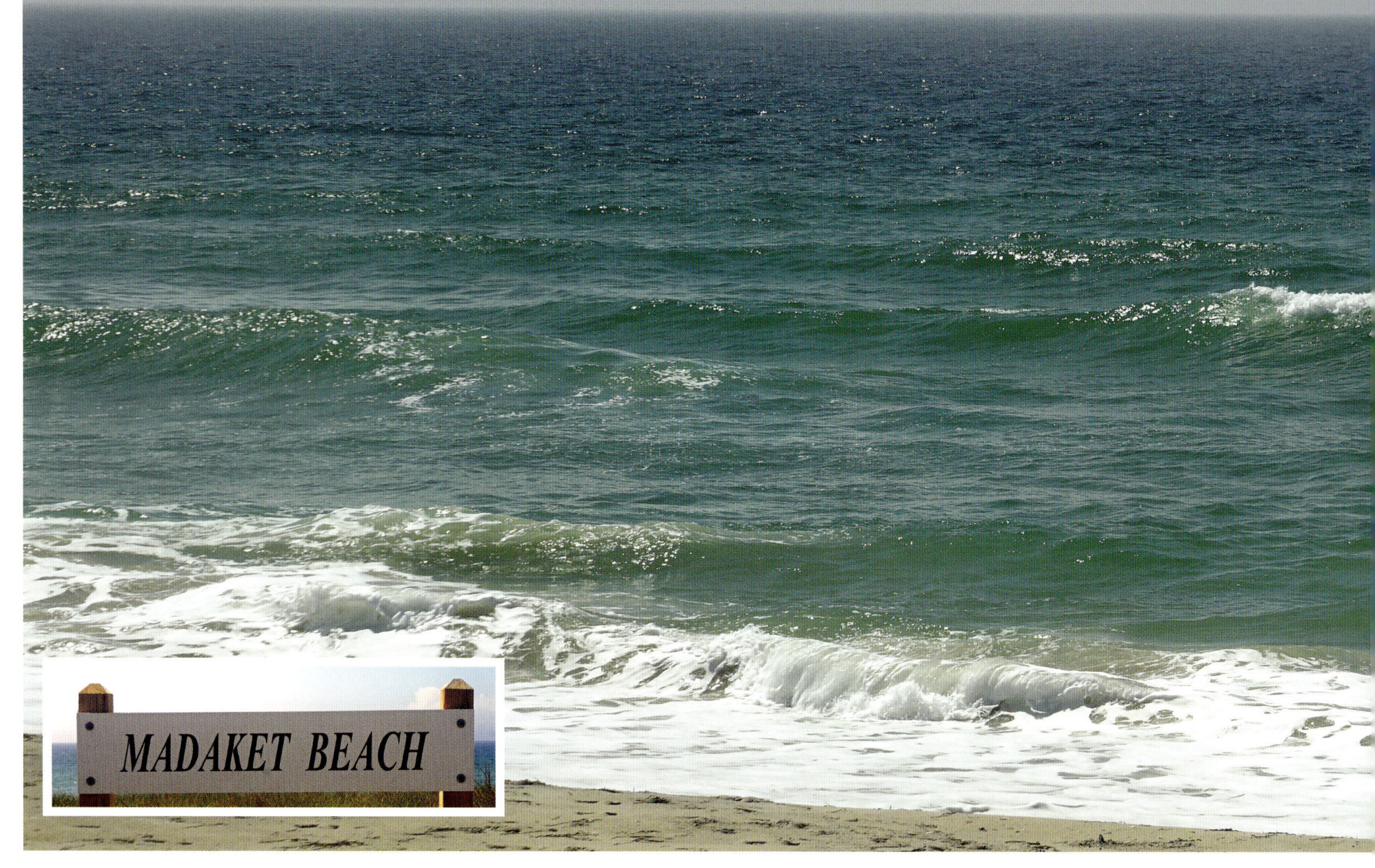
MADAKET BEACH

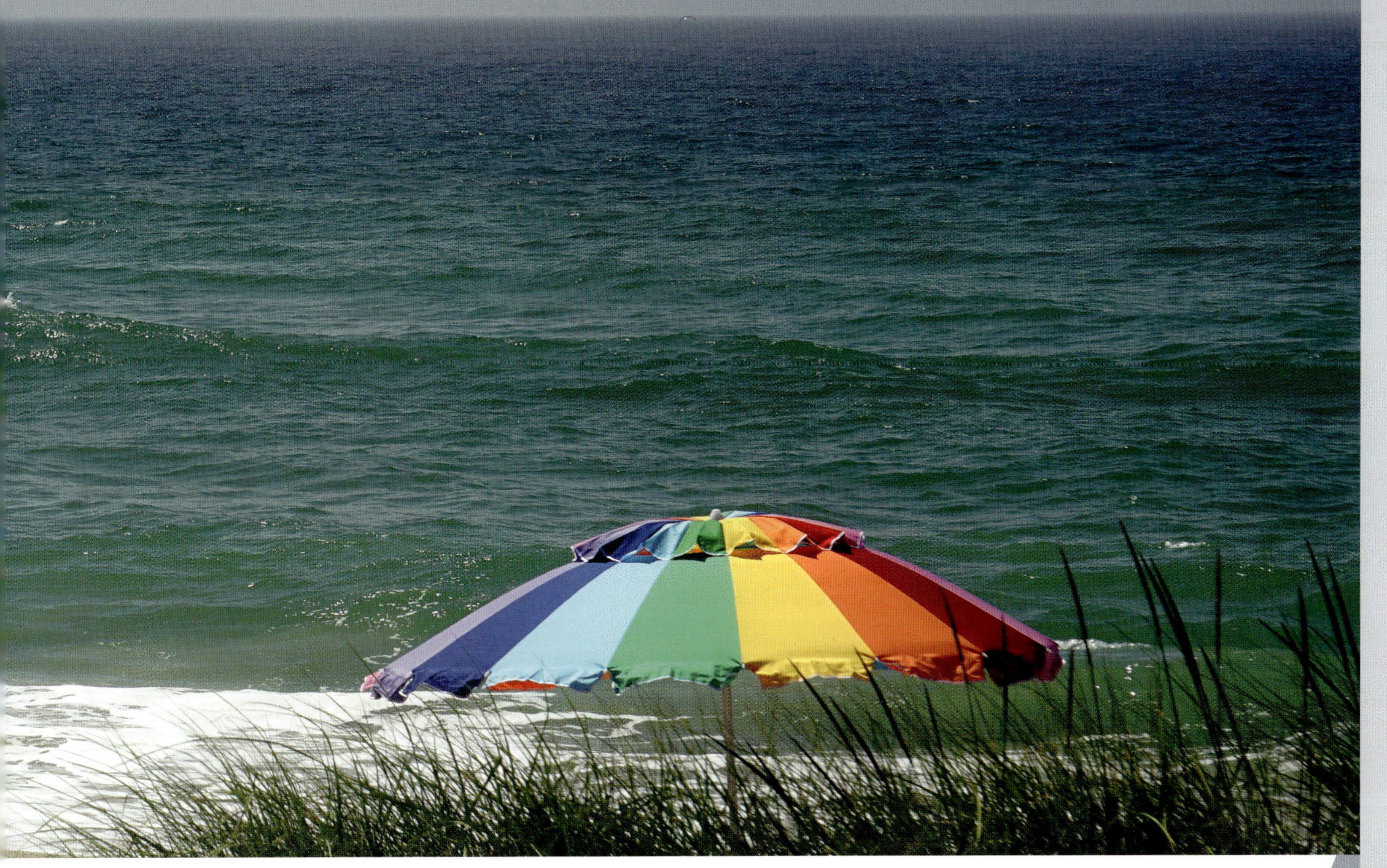

A bright umbrella on Madaket Beach.

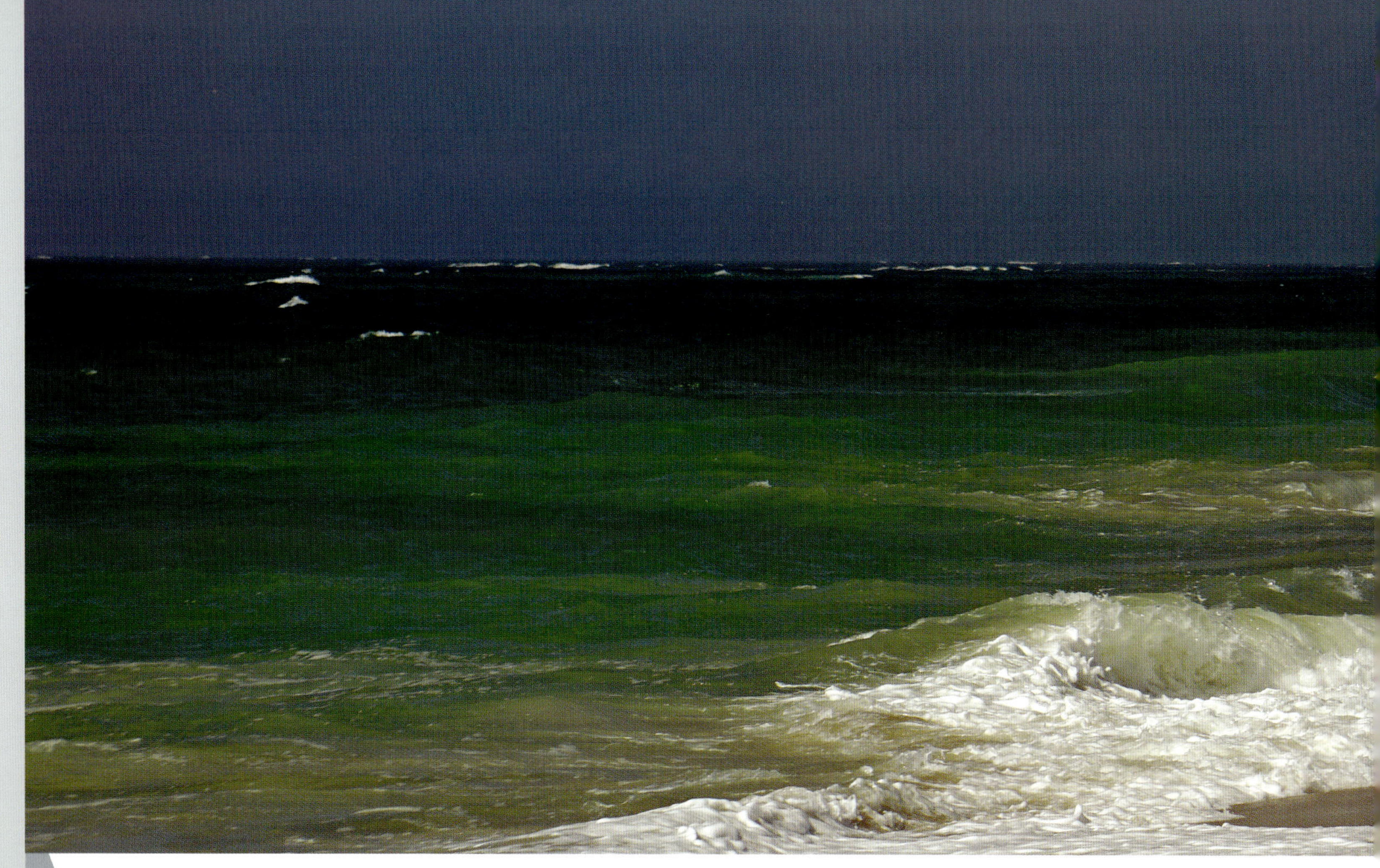

Waves from the Atlantic Ocean and walkers on Madaket Beach meet along the surf line.

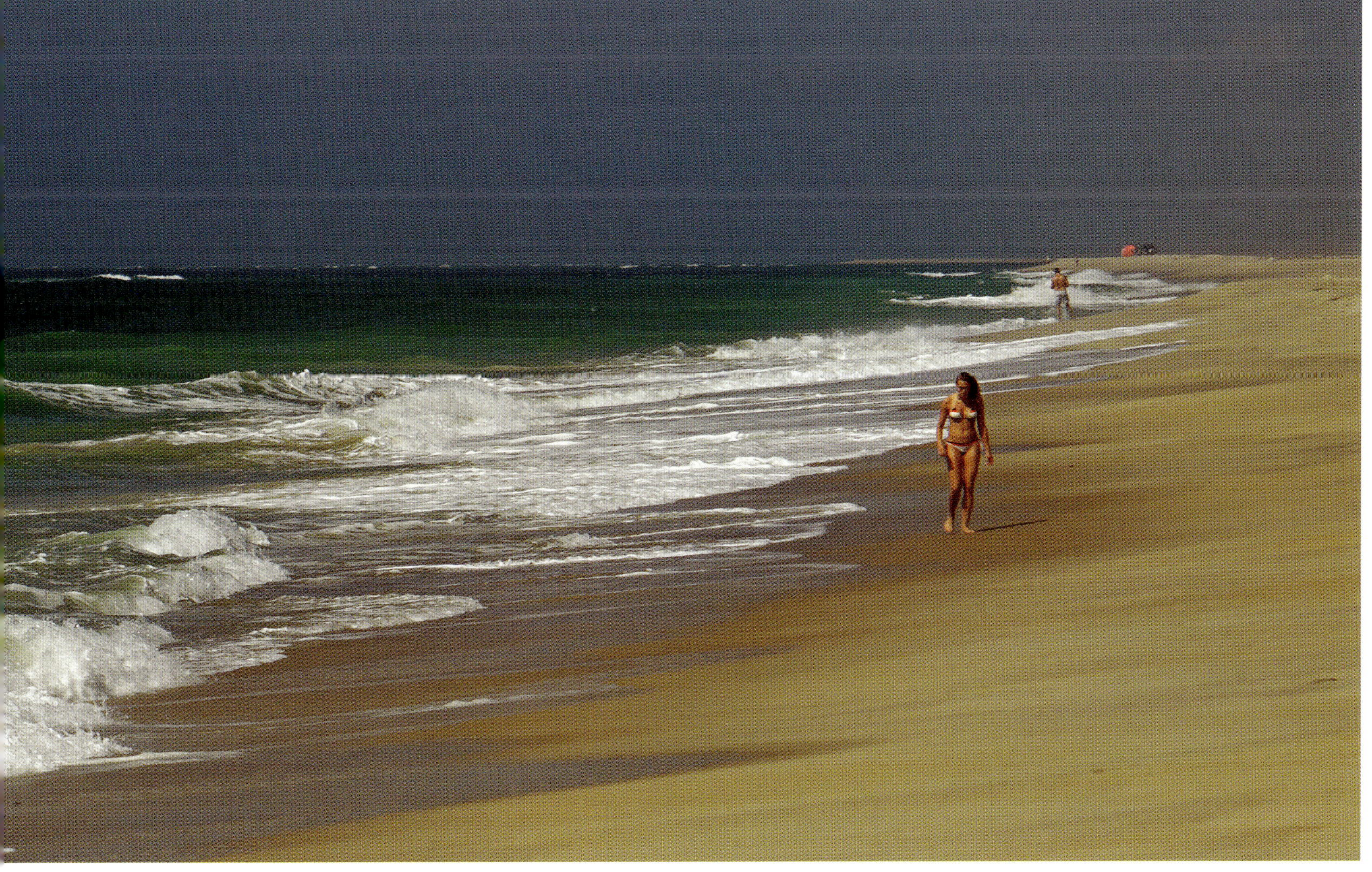

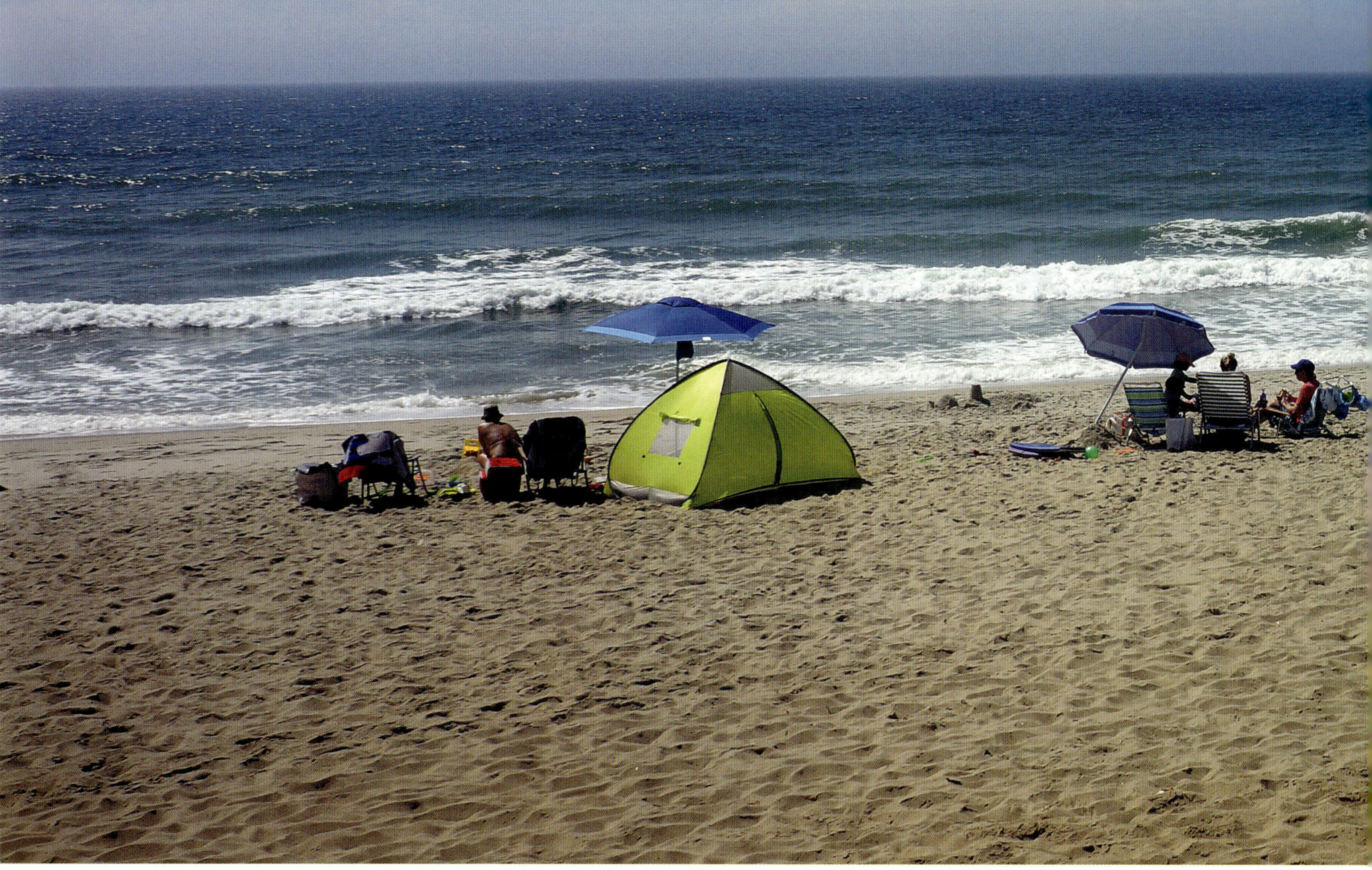

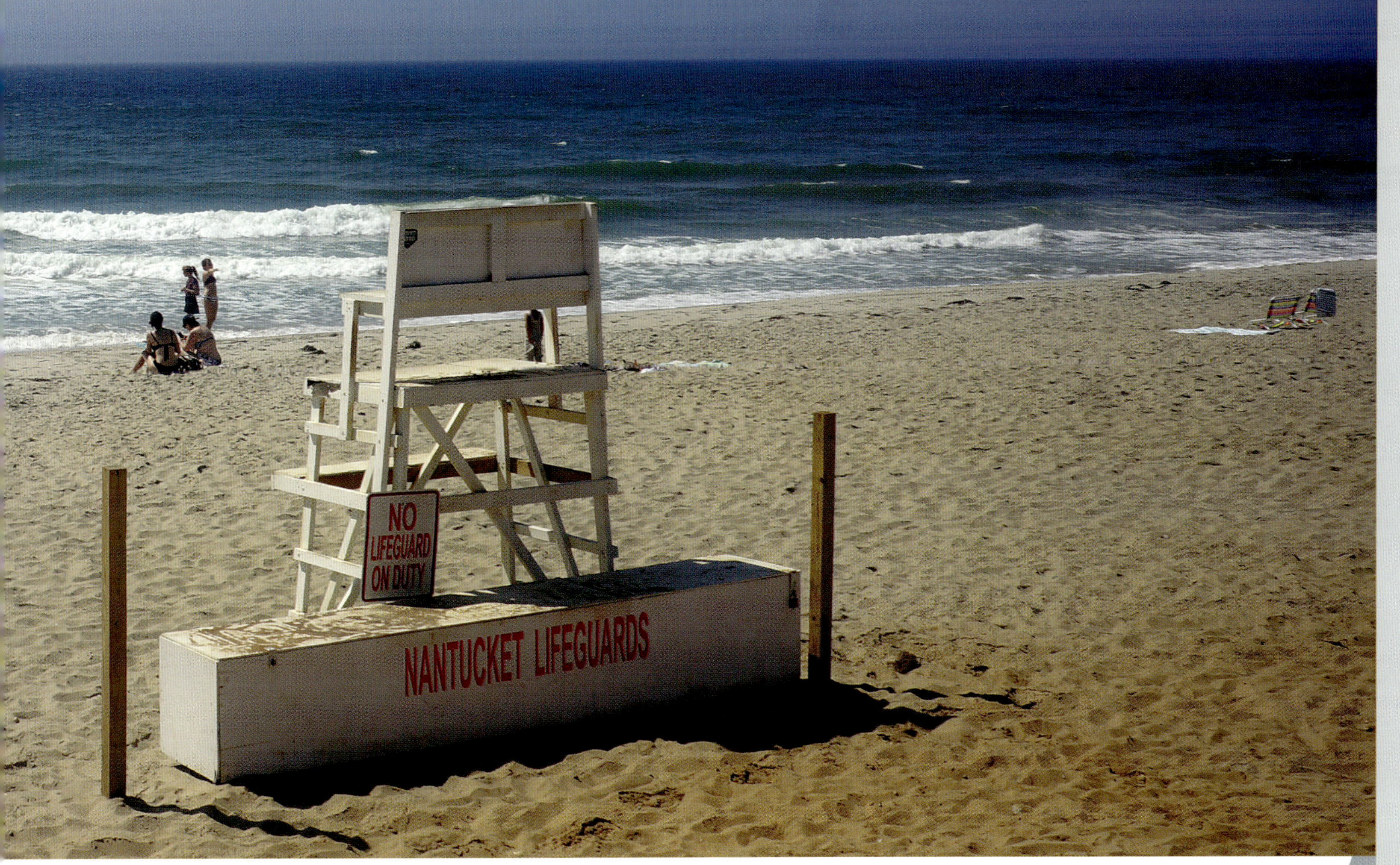

No lifeguard on duty at Cisco Beach.

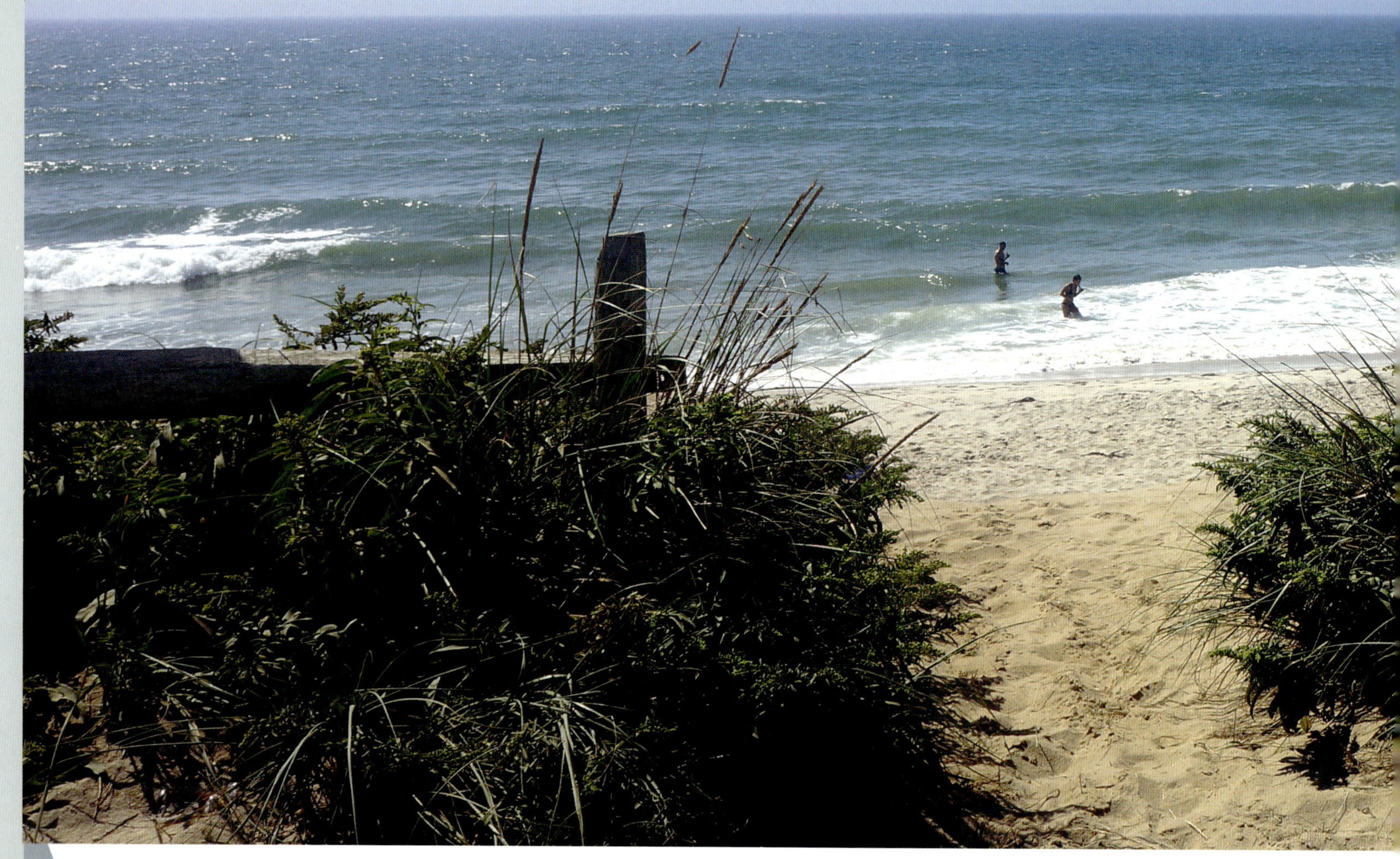

Enjoying the surf at Cisco Beach.

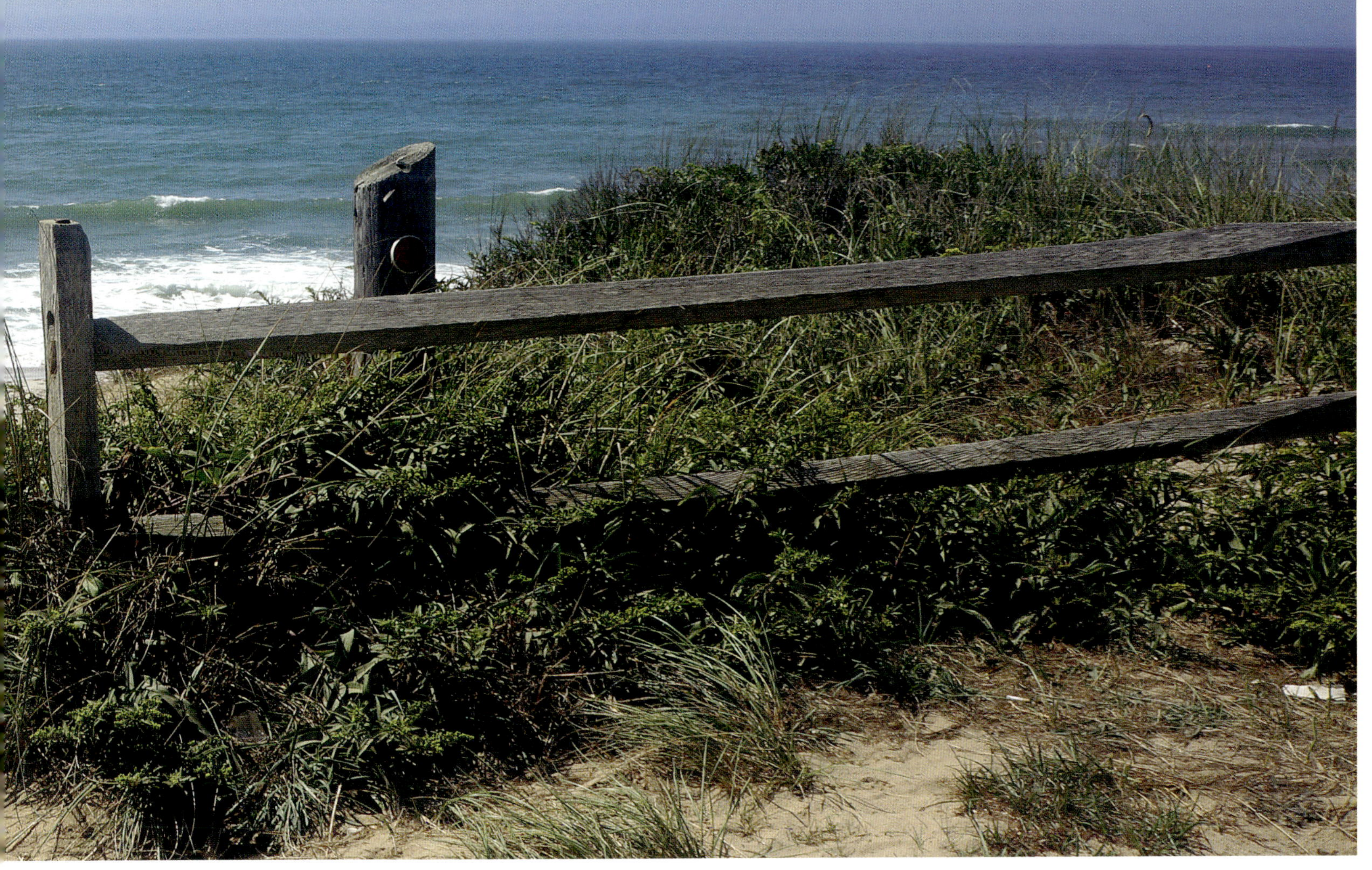

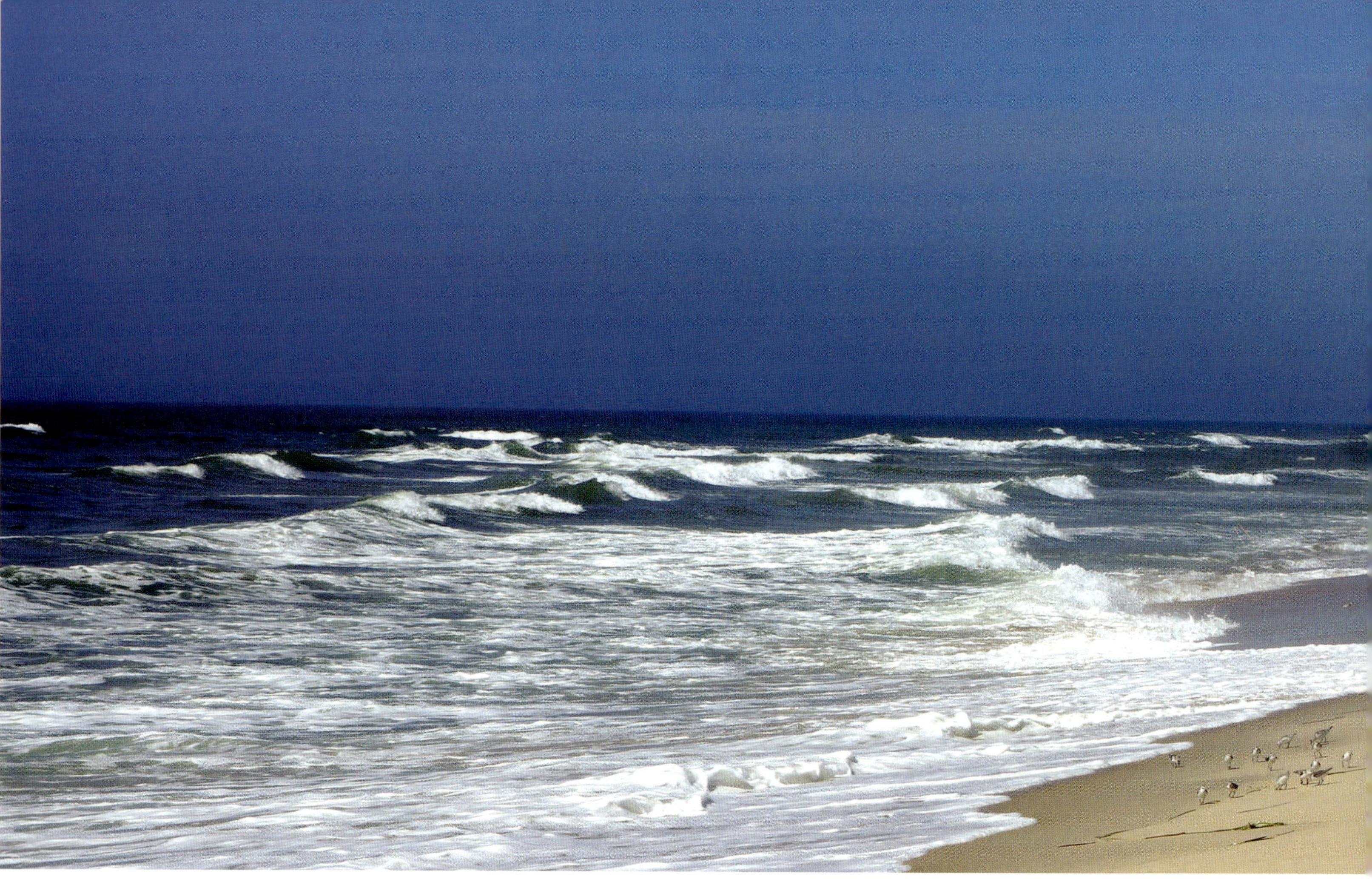

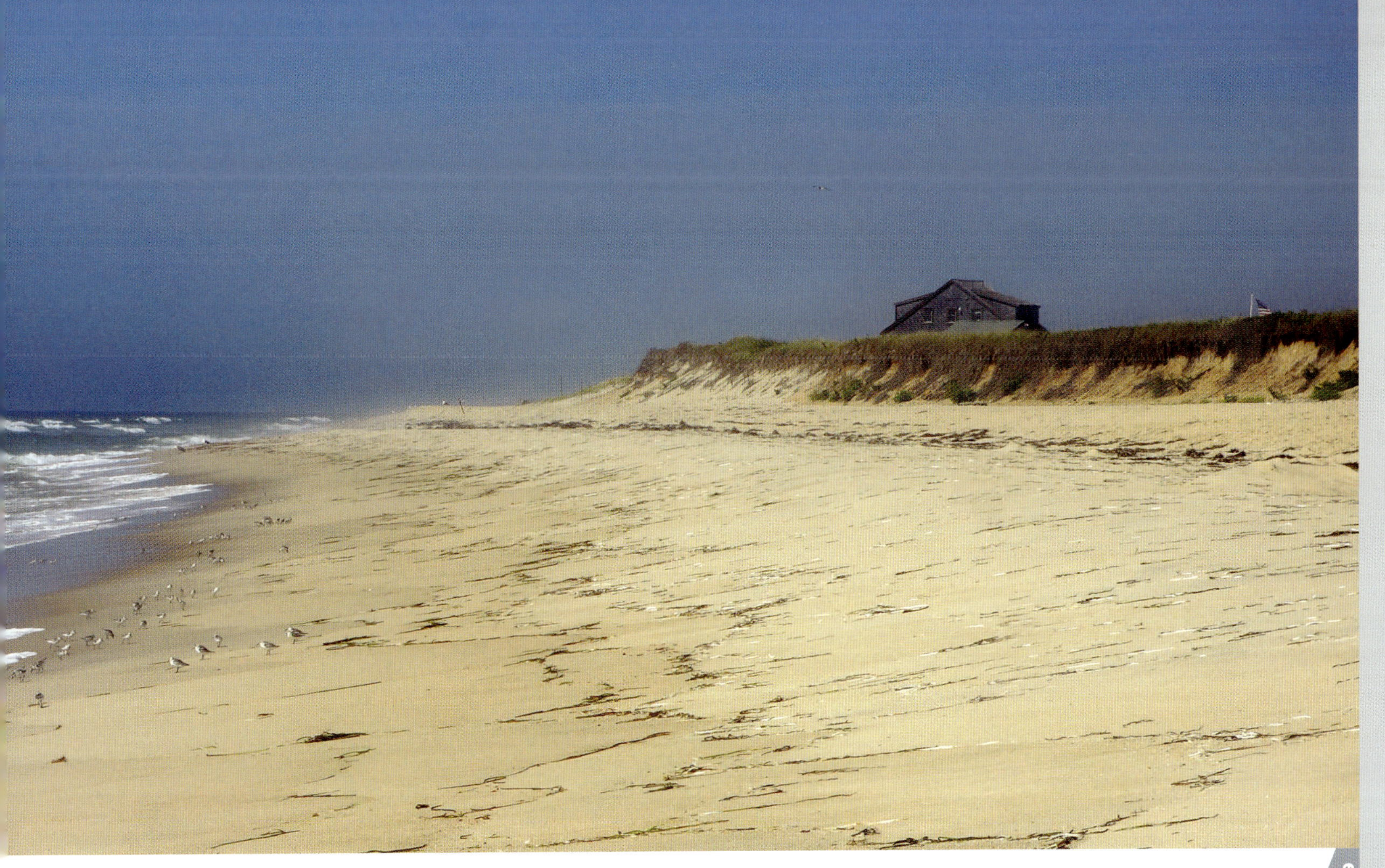

Shorebirds walk the surf just west of Cisco Beach.

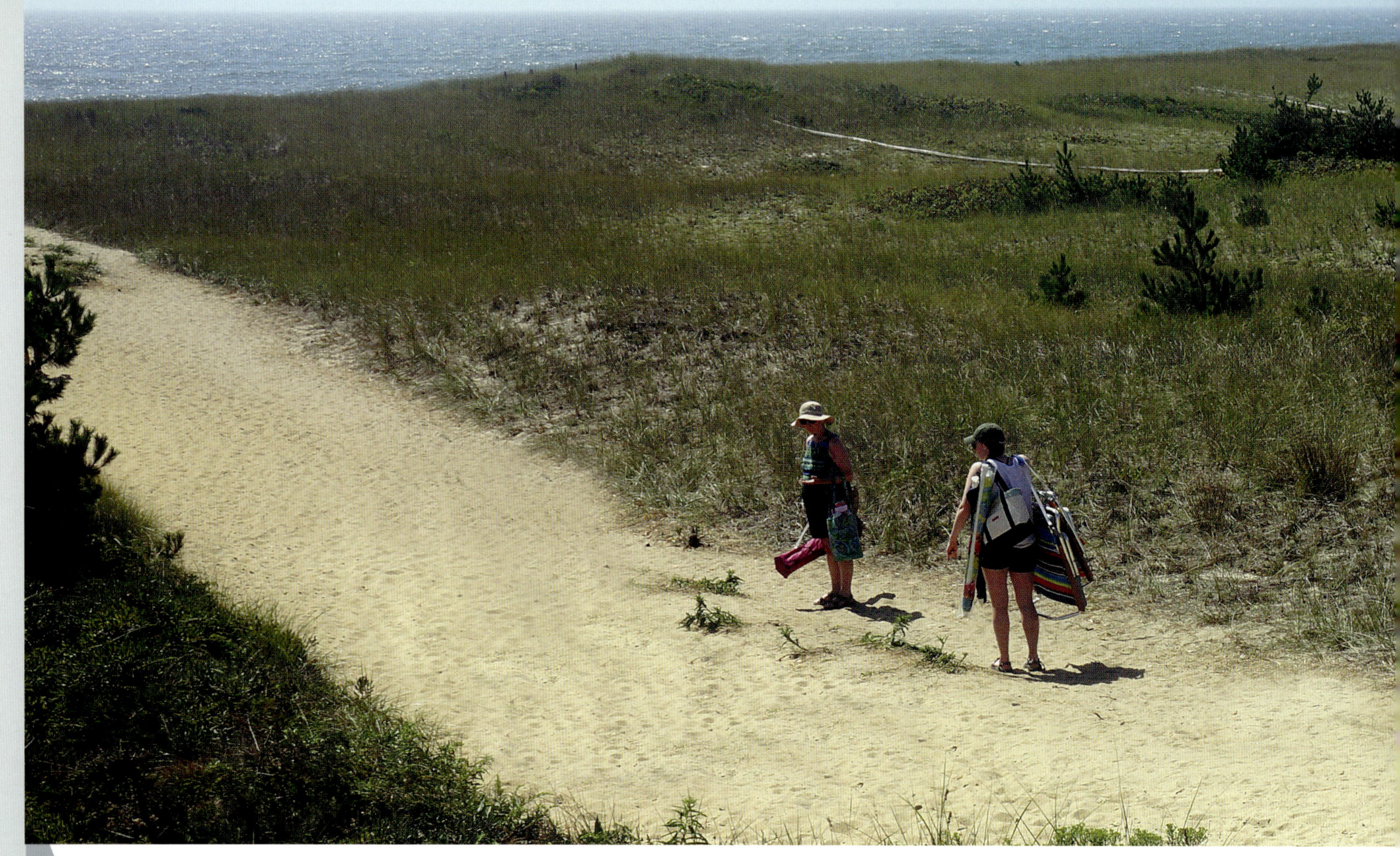

It's a short walk across the dunes to Surfside Beach.

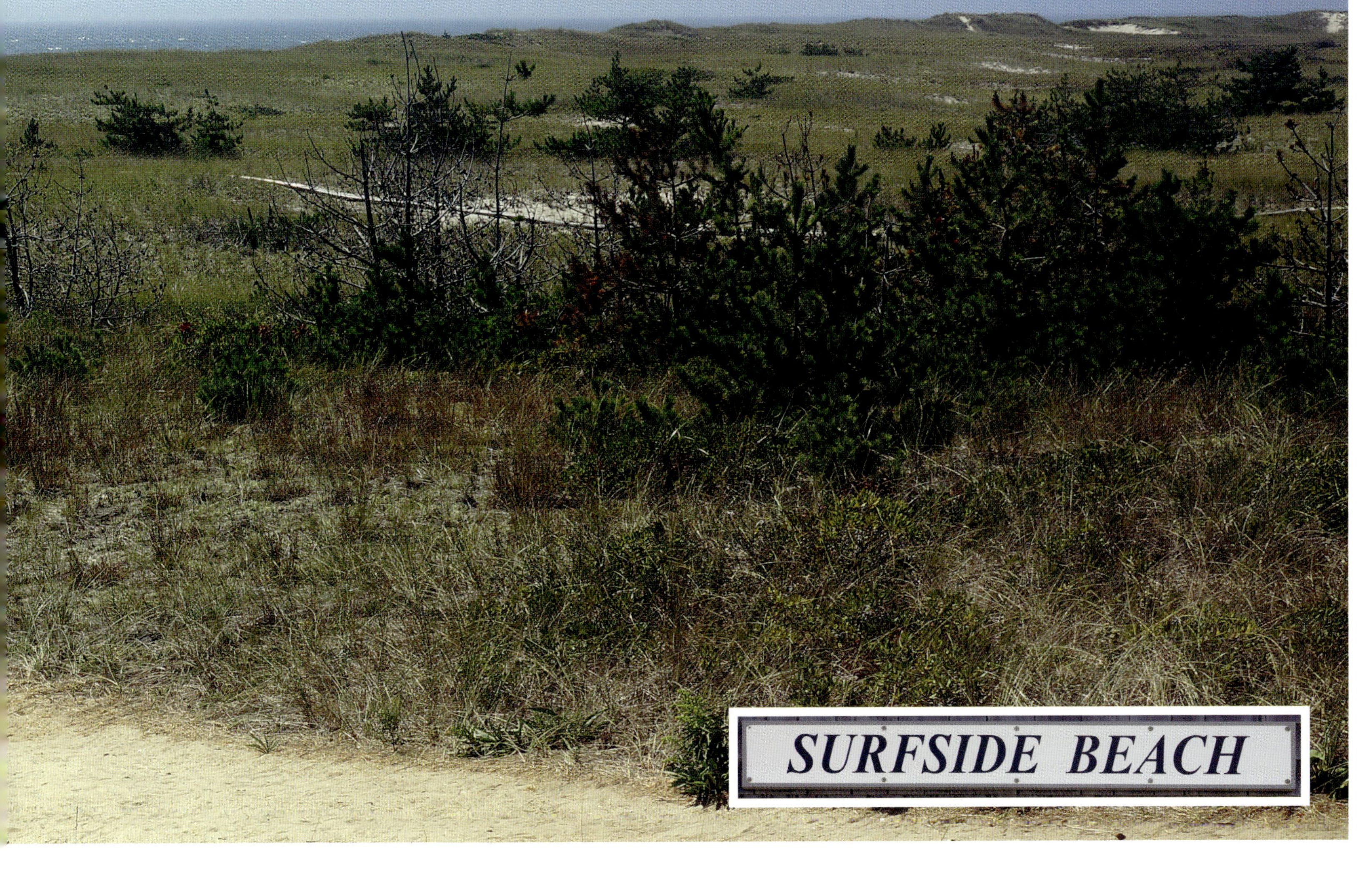
SURFSIDE BEACH

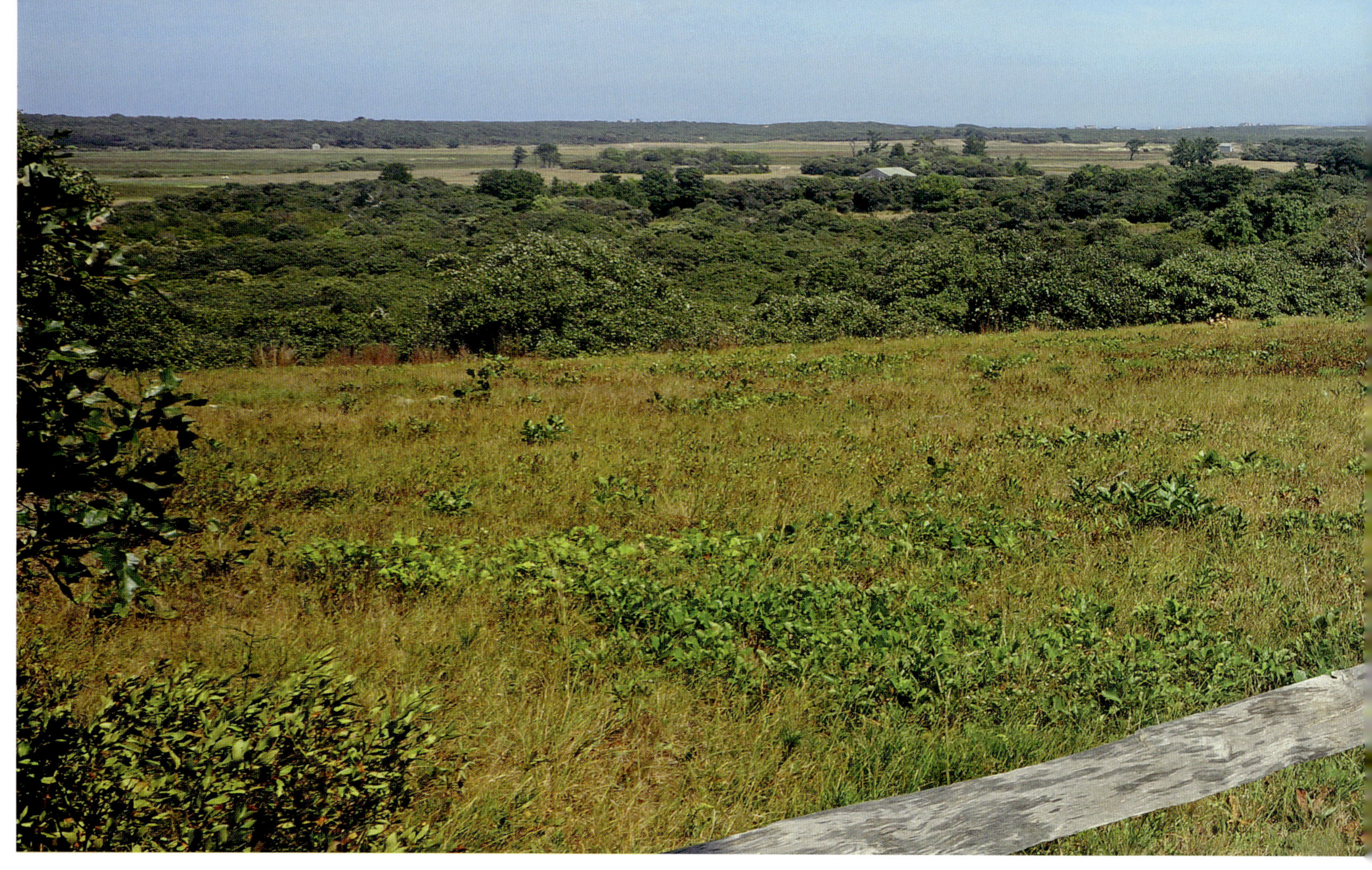

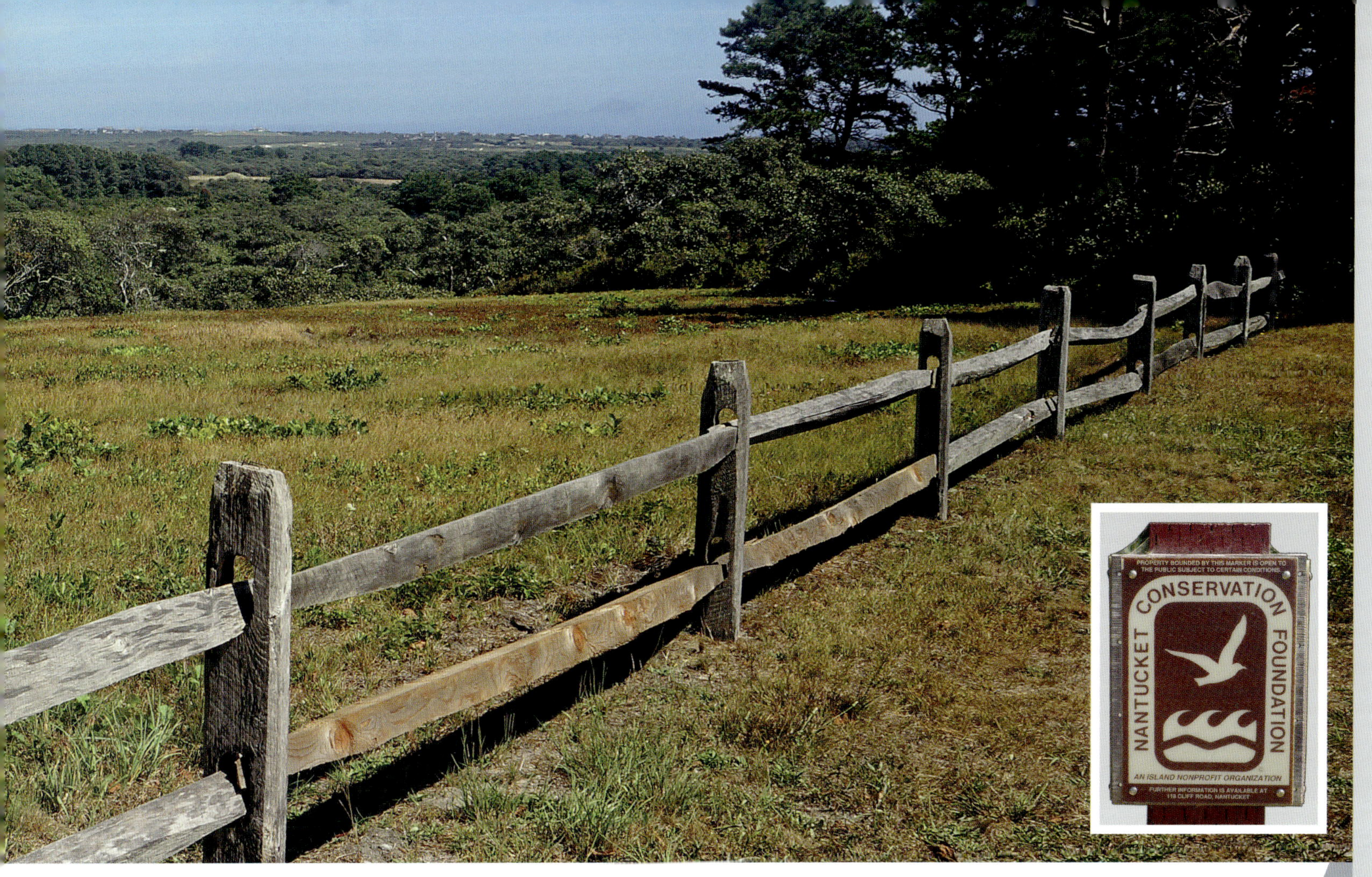

Seen from an overlook, the Middle Moors near Milestone Road comprise more than three thousand acres of conservation land.

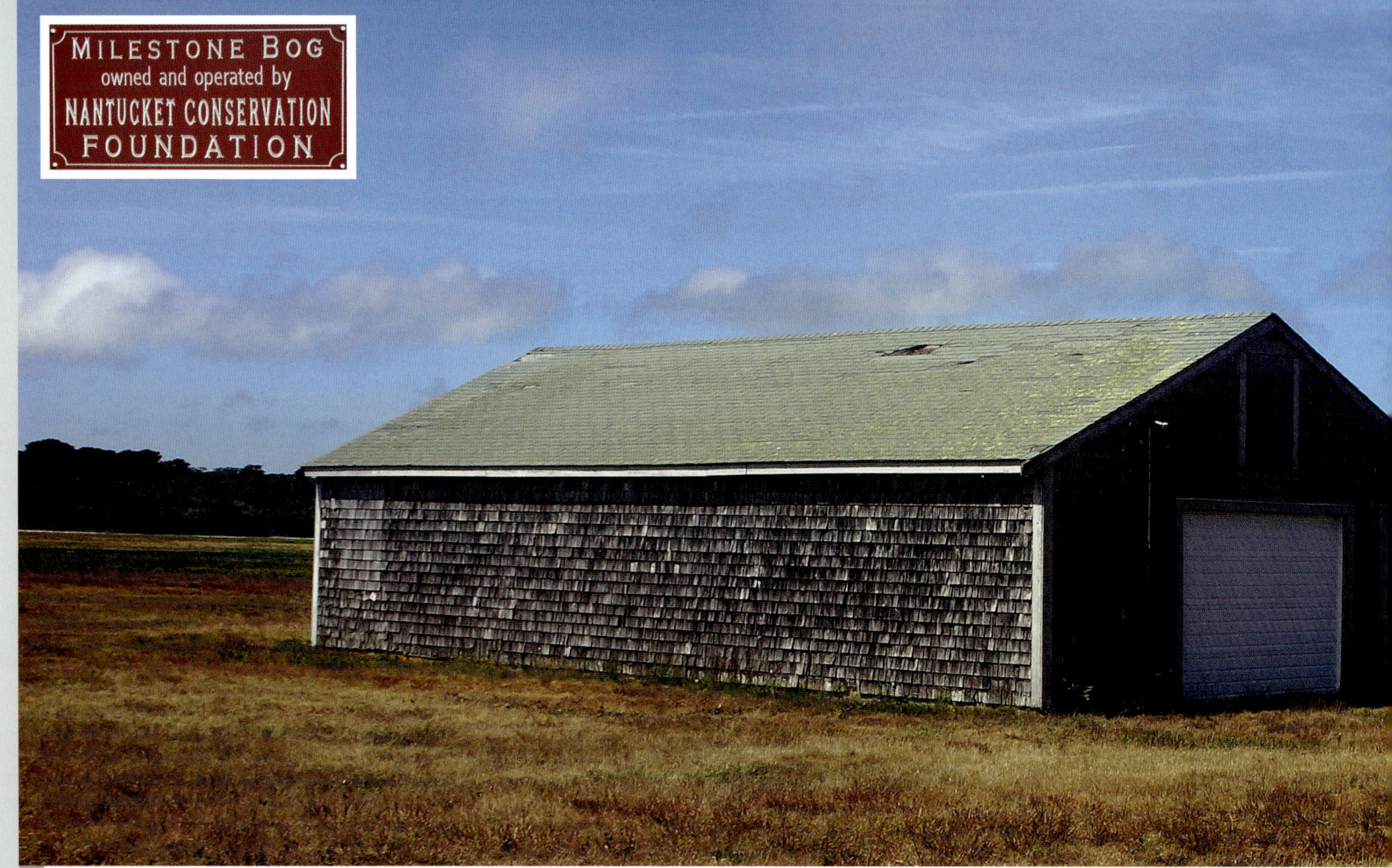

A view across the moors. The barn is used primarily during the cranberry season.

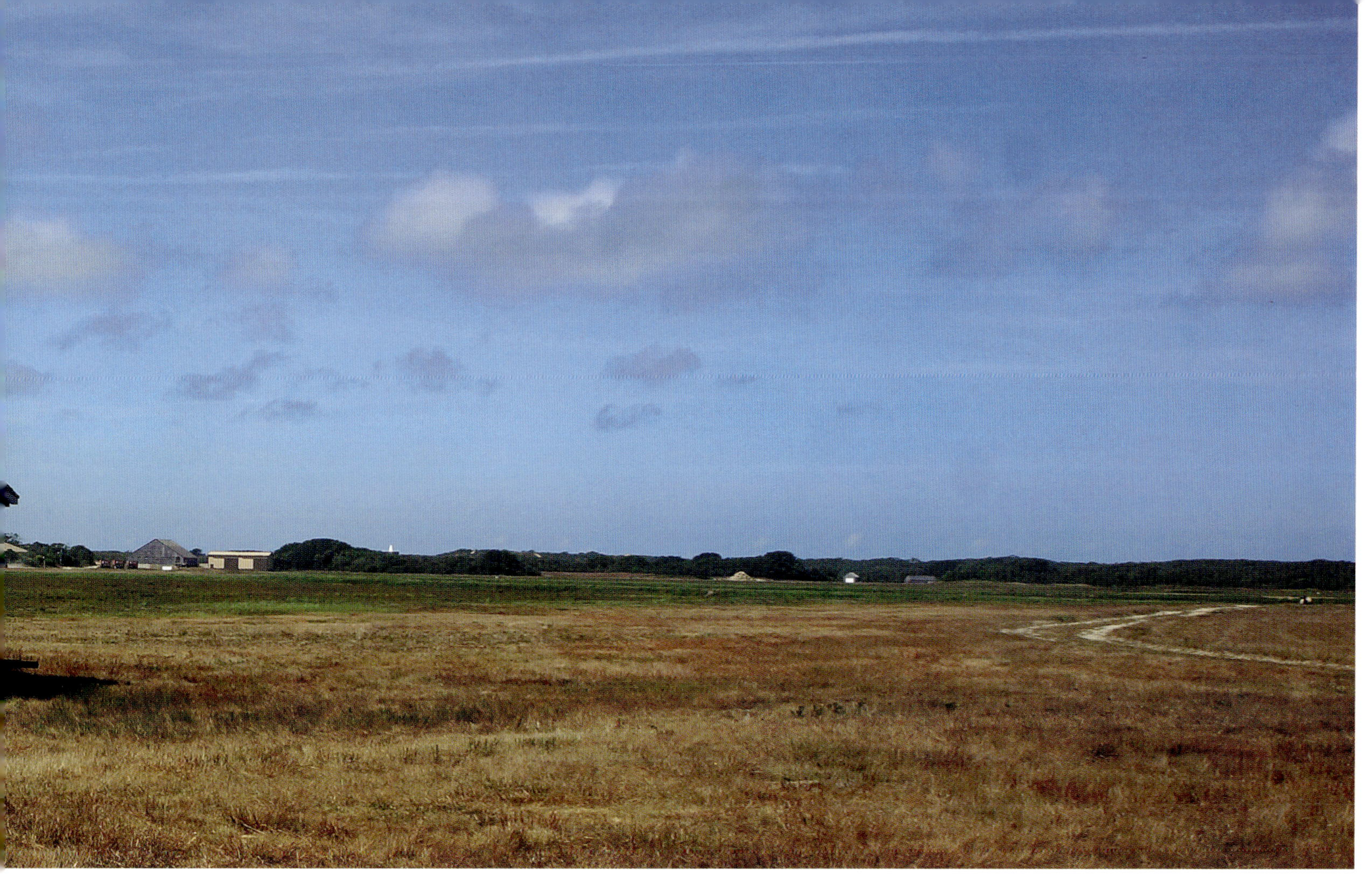

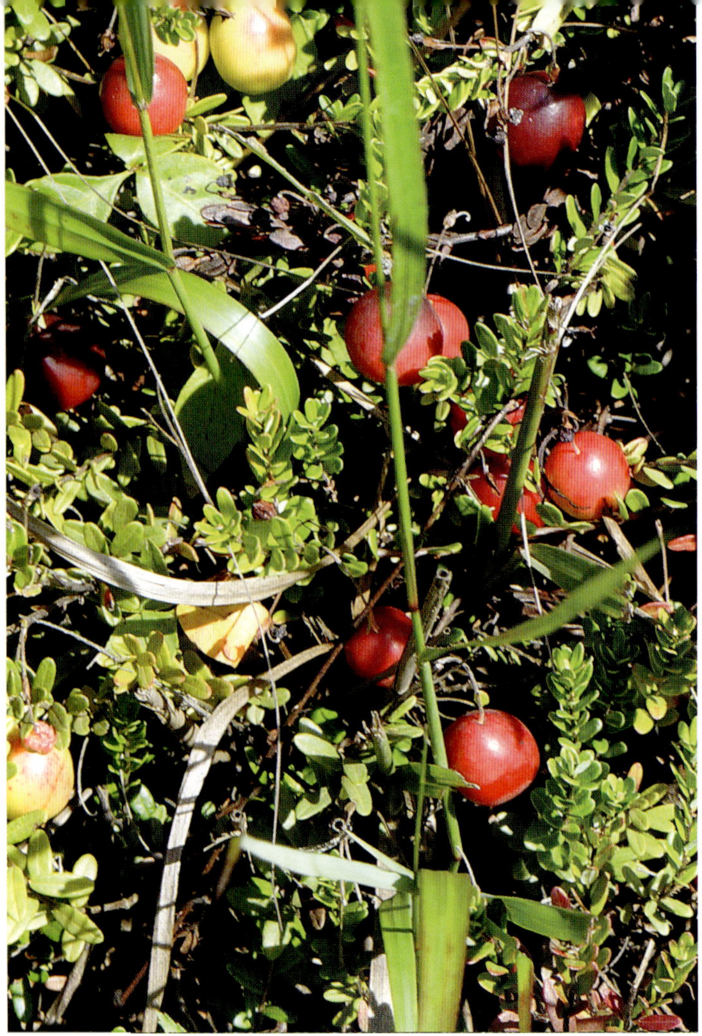

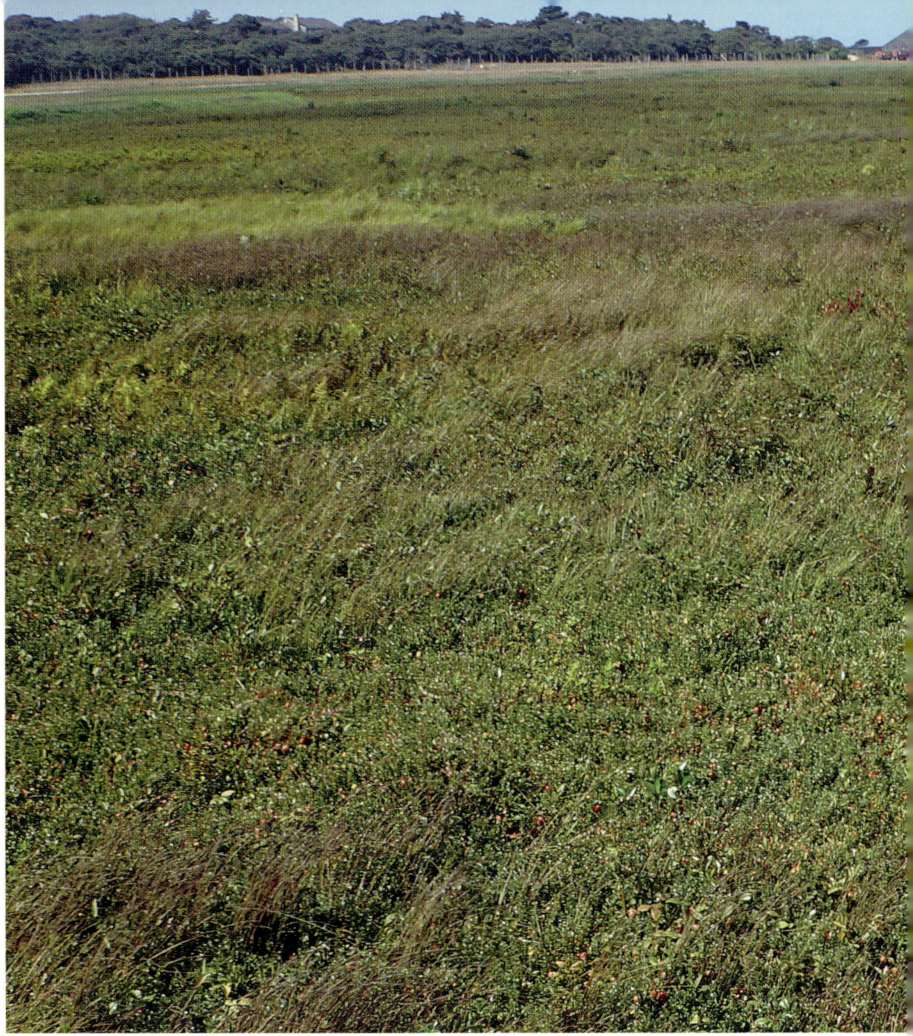

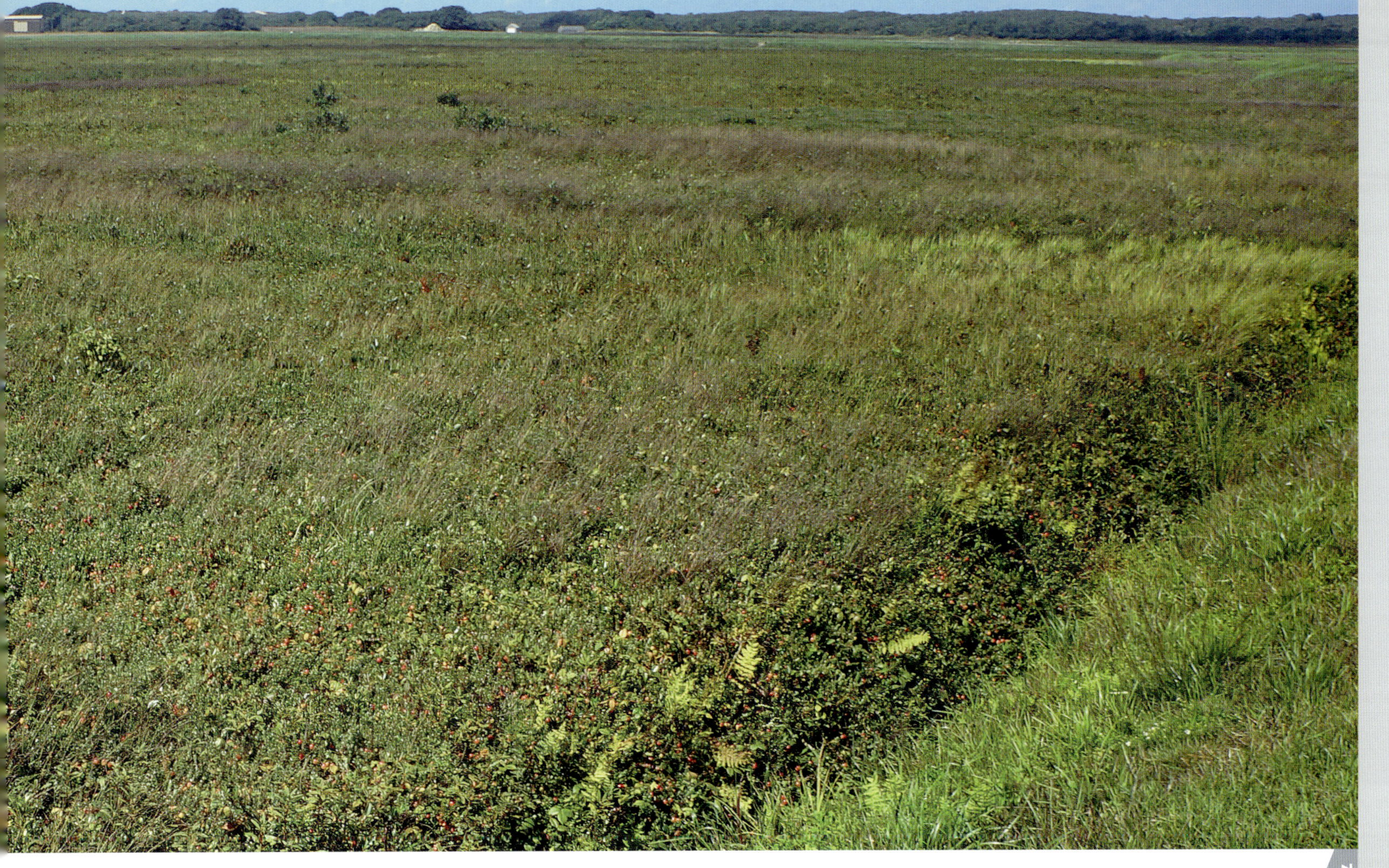

Acres of cranberry bogs produce vibrant red berries in the fall.

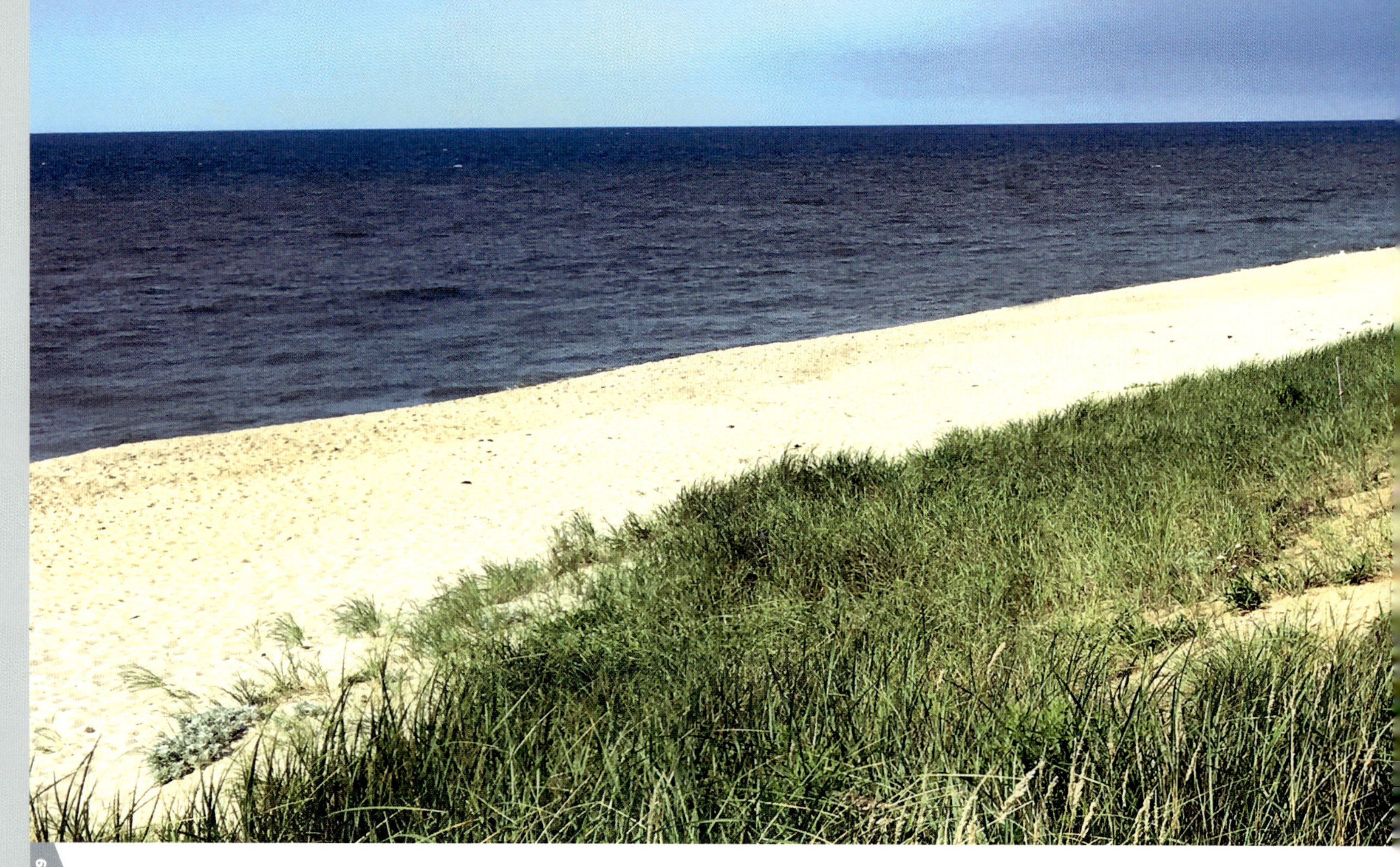

A quiet beach along the south shore.

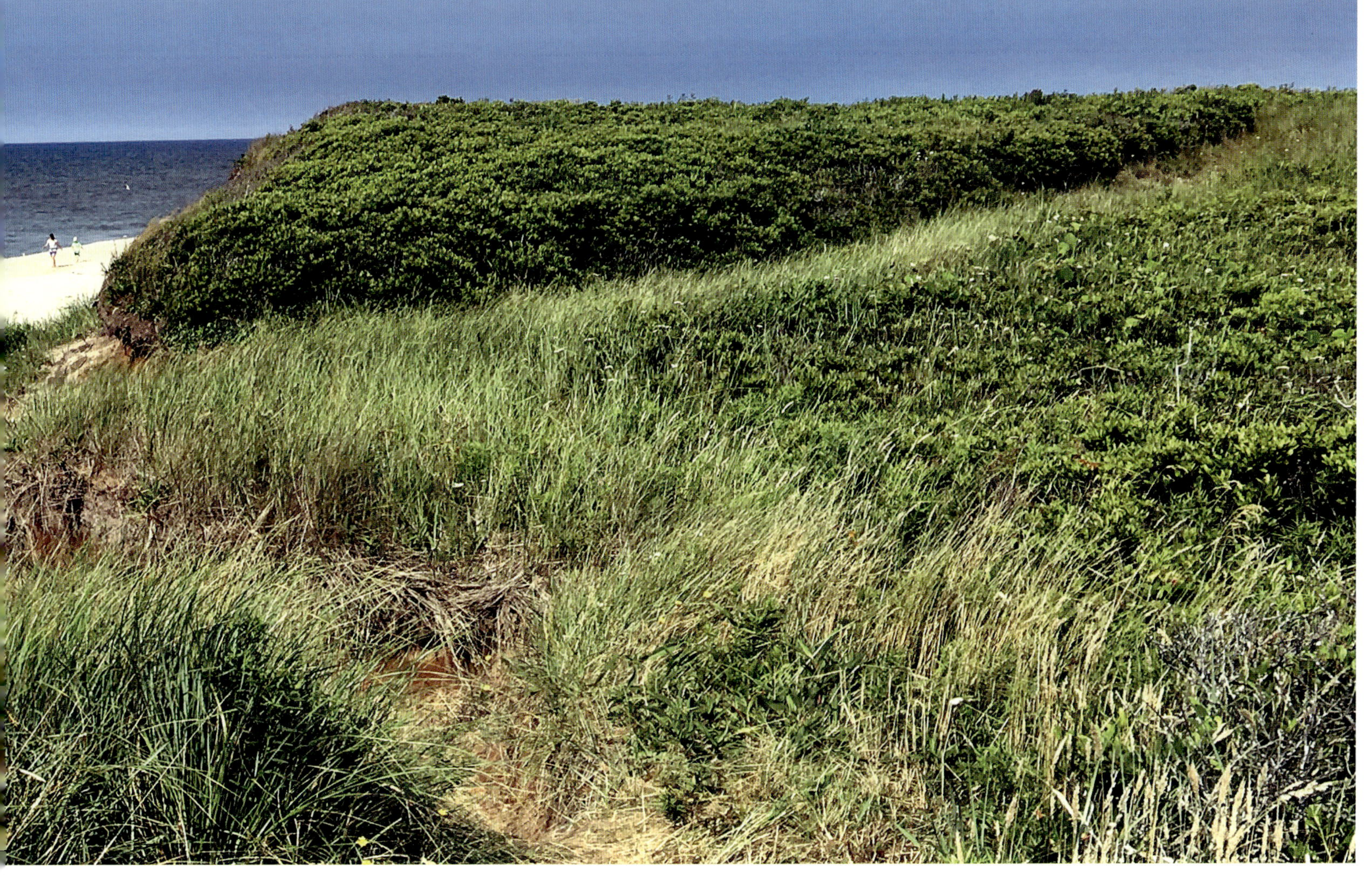

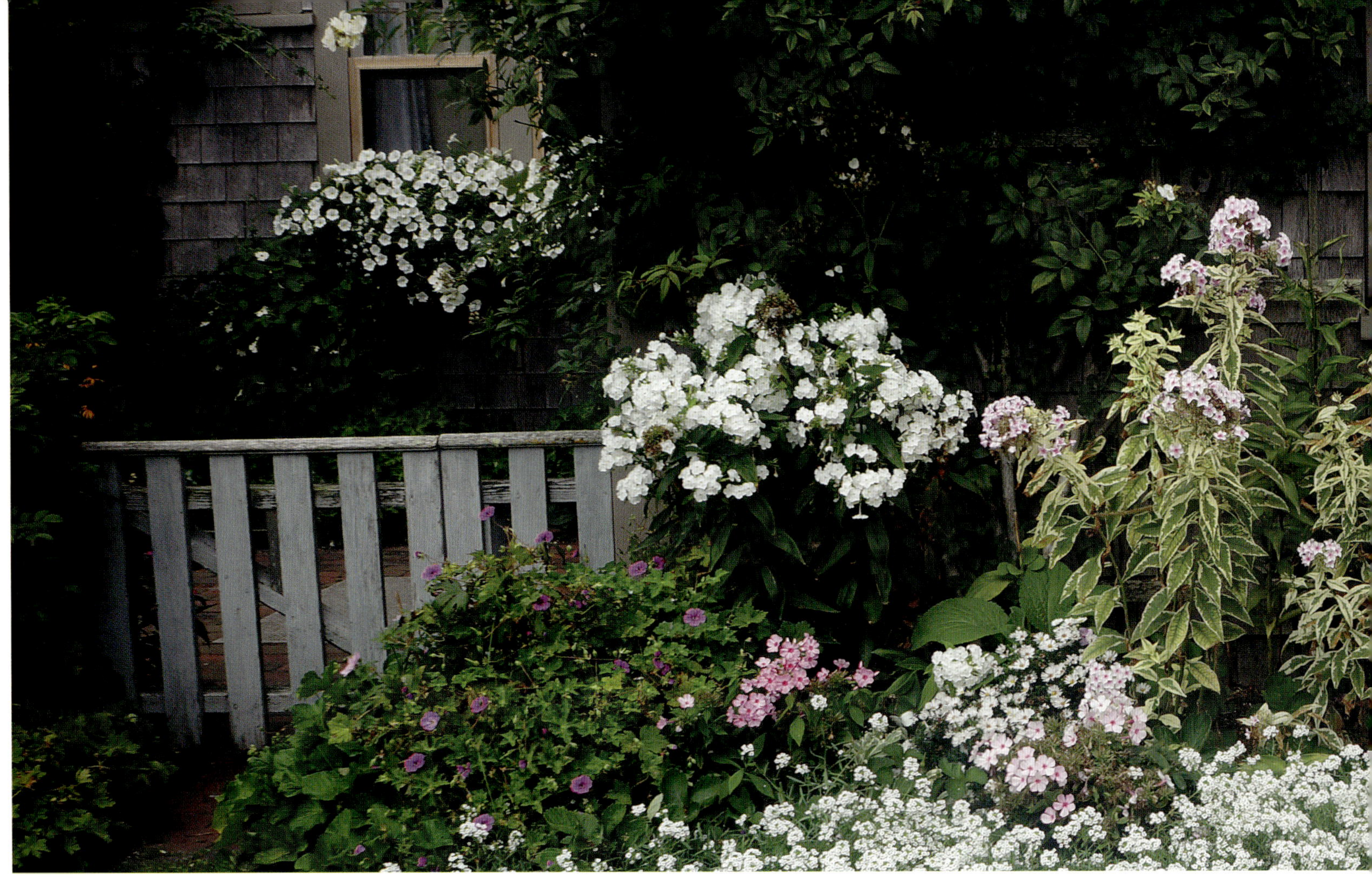

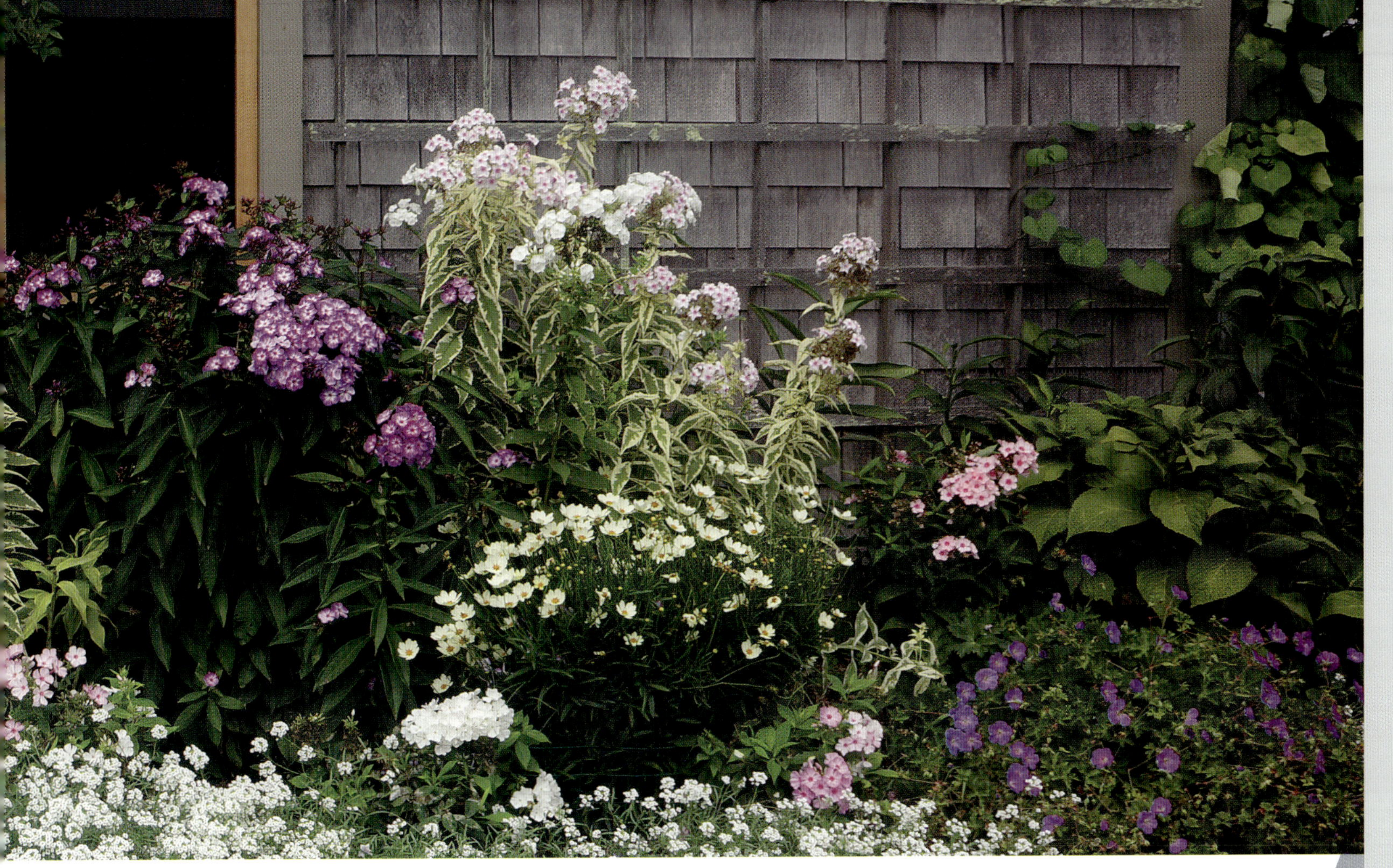

Flowers decorate the front yard of this cottage in Siasconset.

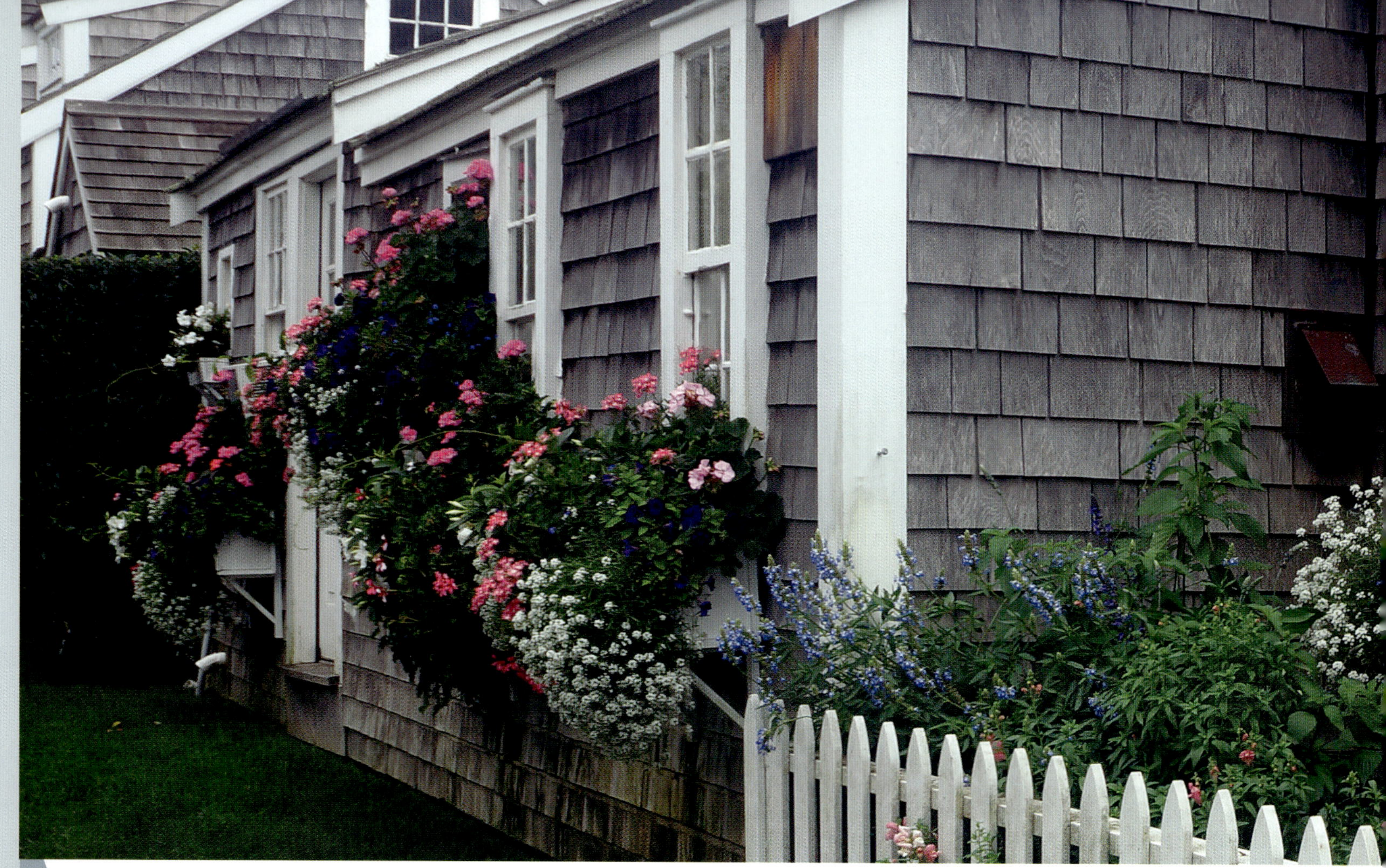

Window boxes brighten this cottage.

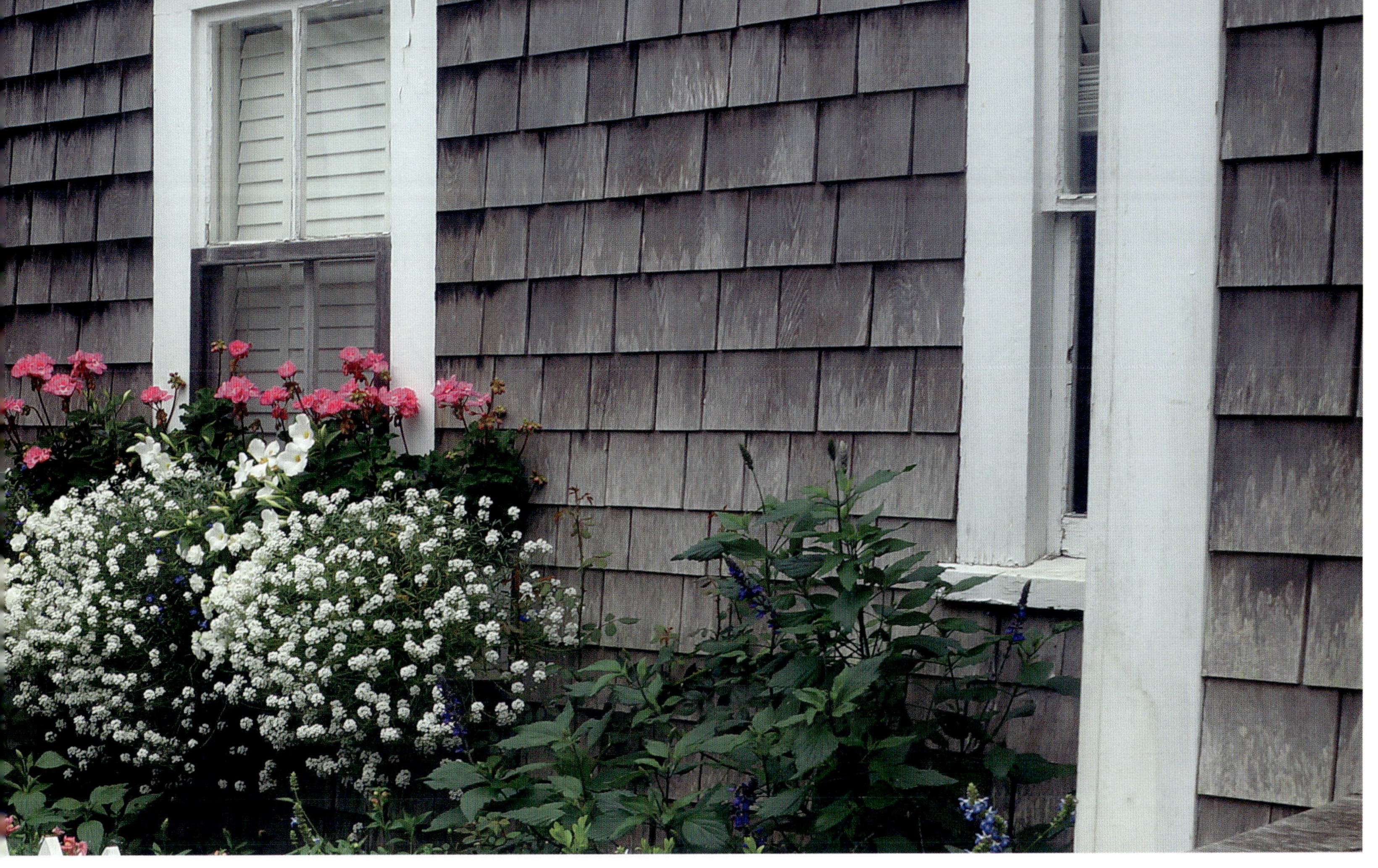

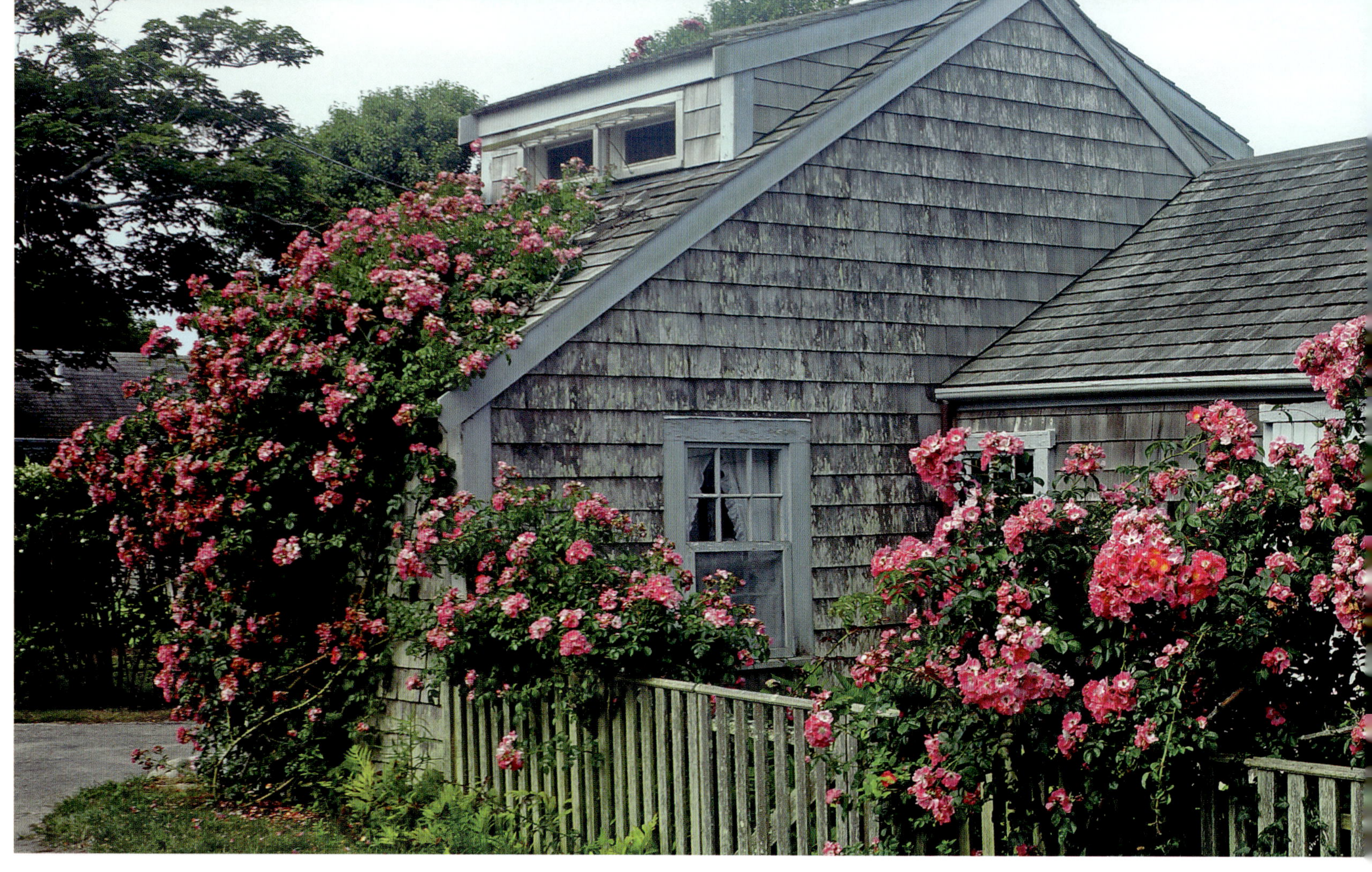

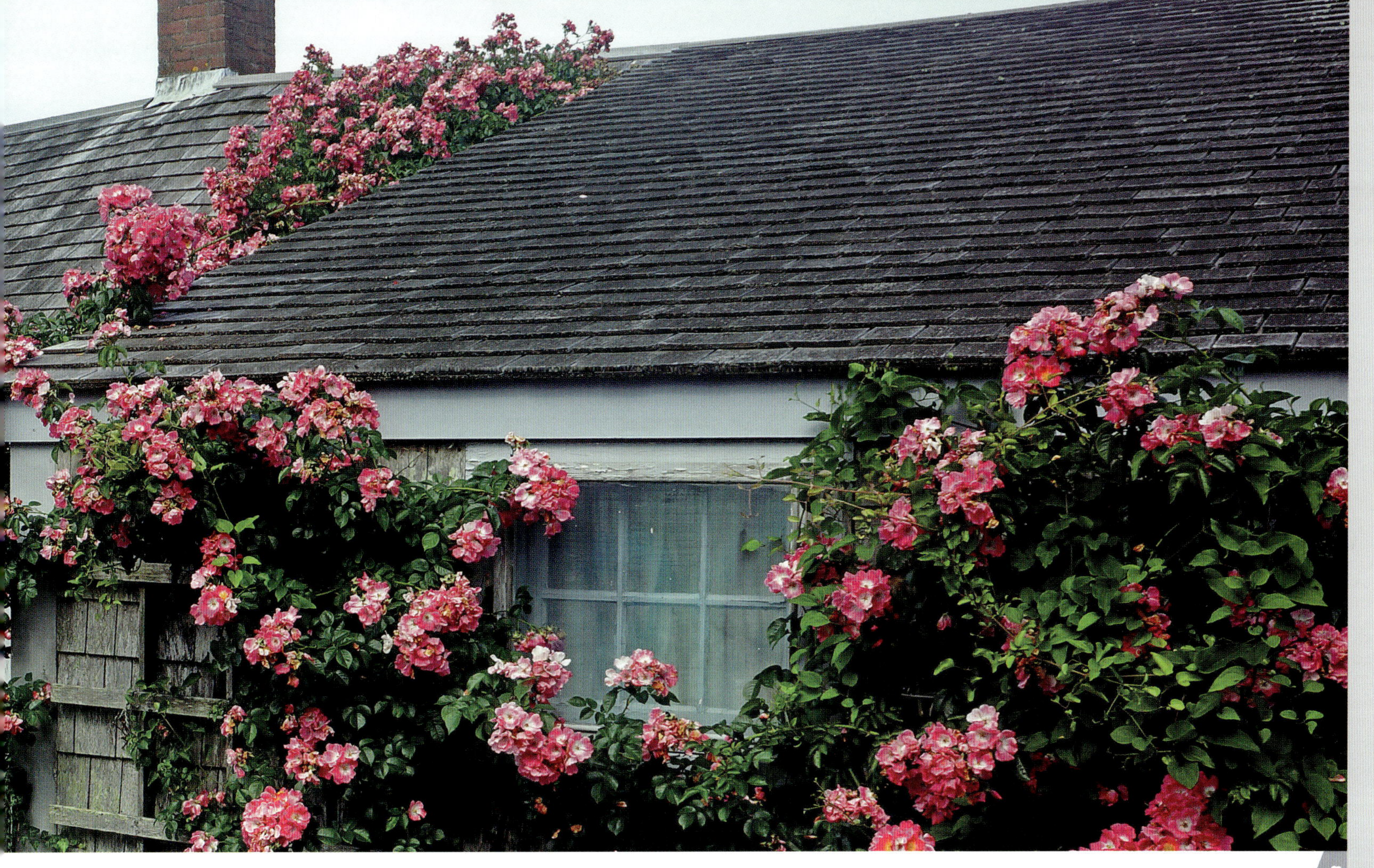

Siasconset quietly hosts many charming homes.

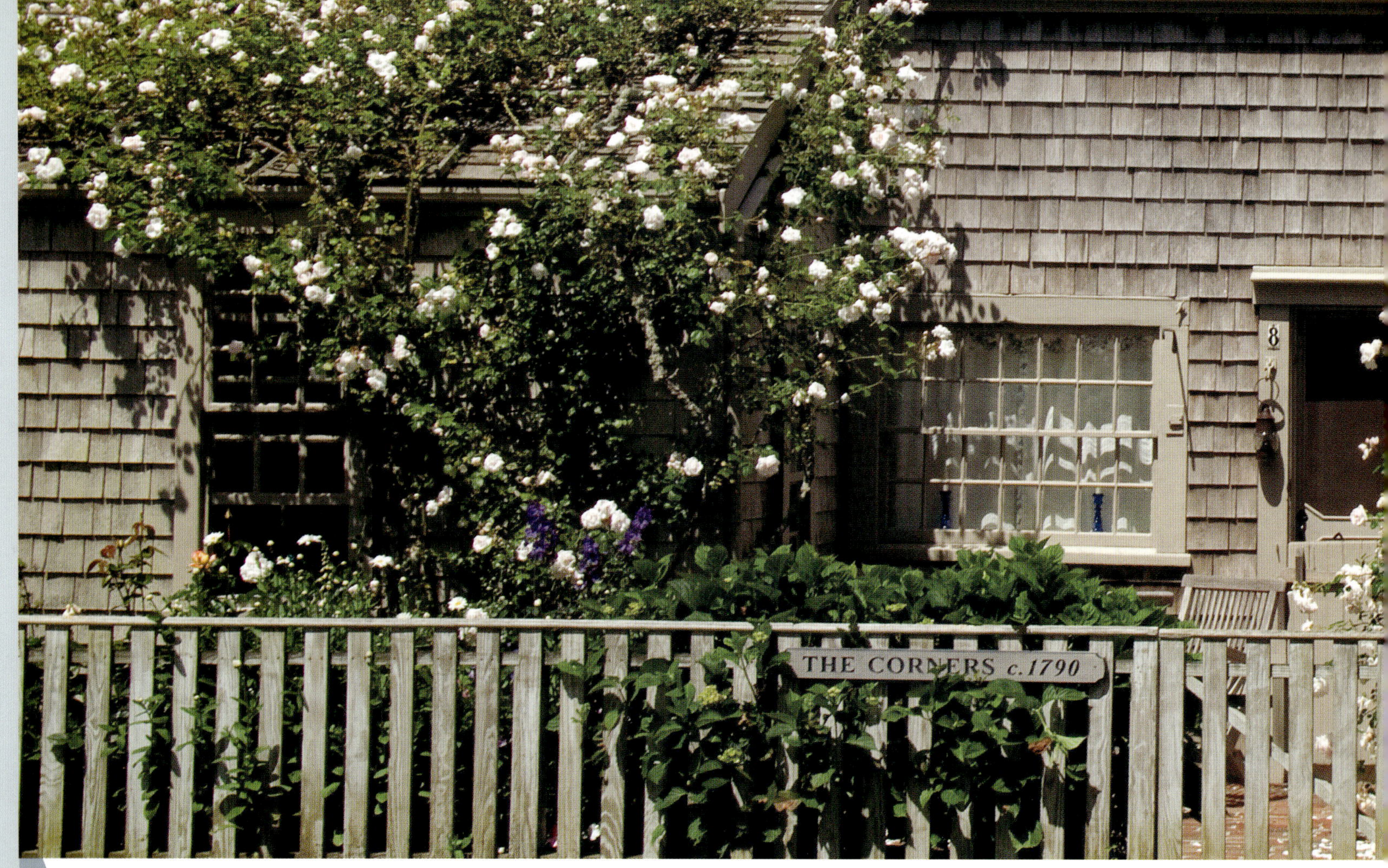

White and red roses cover an almost-hidden cottage.

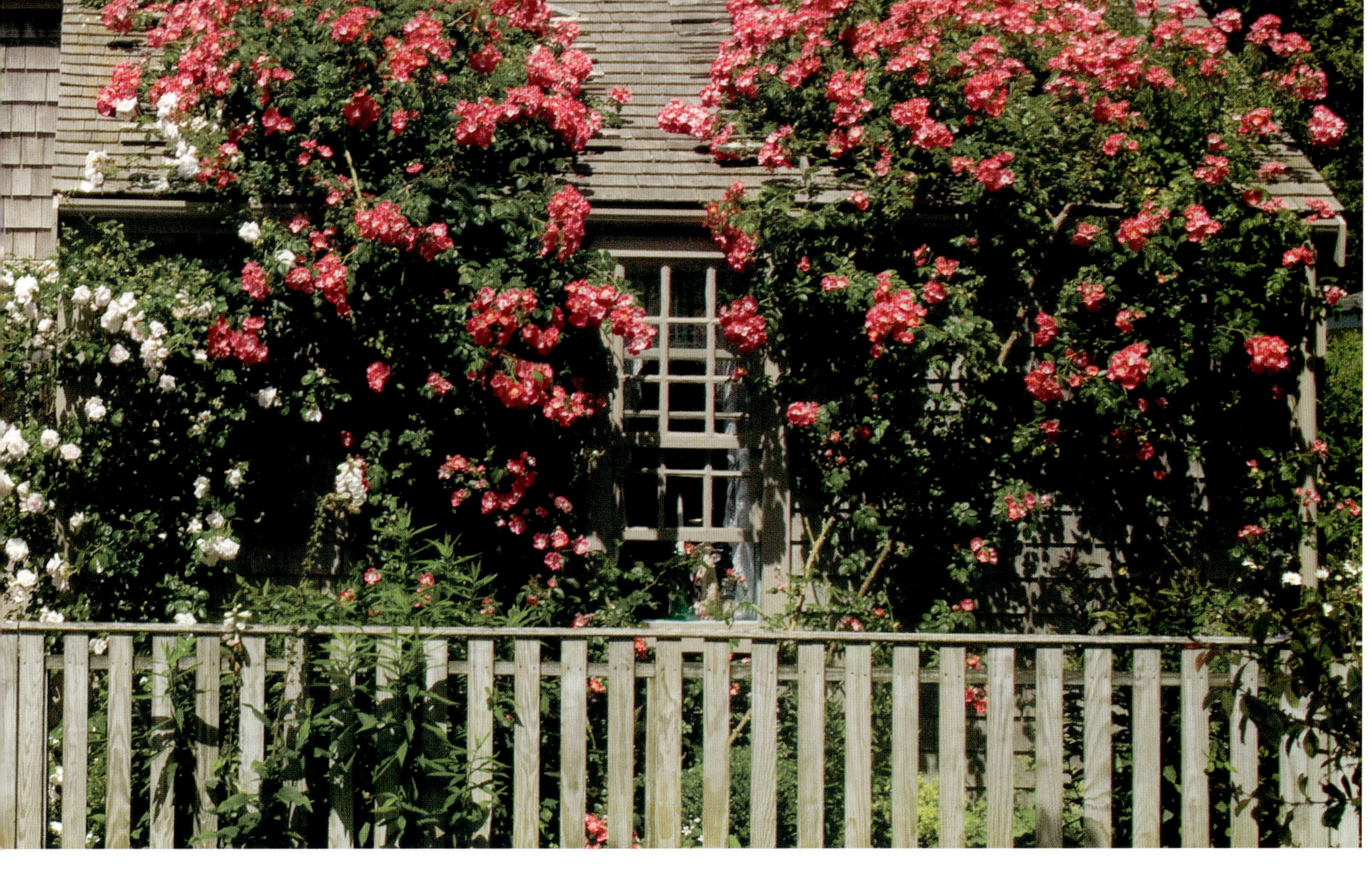

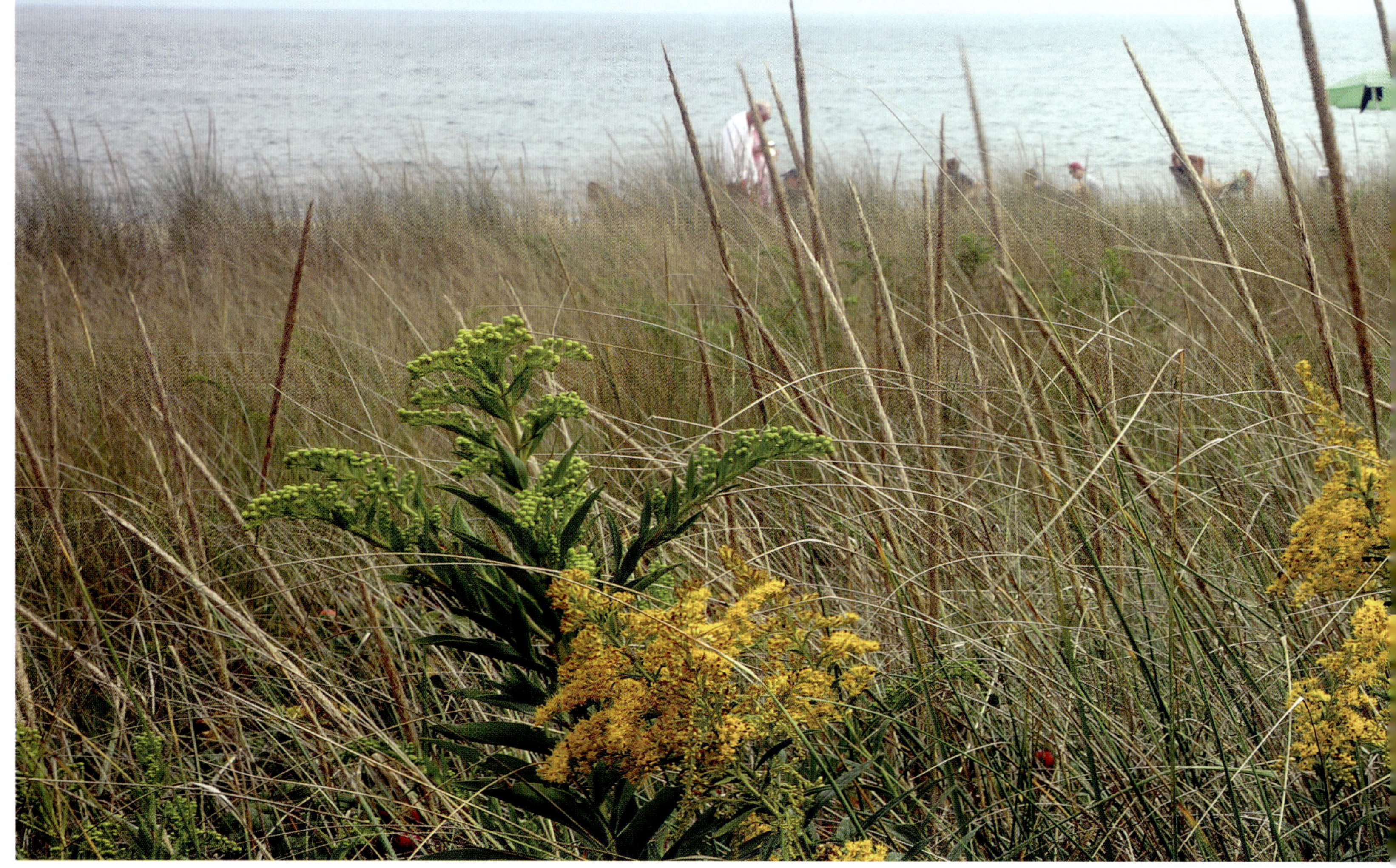

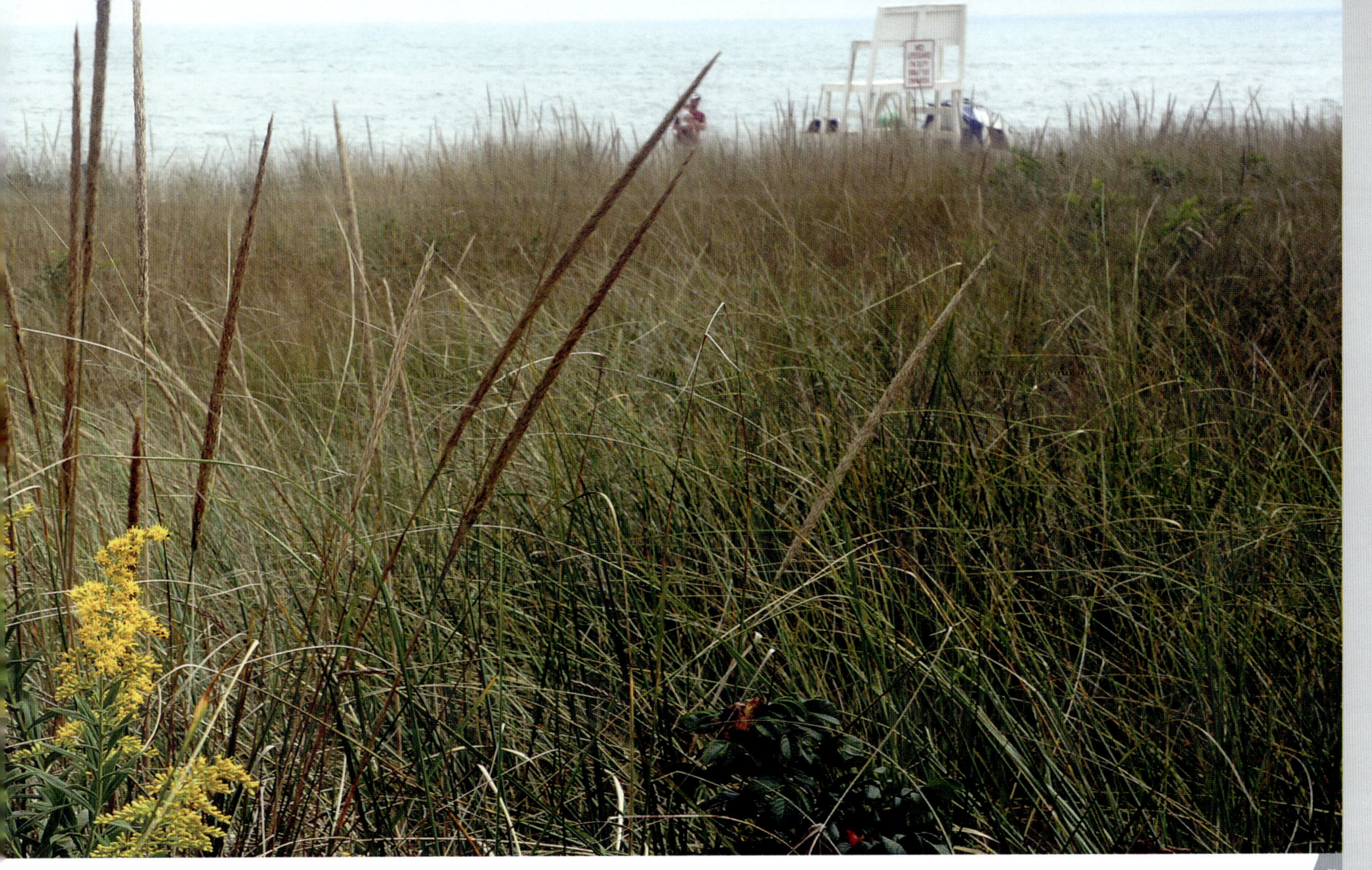

Siasconset Beach, on the Atlantic Ocean, is just beyond the grass-covered dunes.

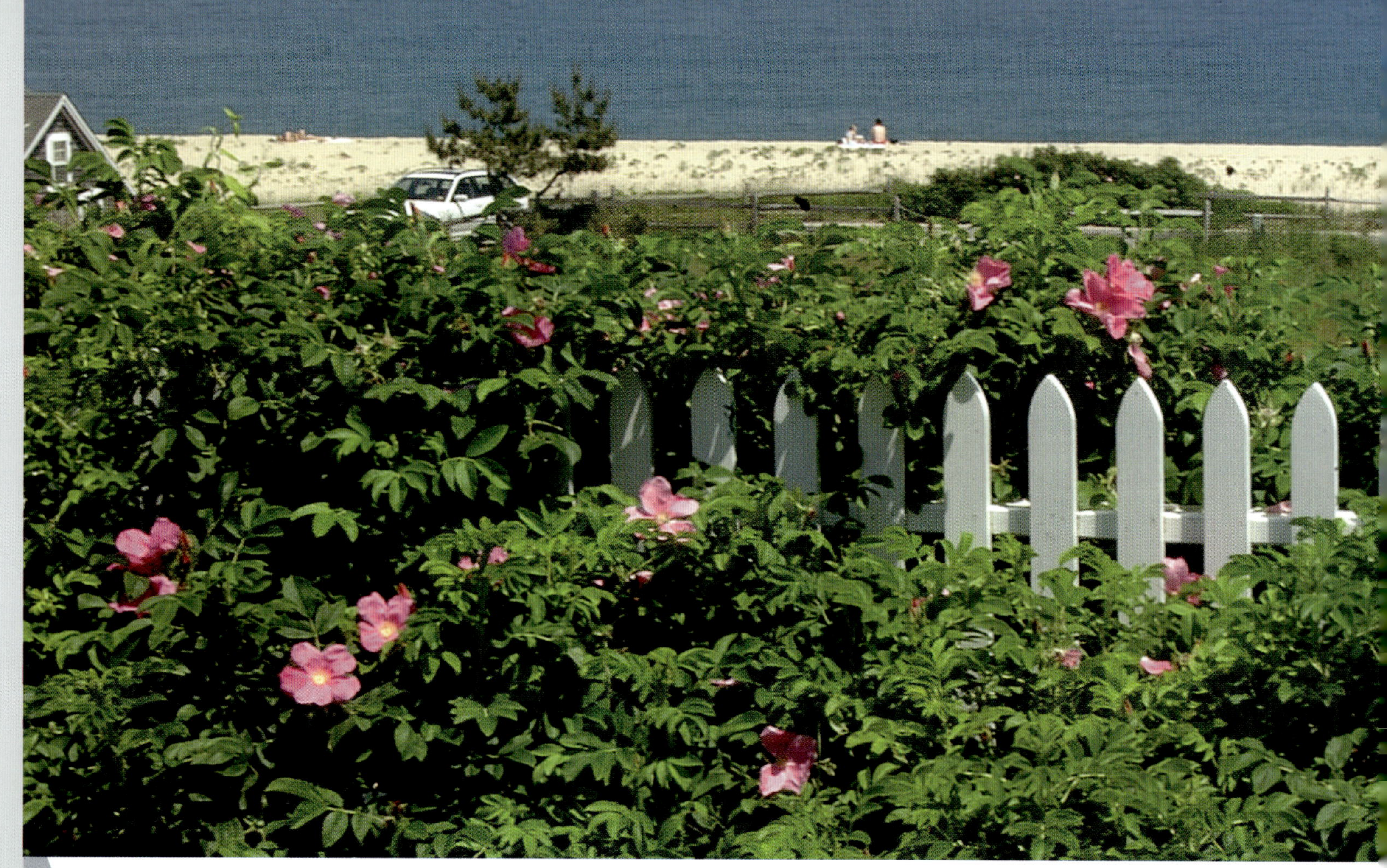

Overlooking the beach on the eastern side of the island.

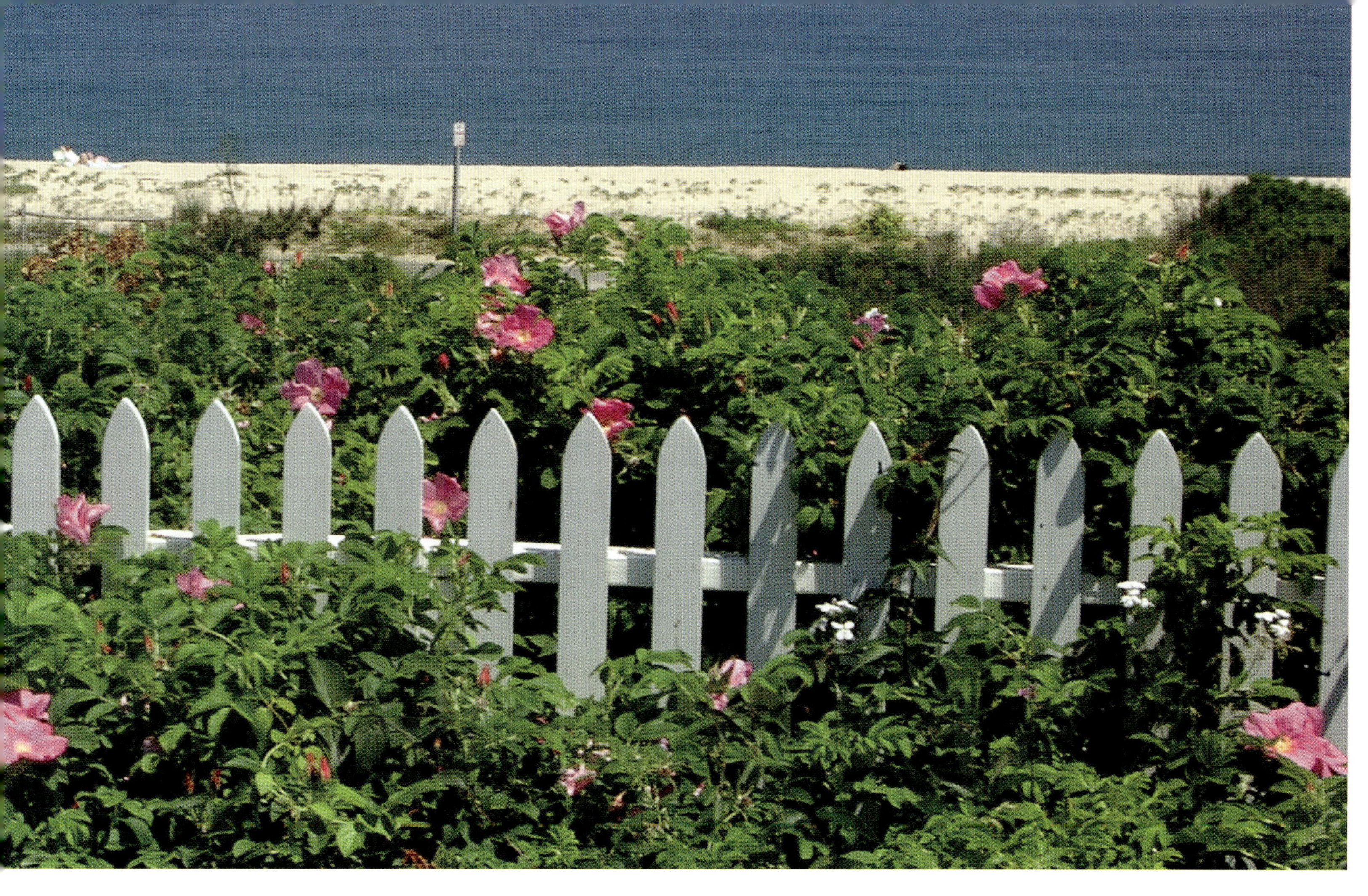

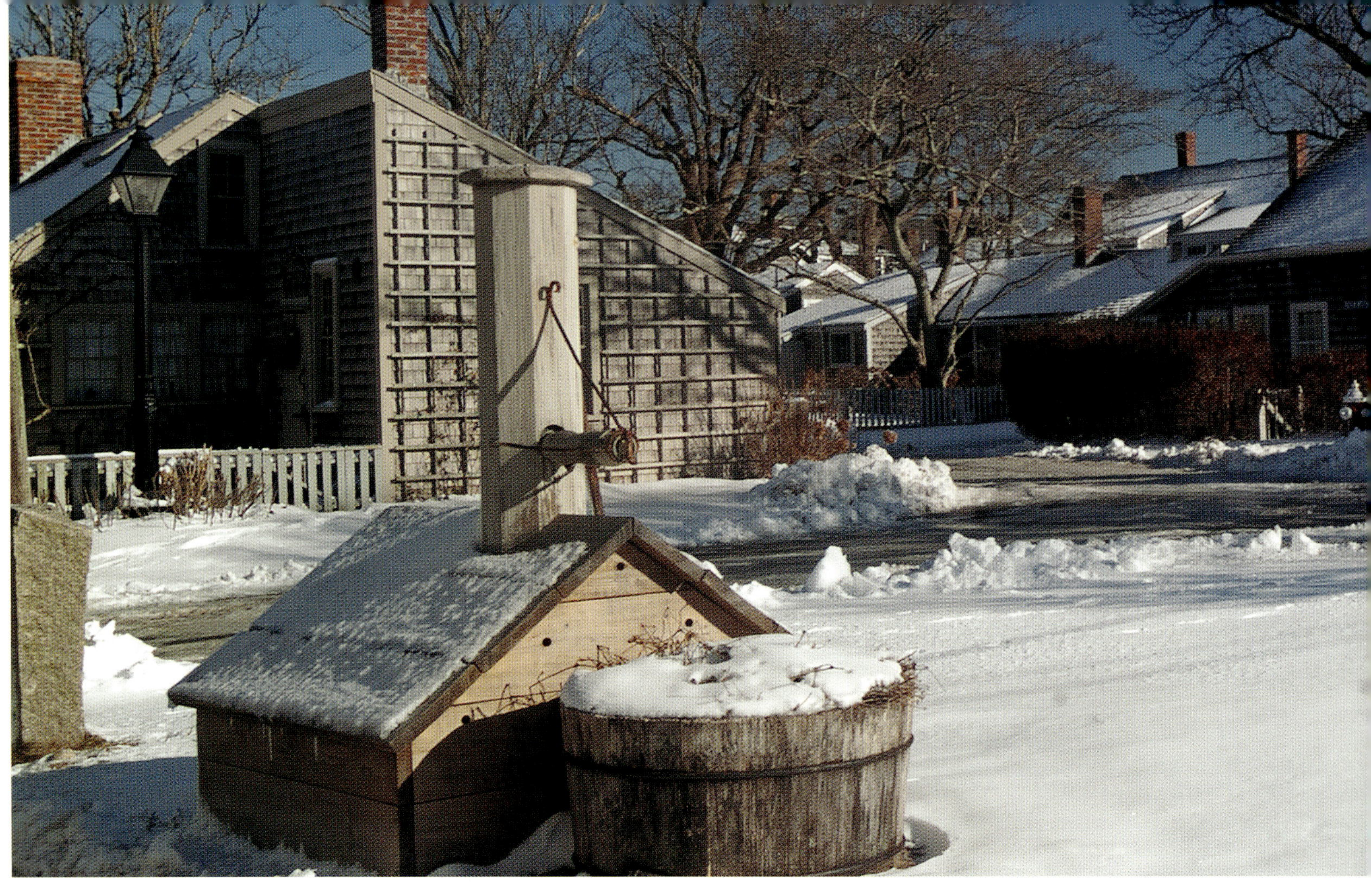

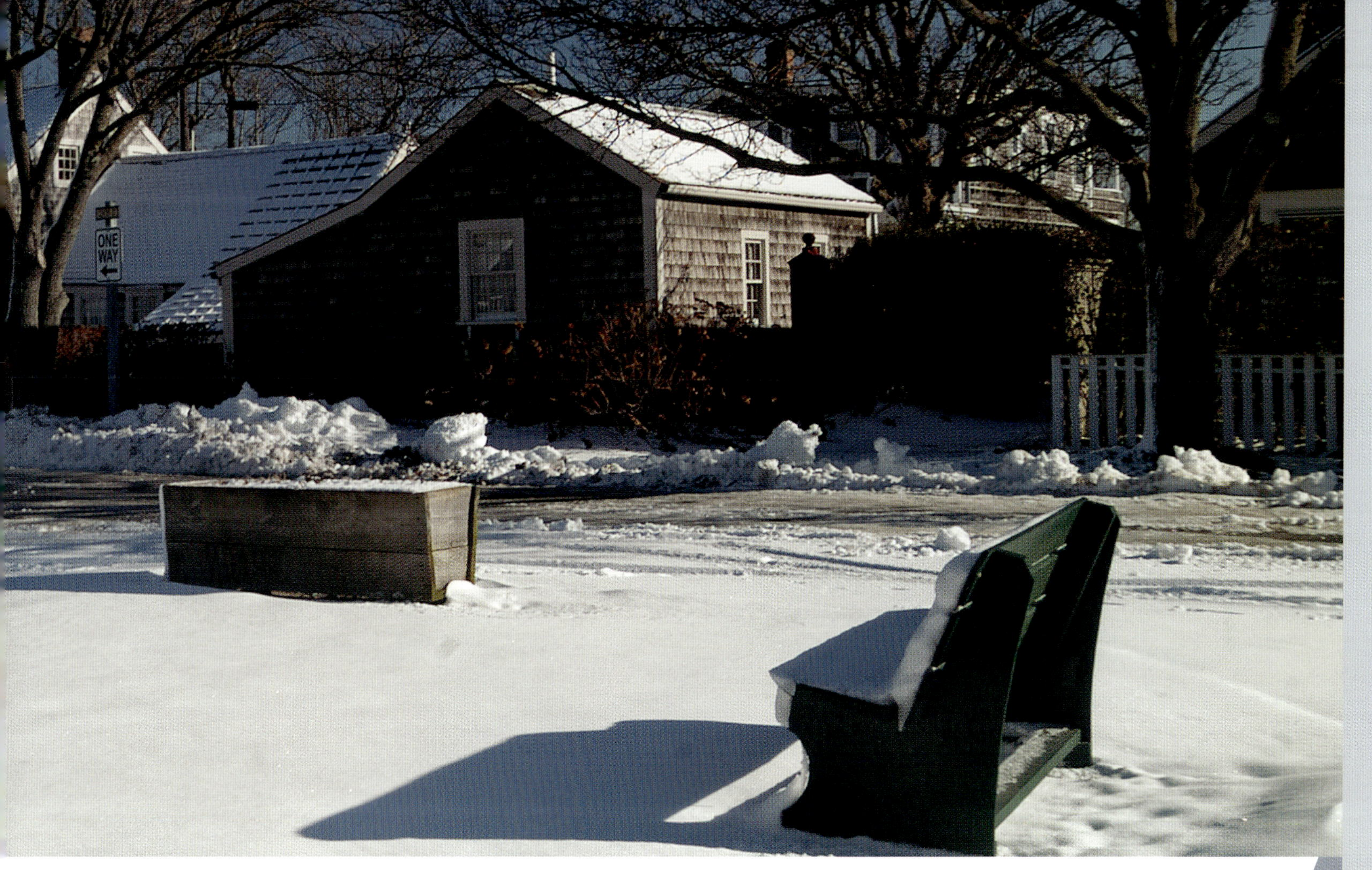

Snow covers the ground in this Siasconset park.

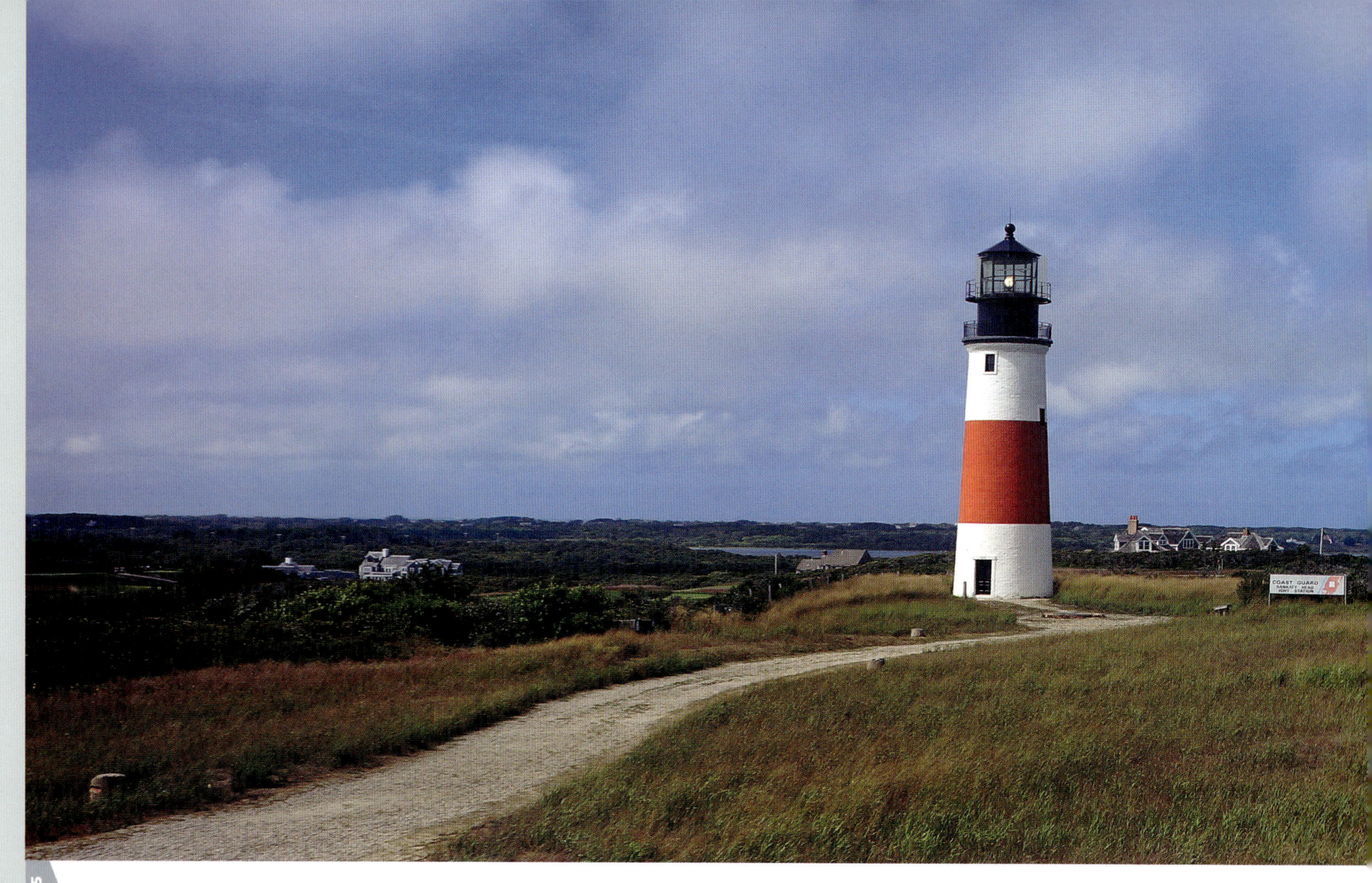

Sankaty Light sits high on the cliffs just north of Siasconset.

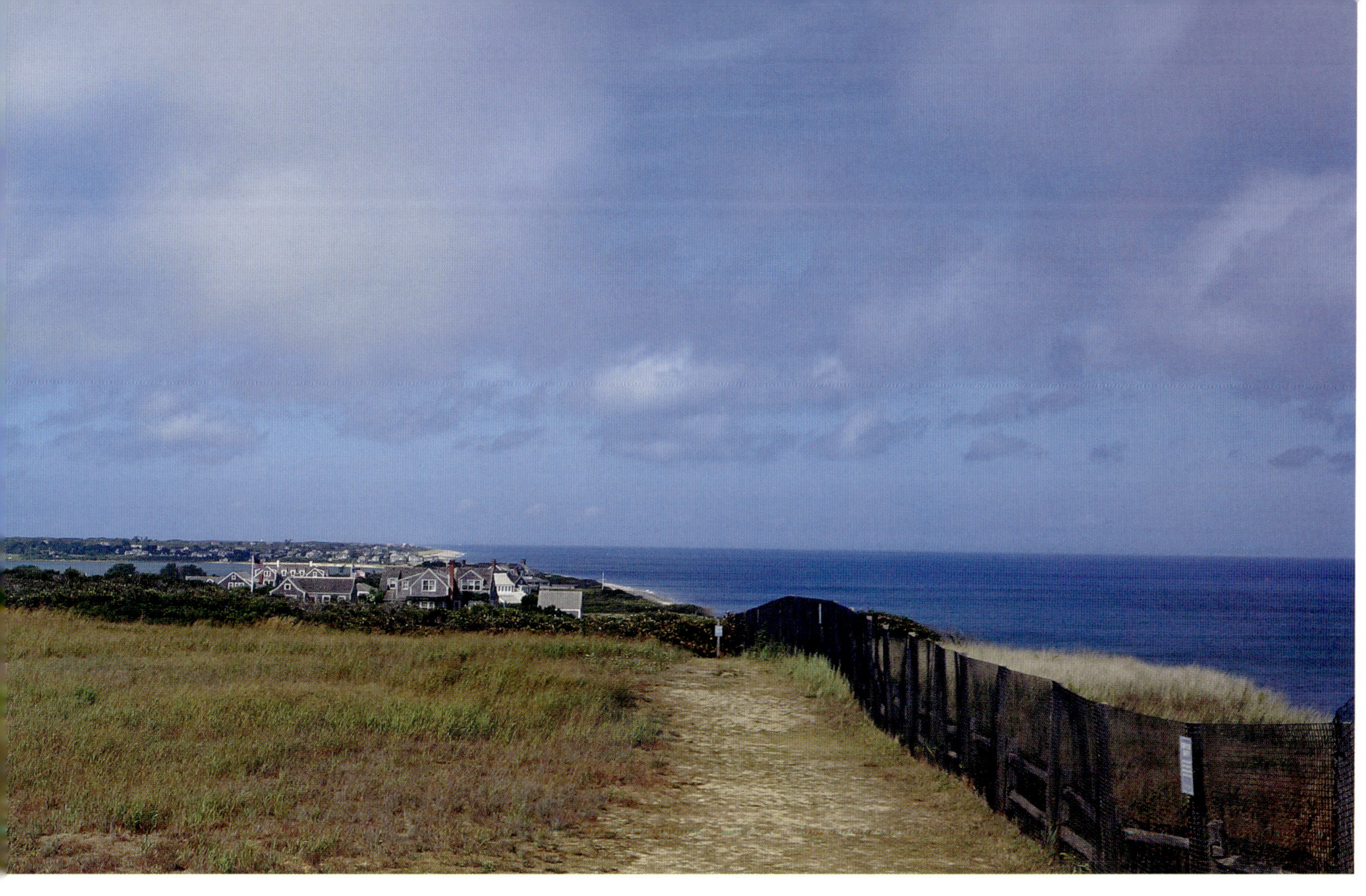

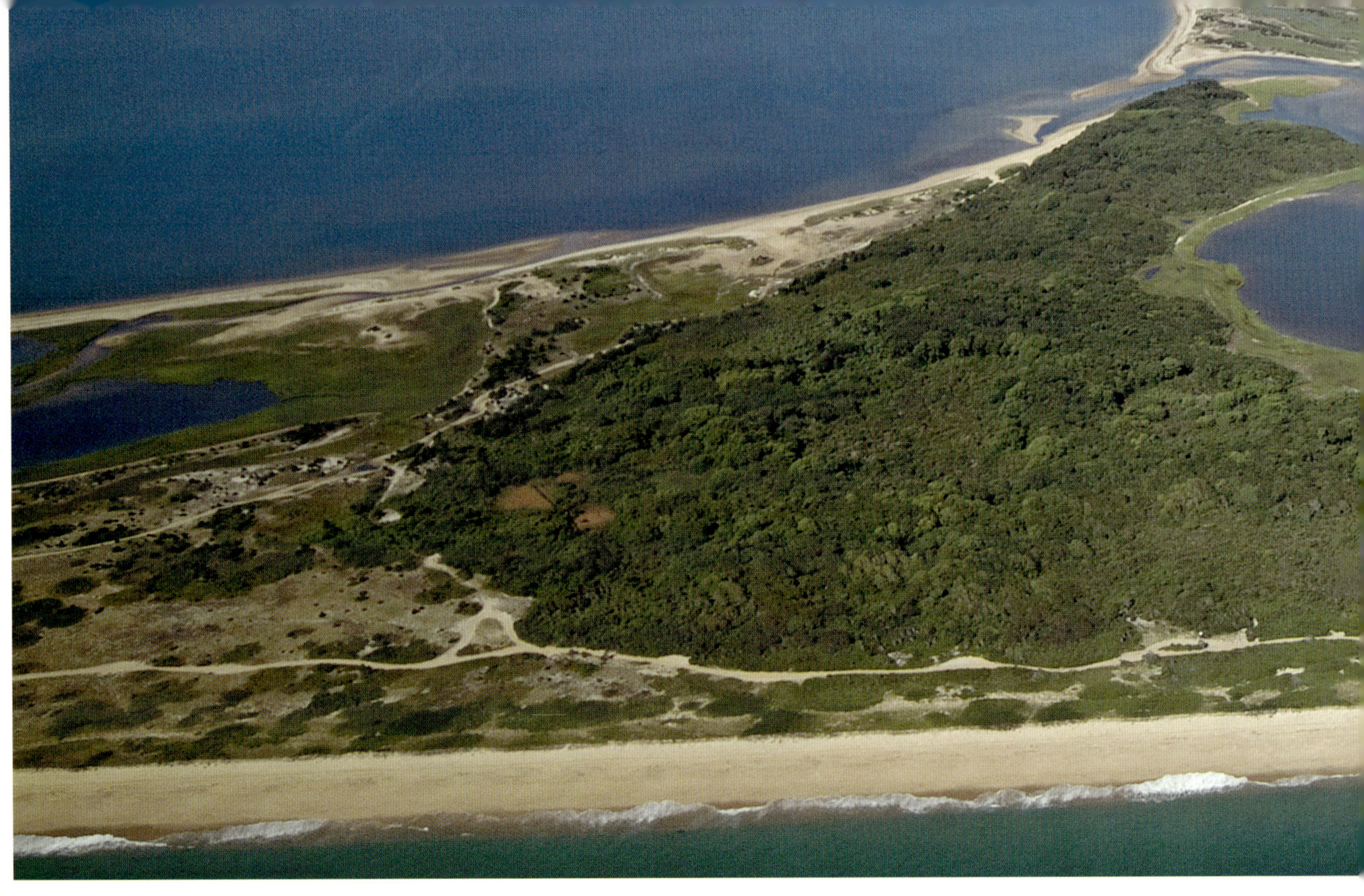

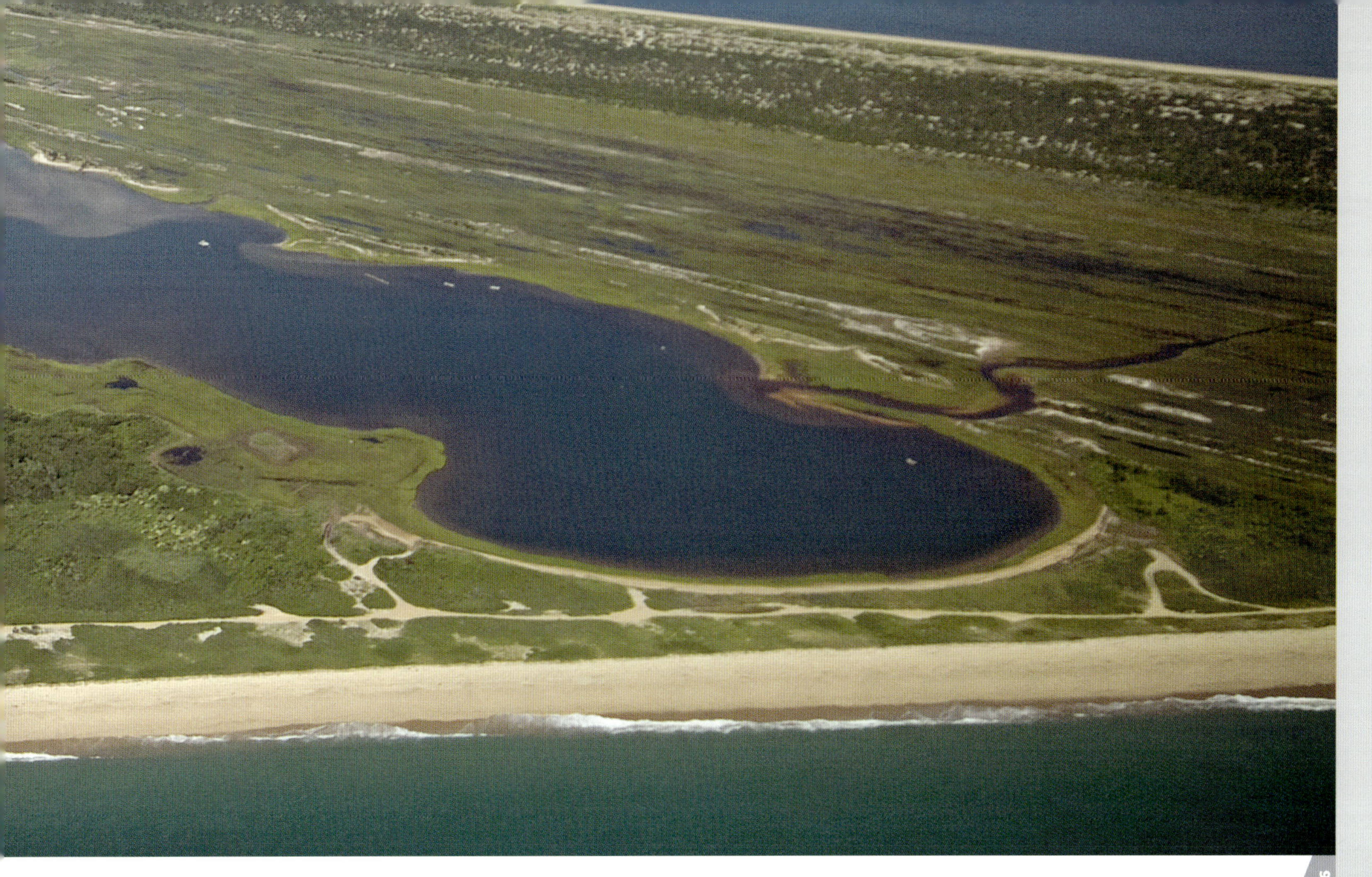

An aerial view of Coskata Pond. The sandy road in front leads to Great Point (unseen, to right of photo).

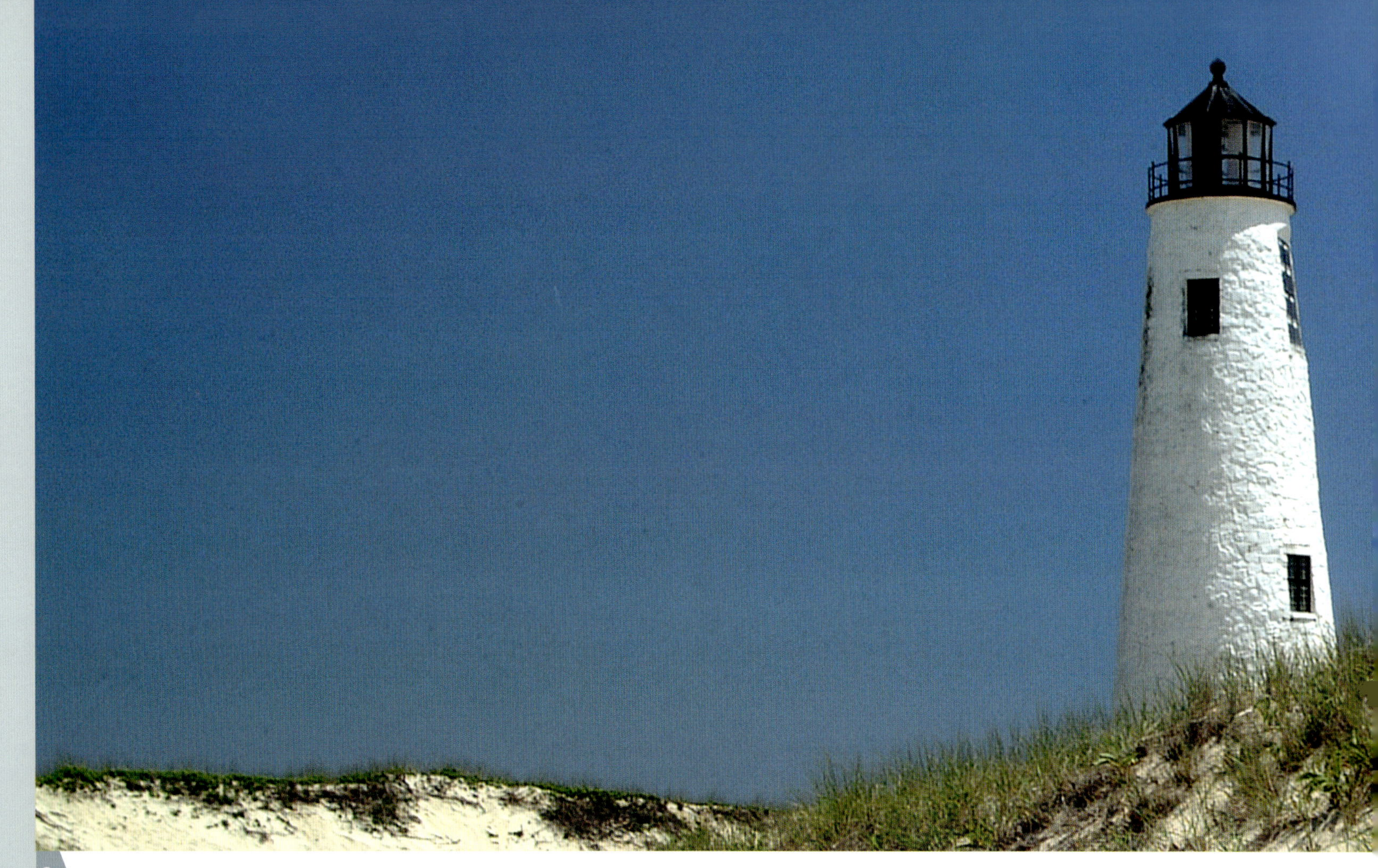

Great Point Lighthouse was rebuilt after the original tower was destroyed in a 1984 storm.

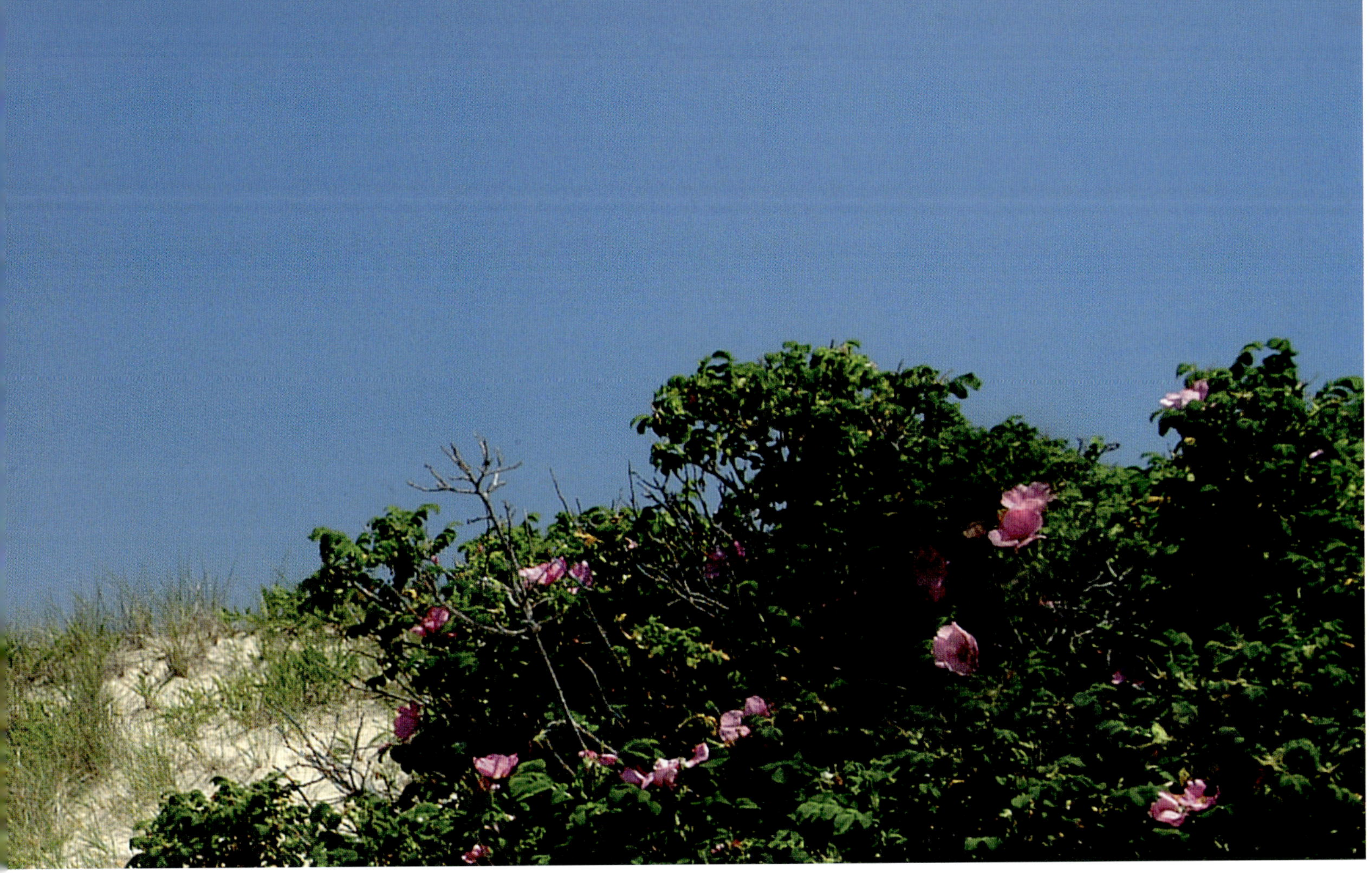

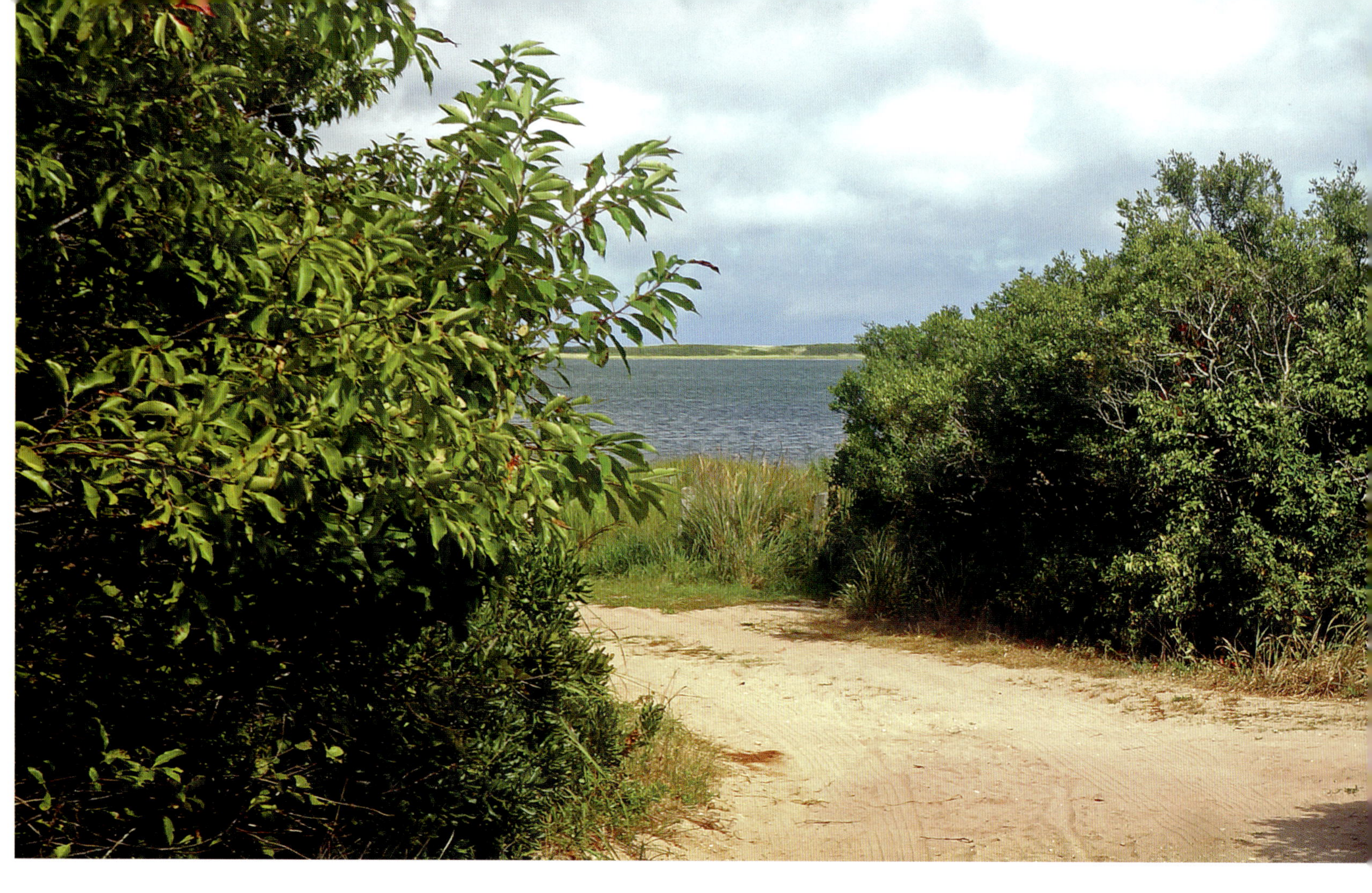

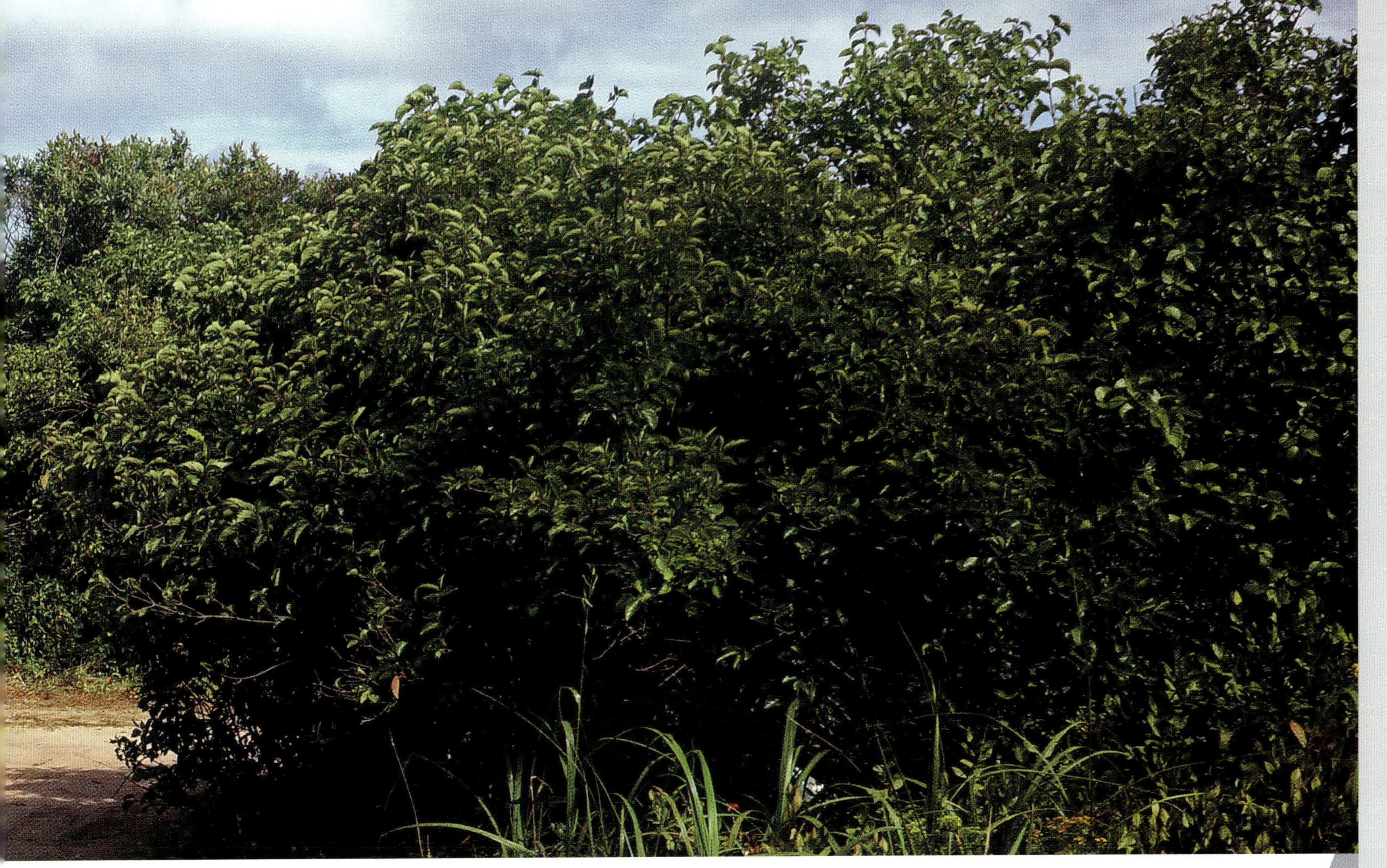

A sandy road leads to a pond that is hidden by trees.

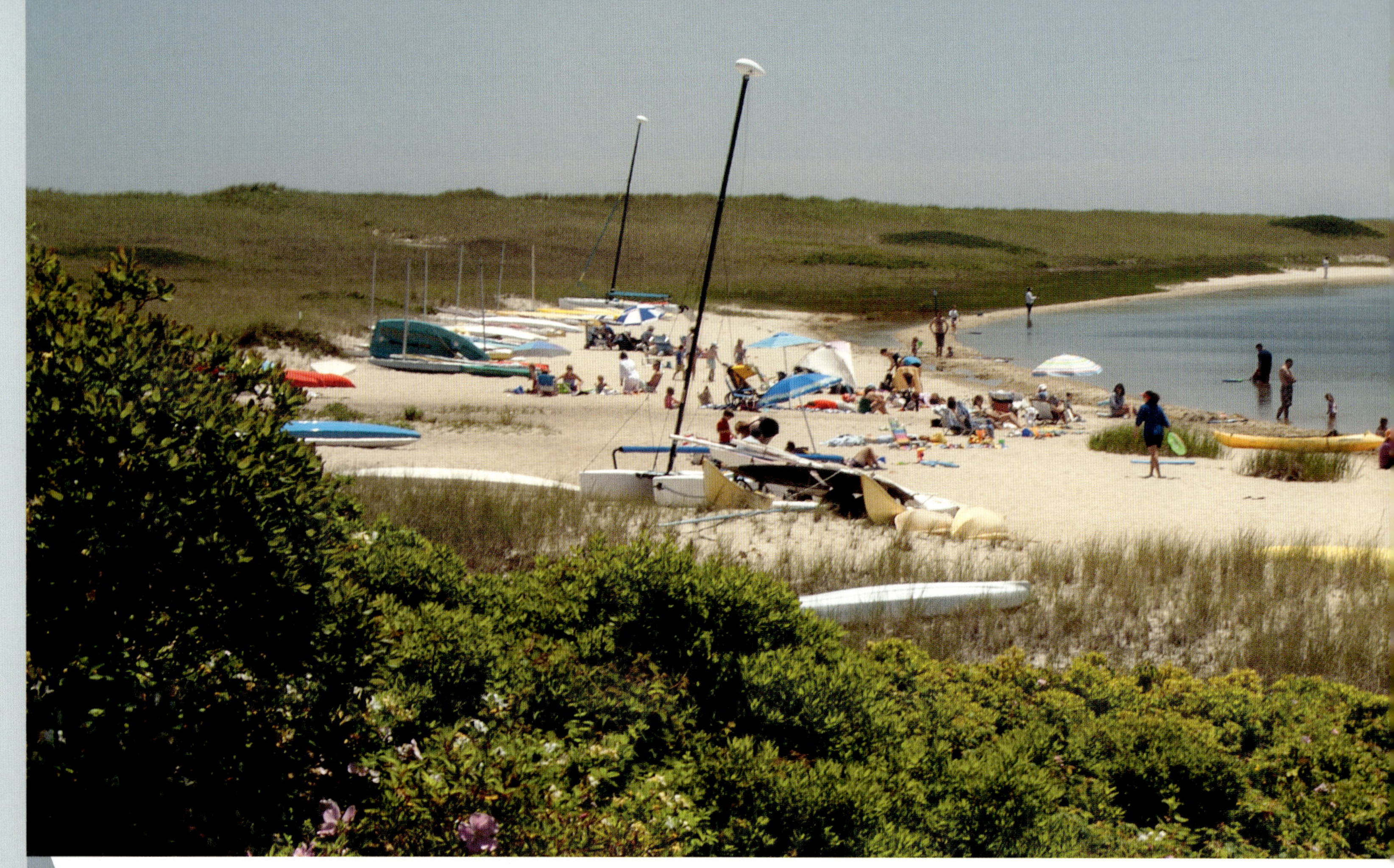

Bathers enjoy Sesachacha Pond in Quidnet.

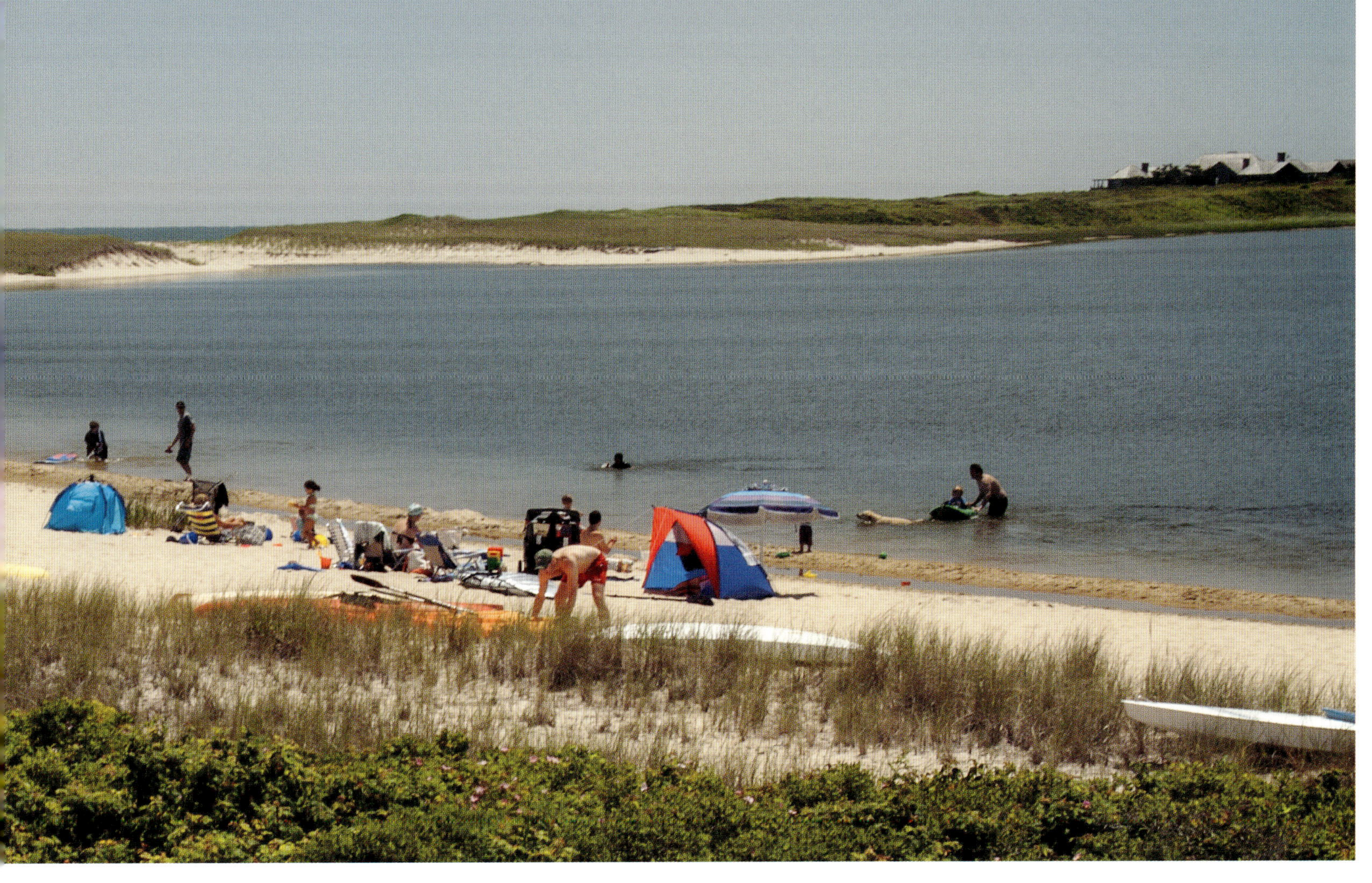

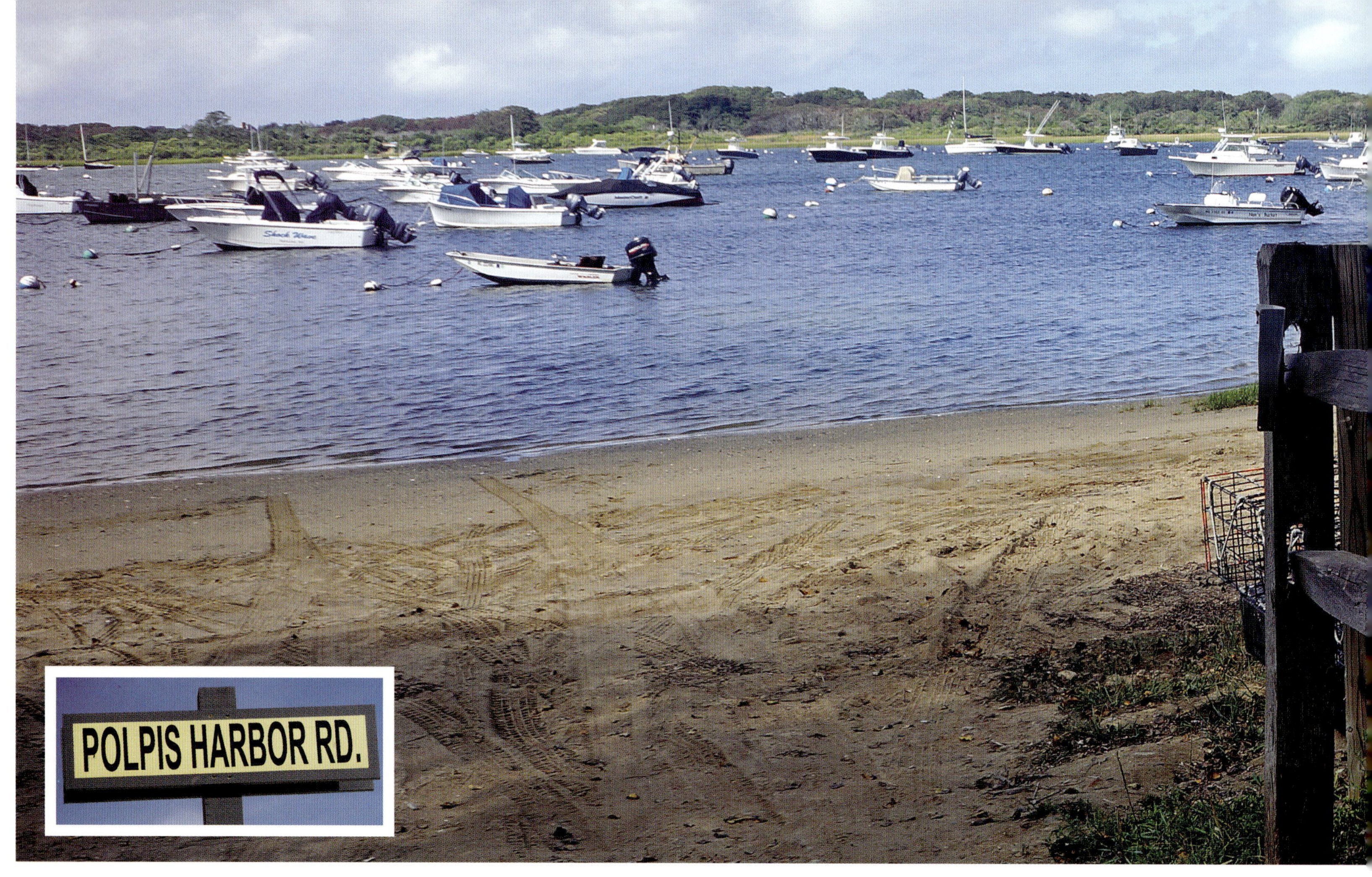
POLPIS HARBOR RD.

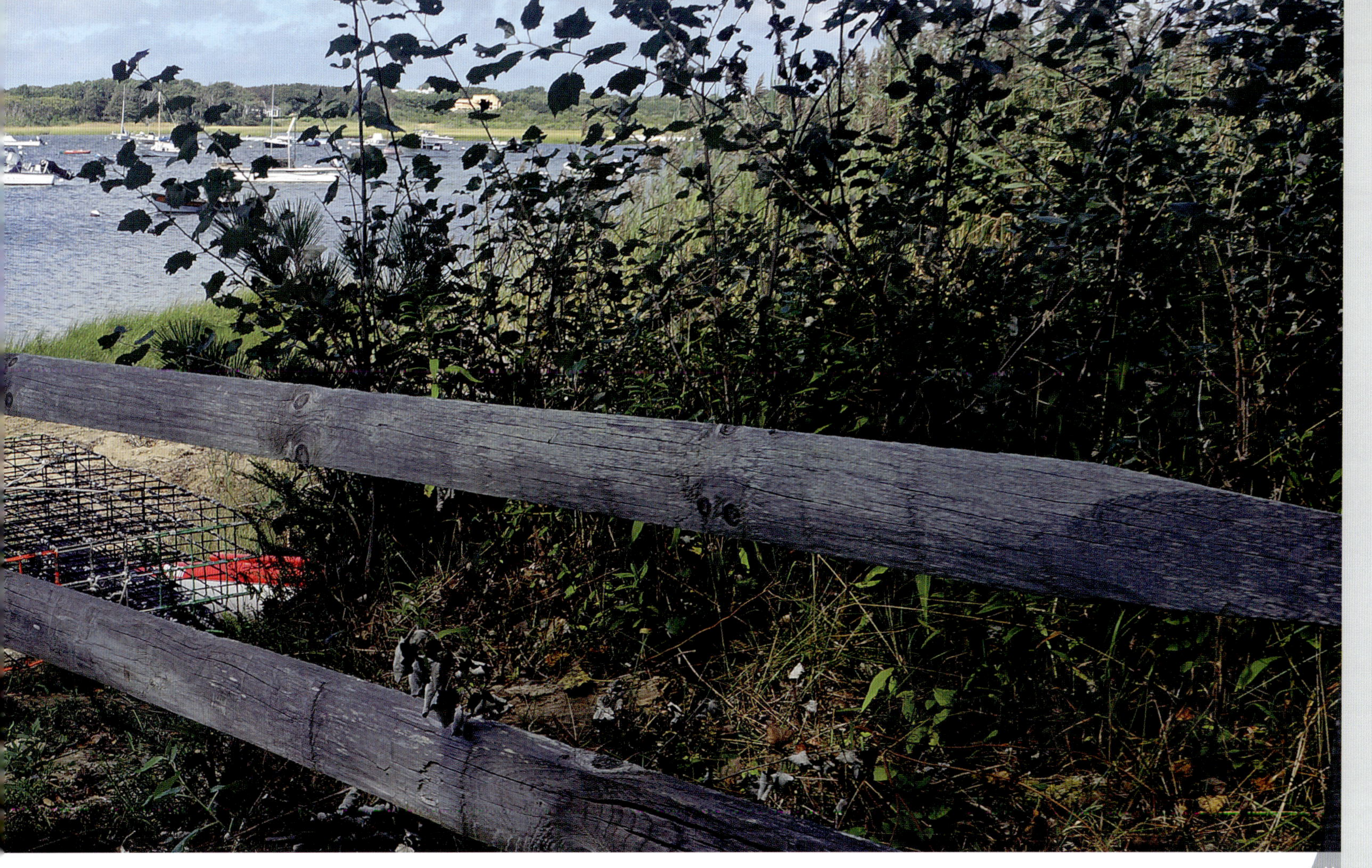

At the end of this road lies Polpis Harbor.

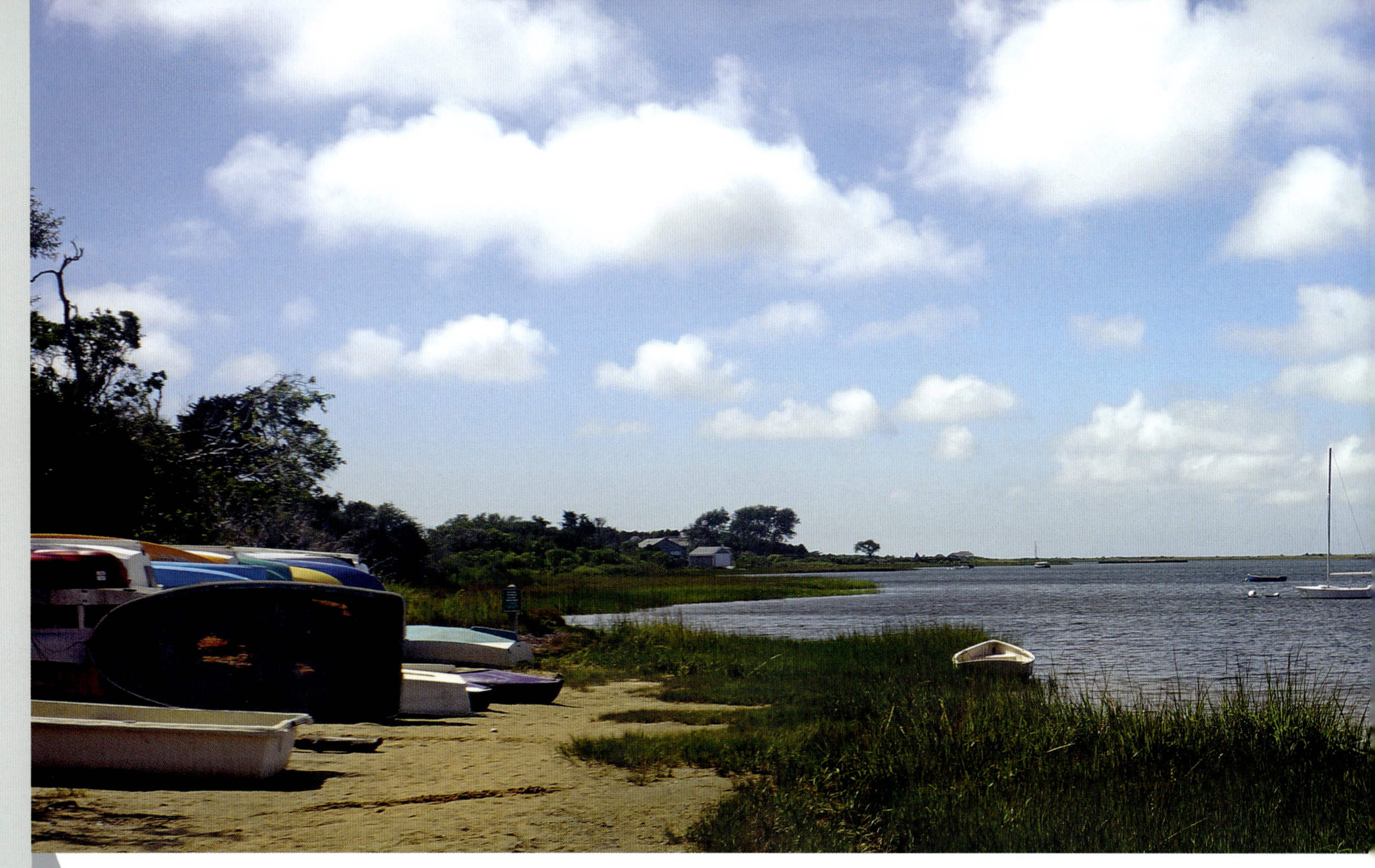

Polpis Harbor looking toward Nantucket Harbor.

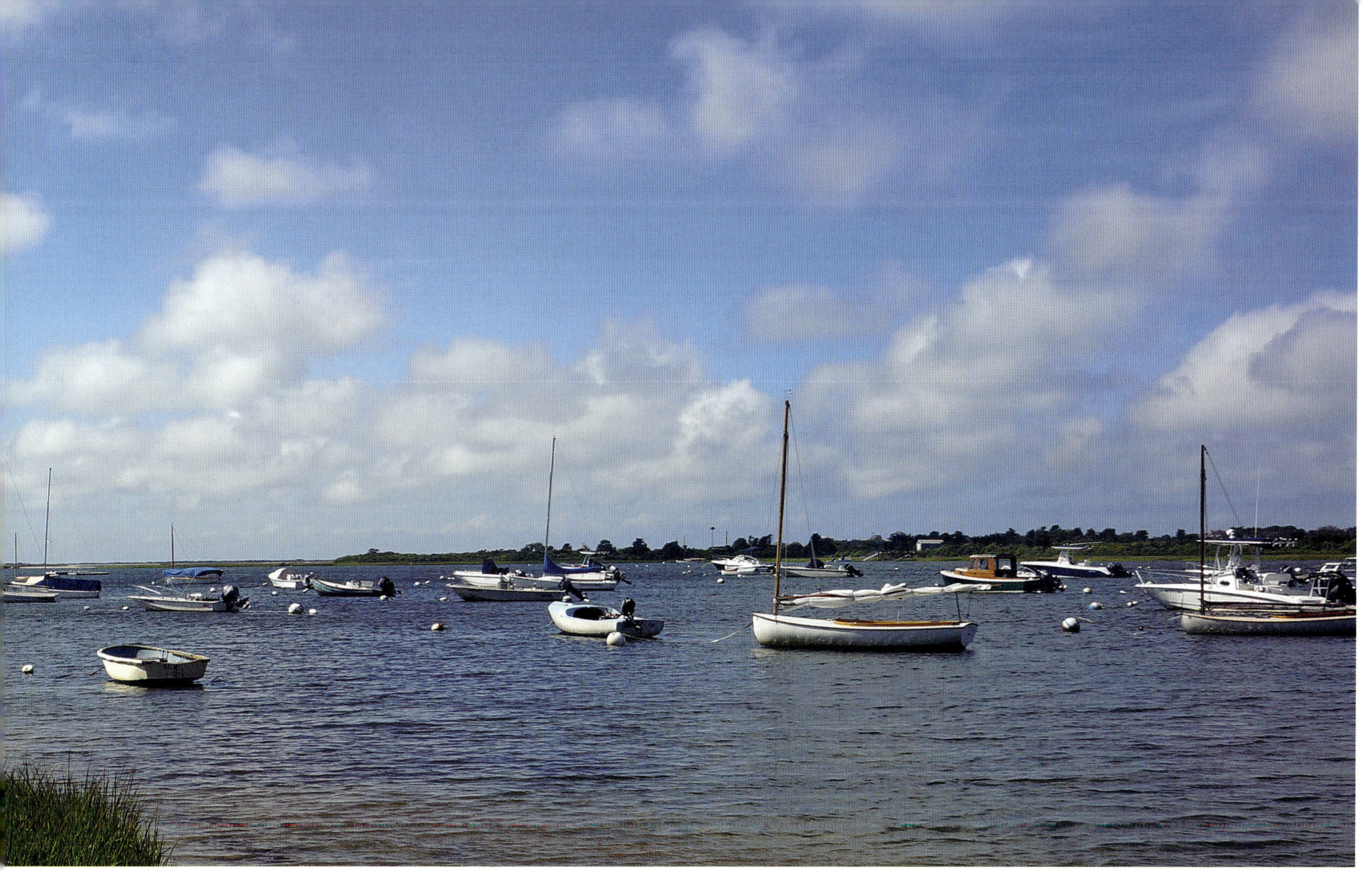

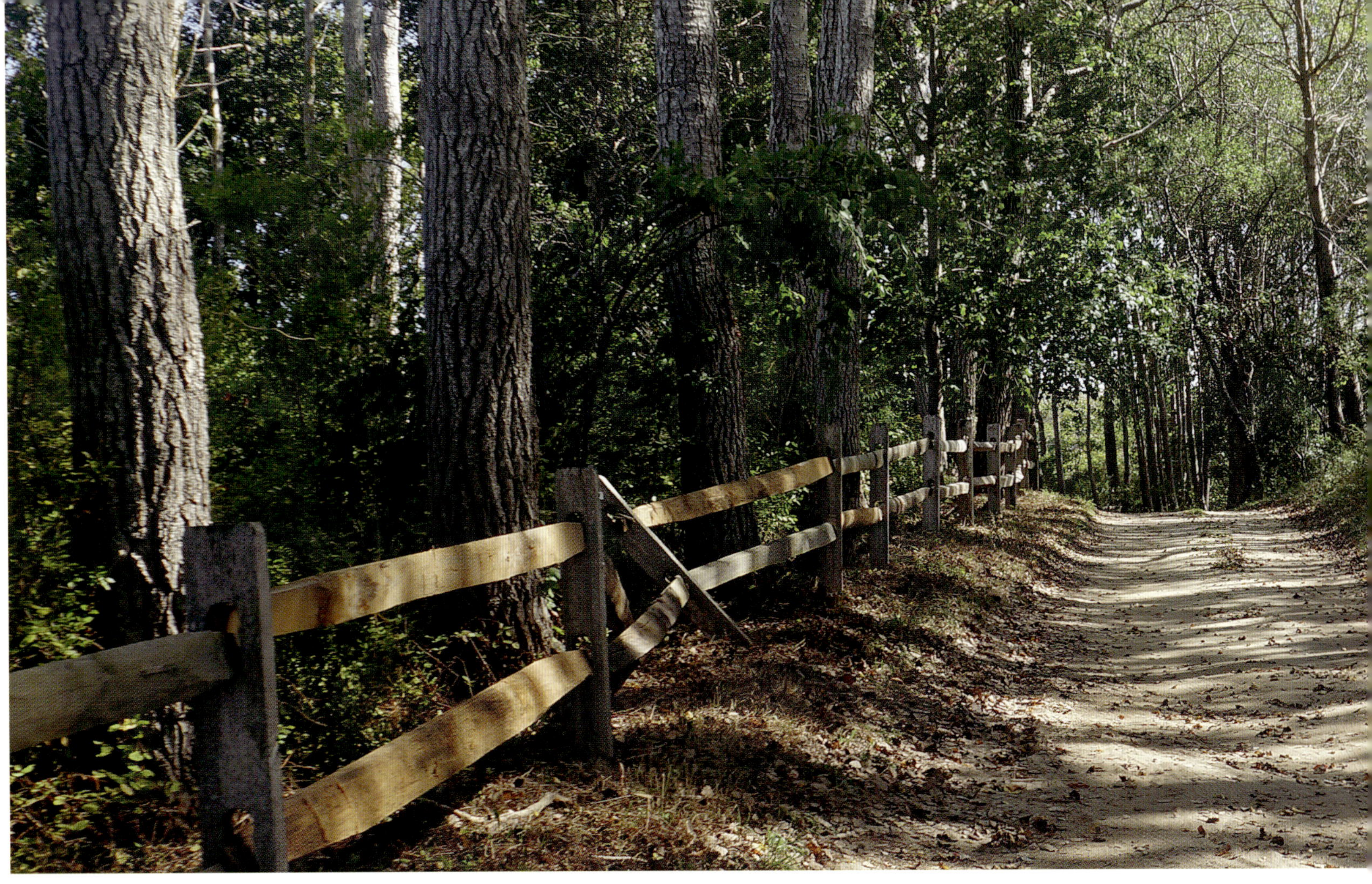

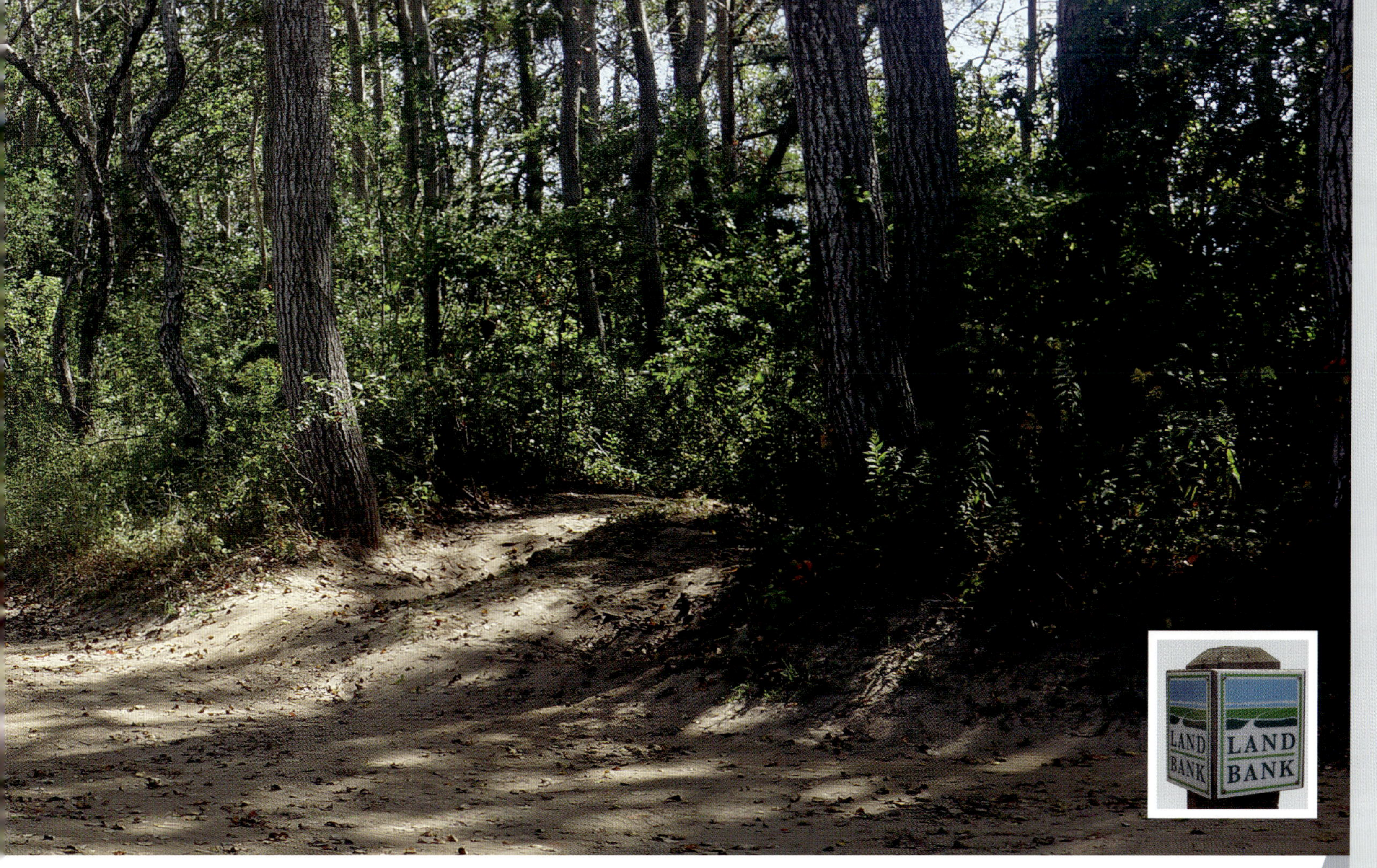

Sandy and narrow roads are common on the island. Many acres of land will be preserved for generations to come.

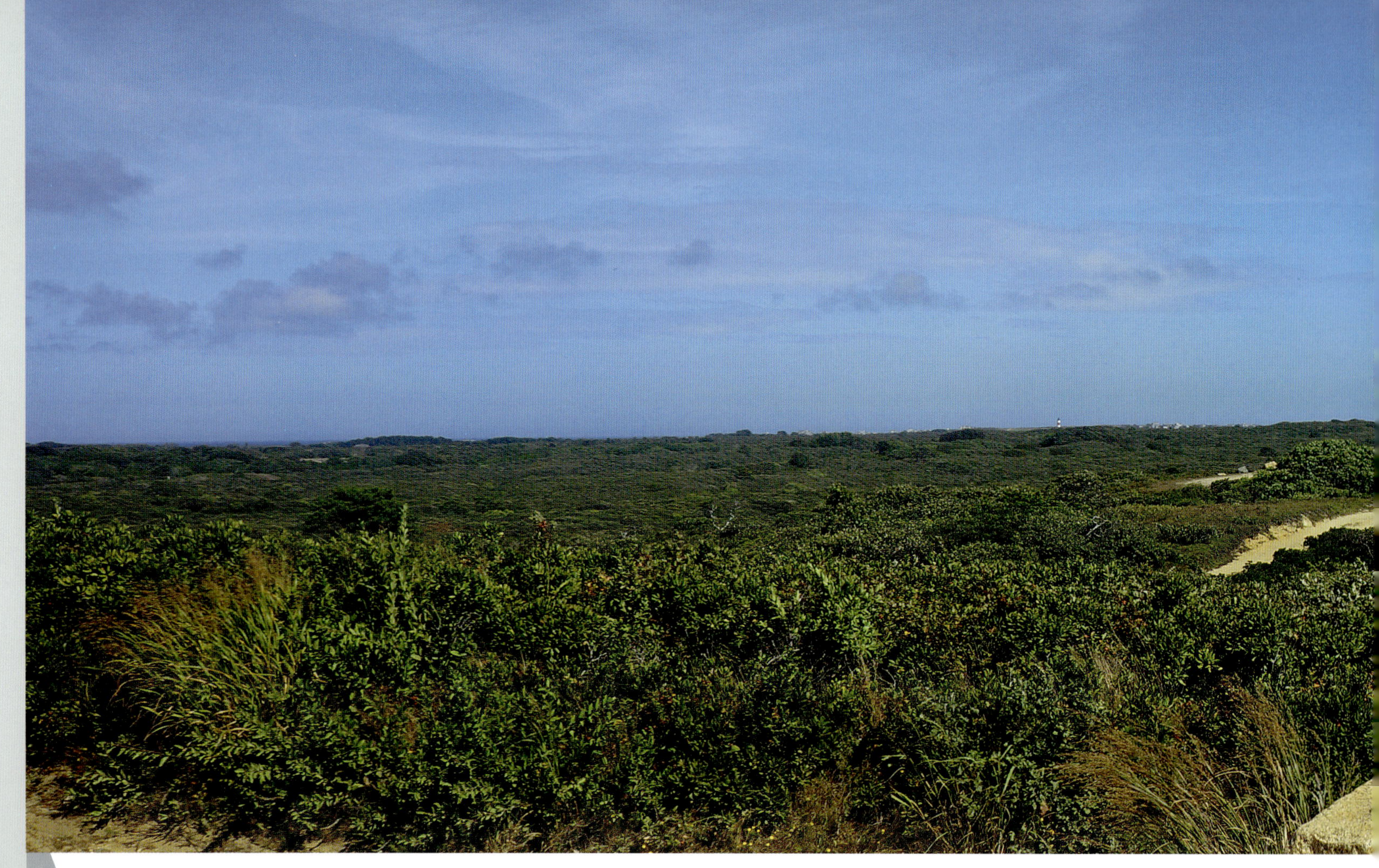

Looking east toward Siasconset from the Altar Rock area, which is the highest point on the island.

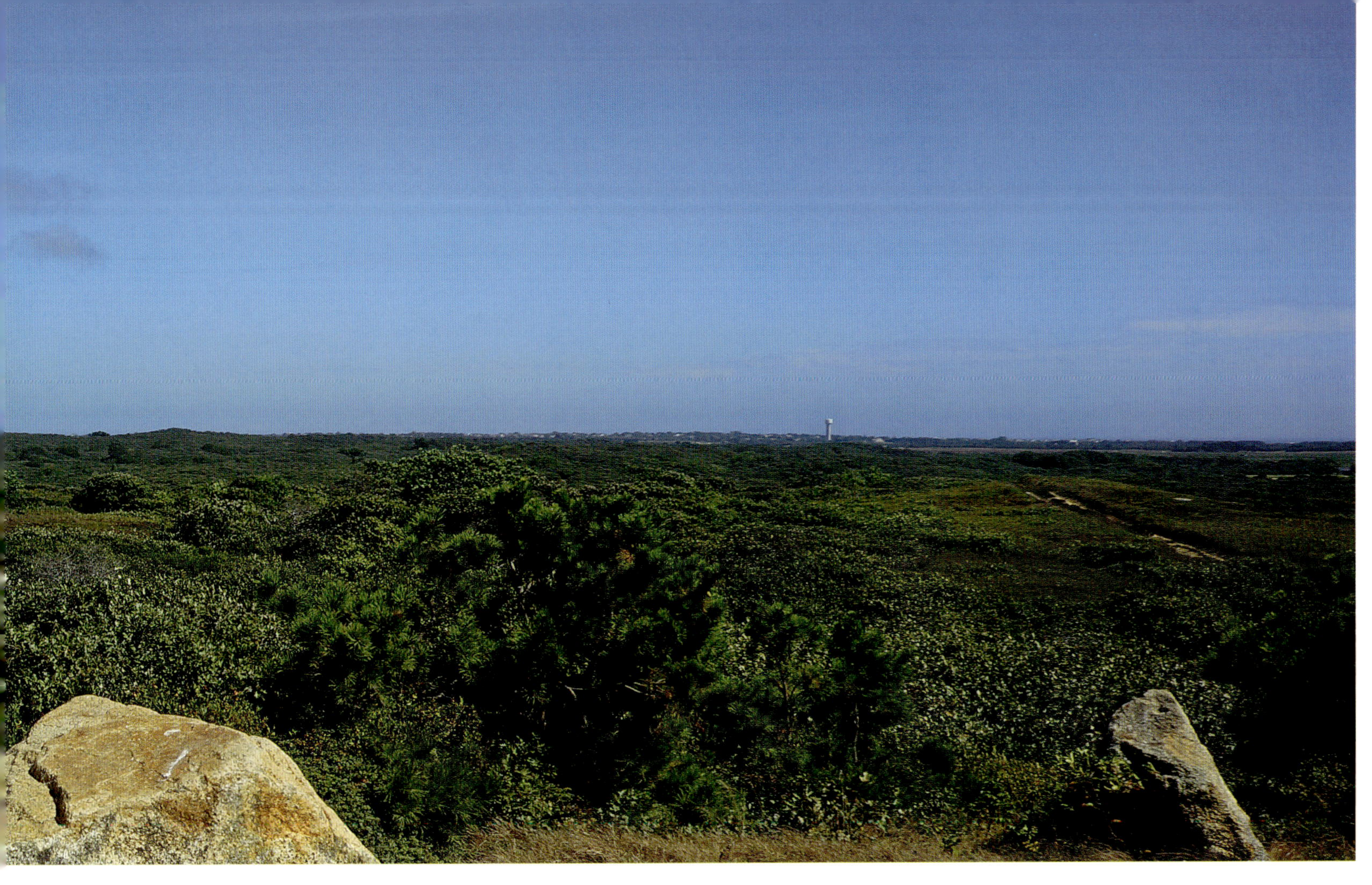

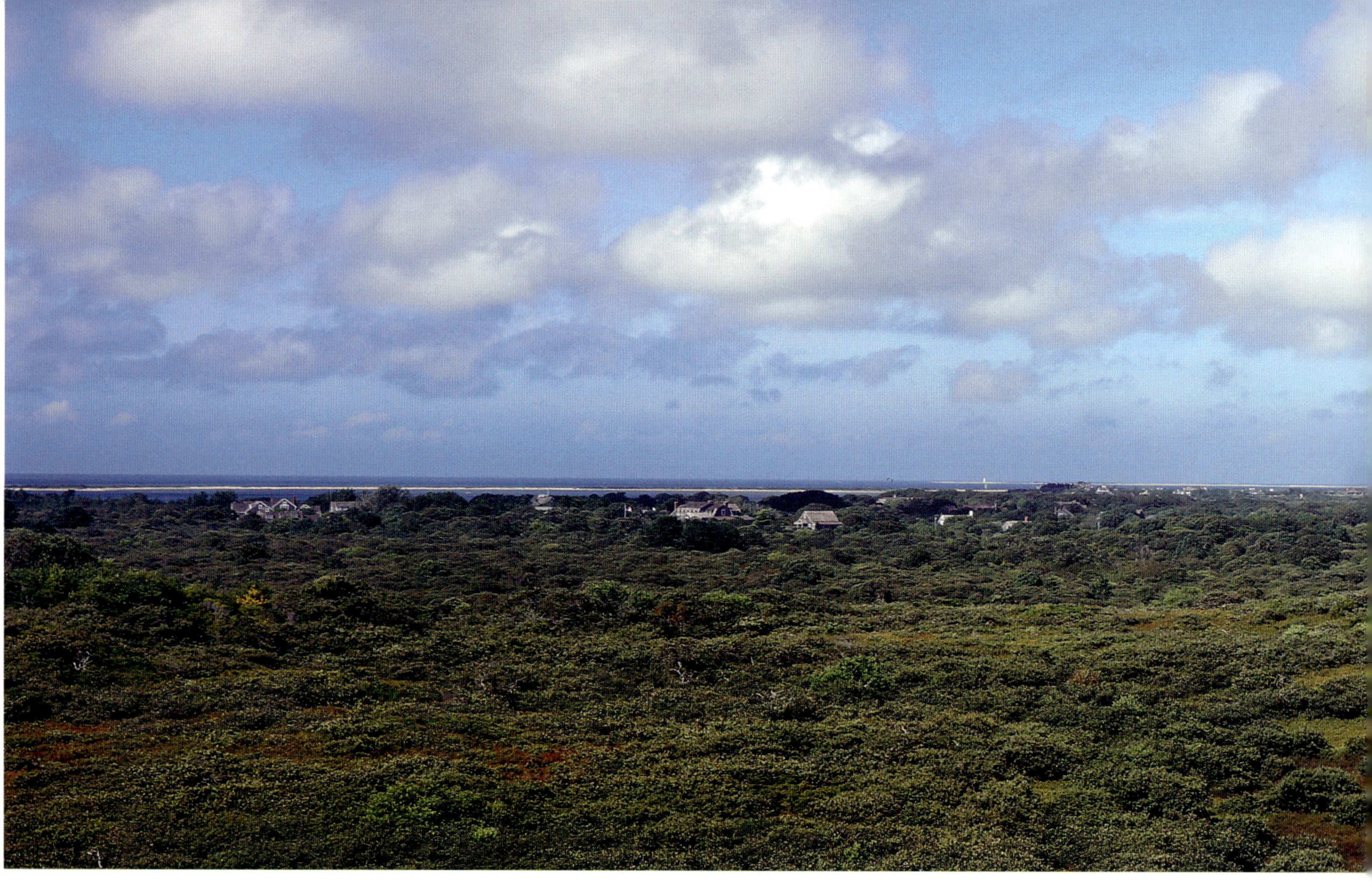

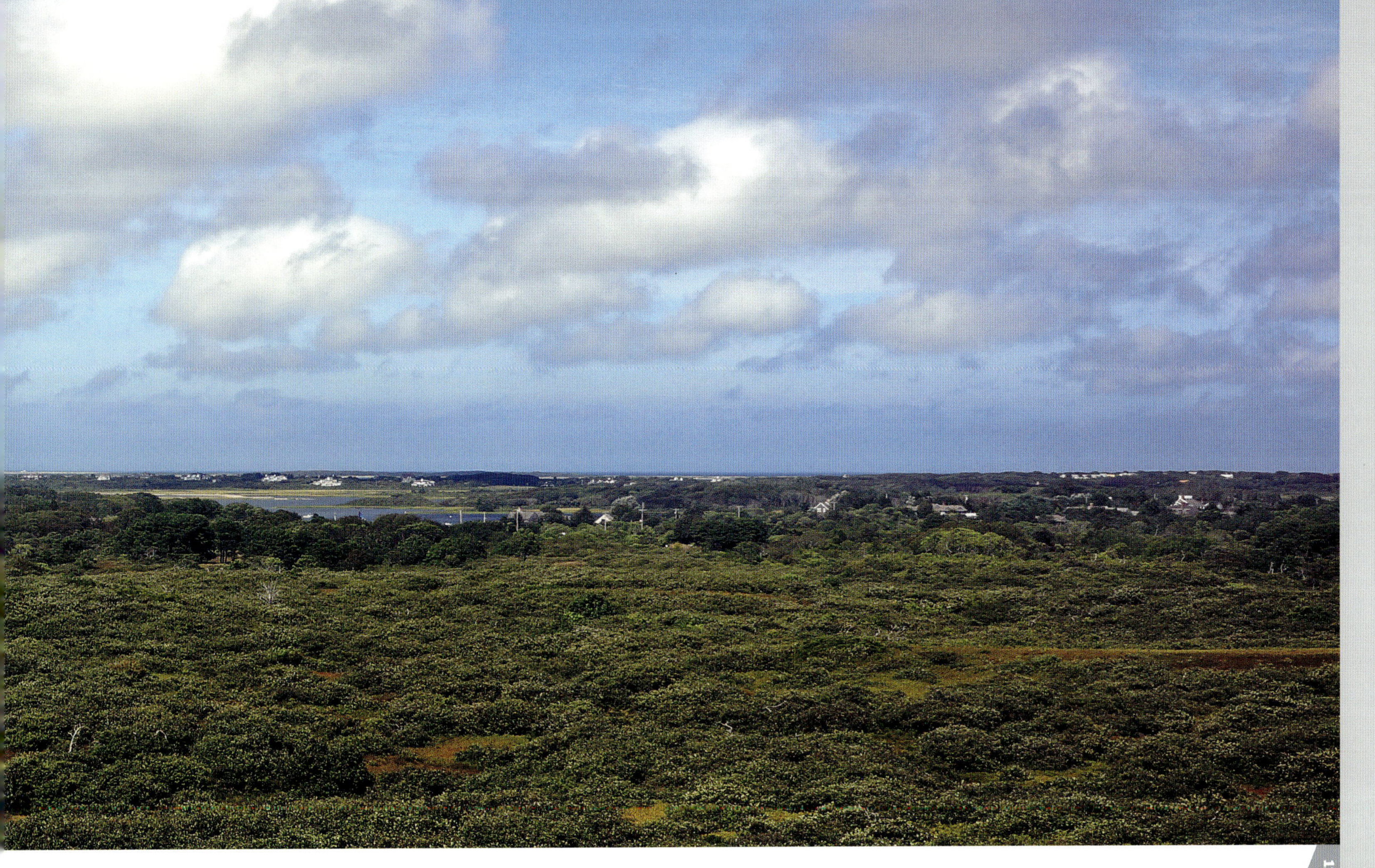

Another view from Altar Rock, this time looking north.

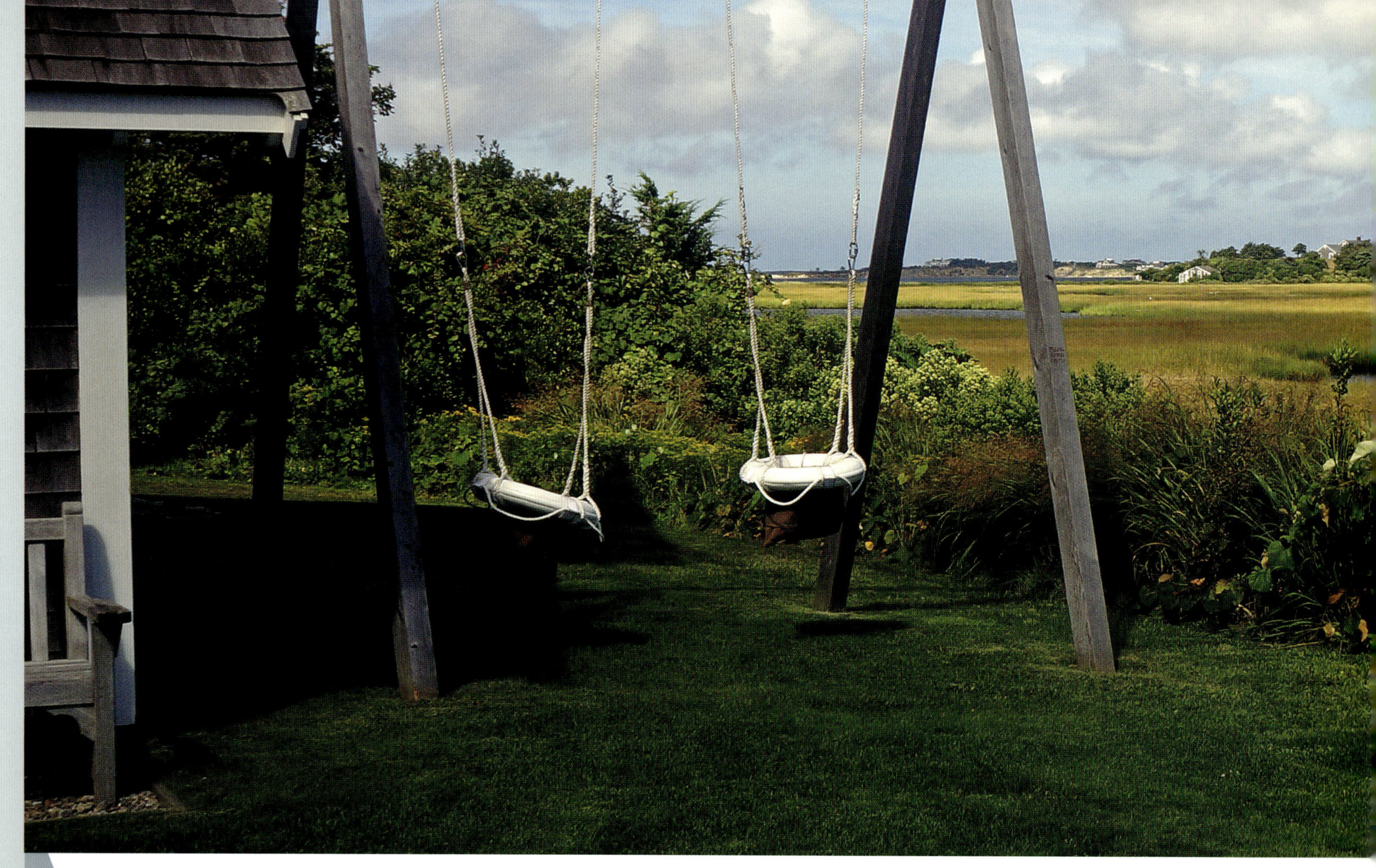

The Breeches Buoy exhibit at the Shipwreck and Lifesaving Museum.

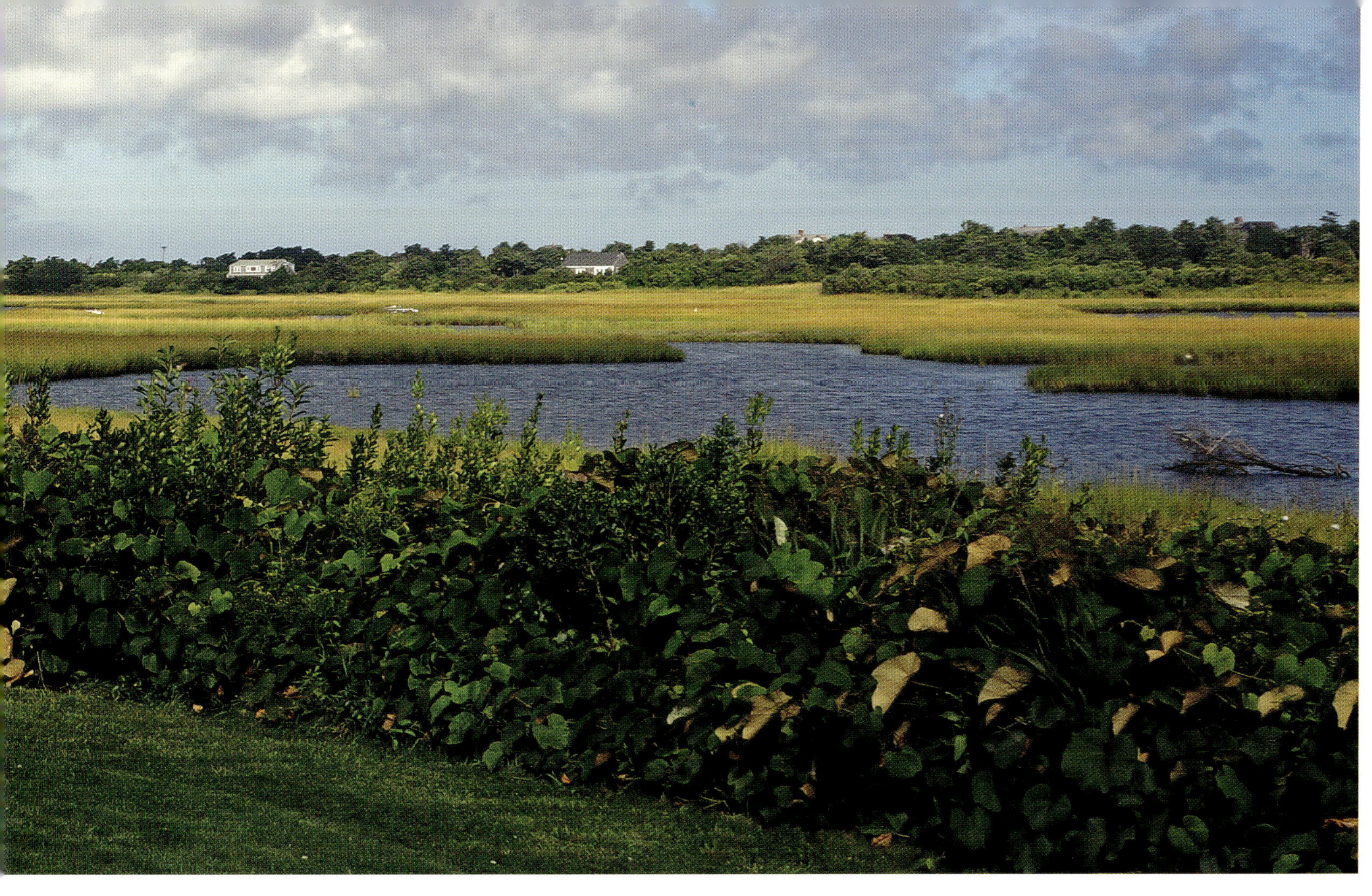

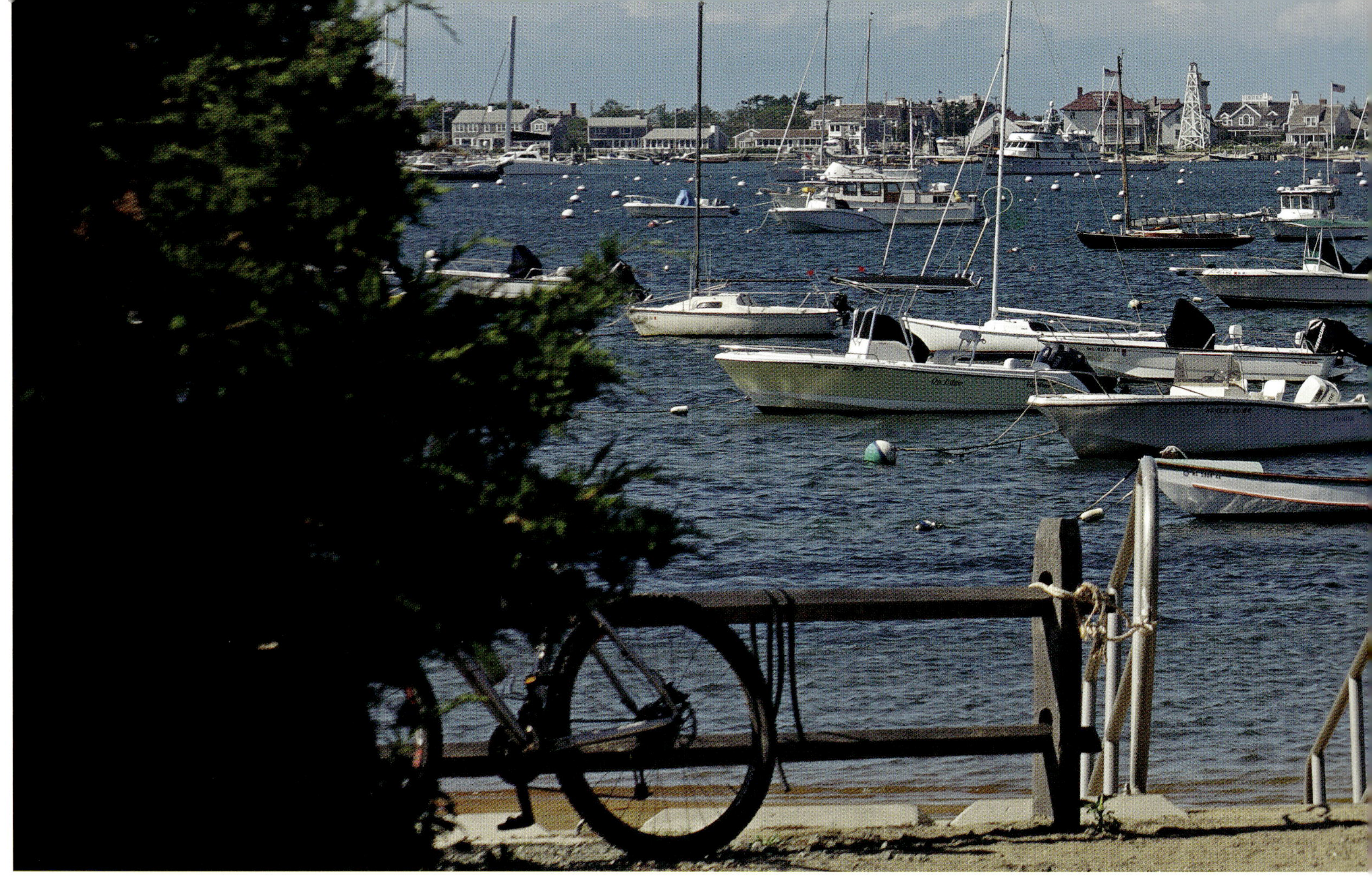

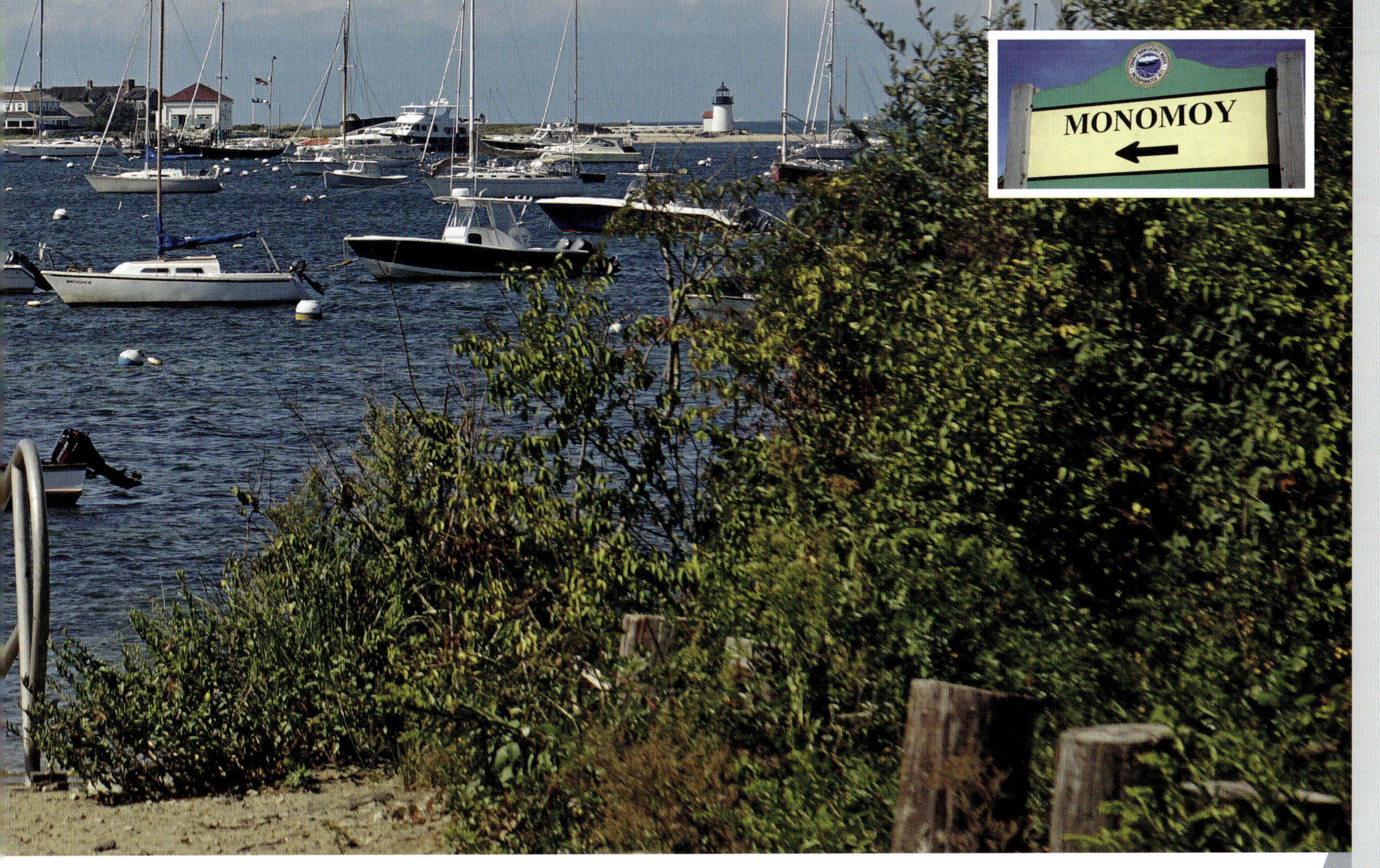

Brant Point Light is visible across the harbor from Monomoy.

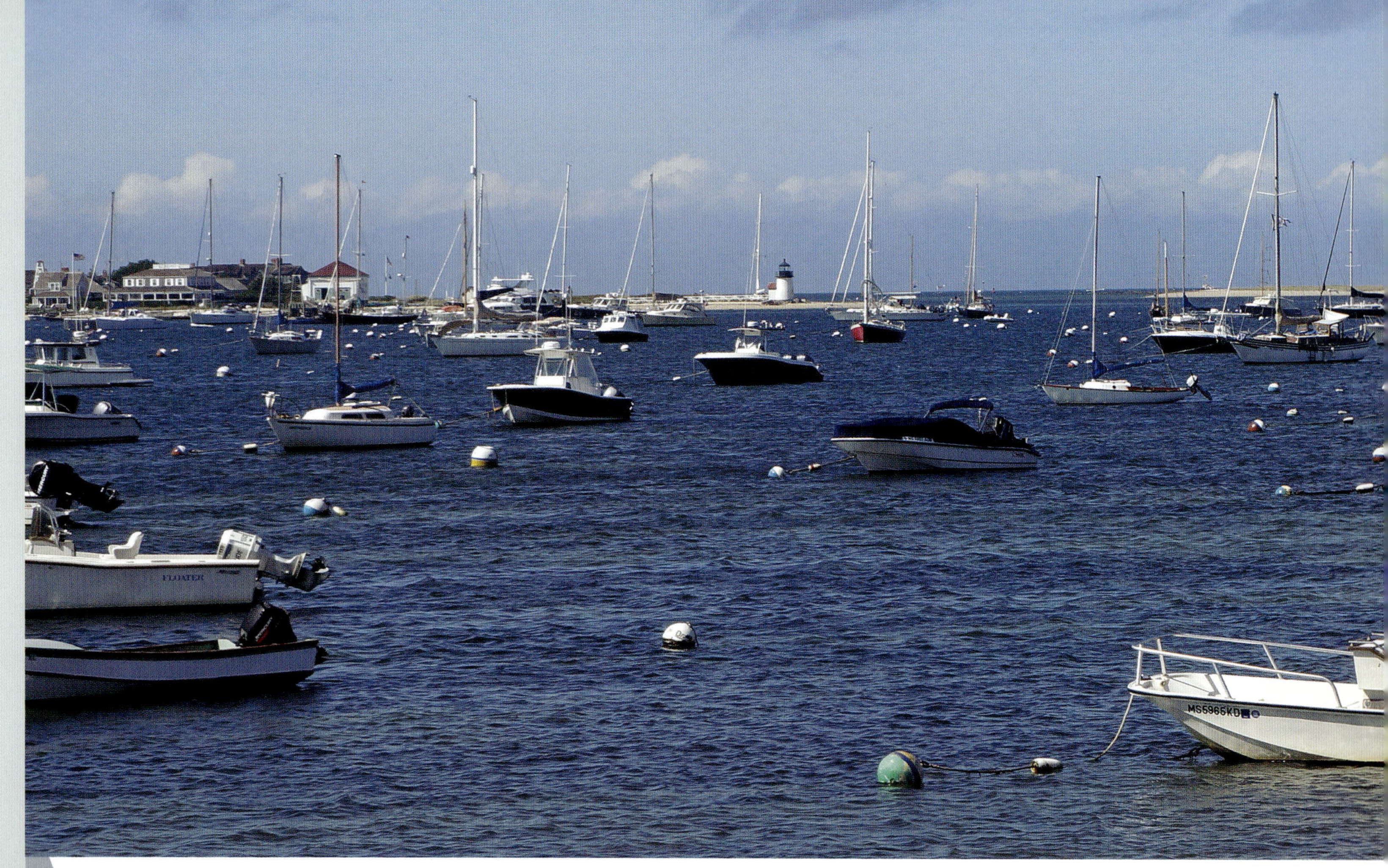

A harbor view from the beach at Monomoy.

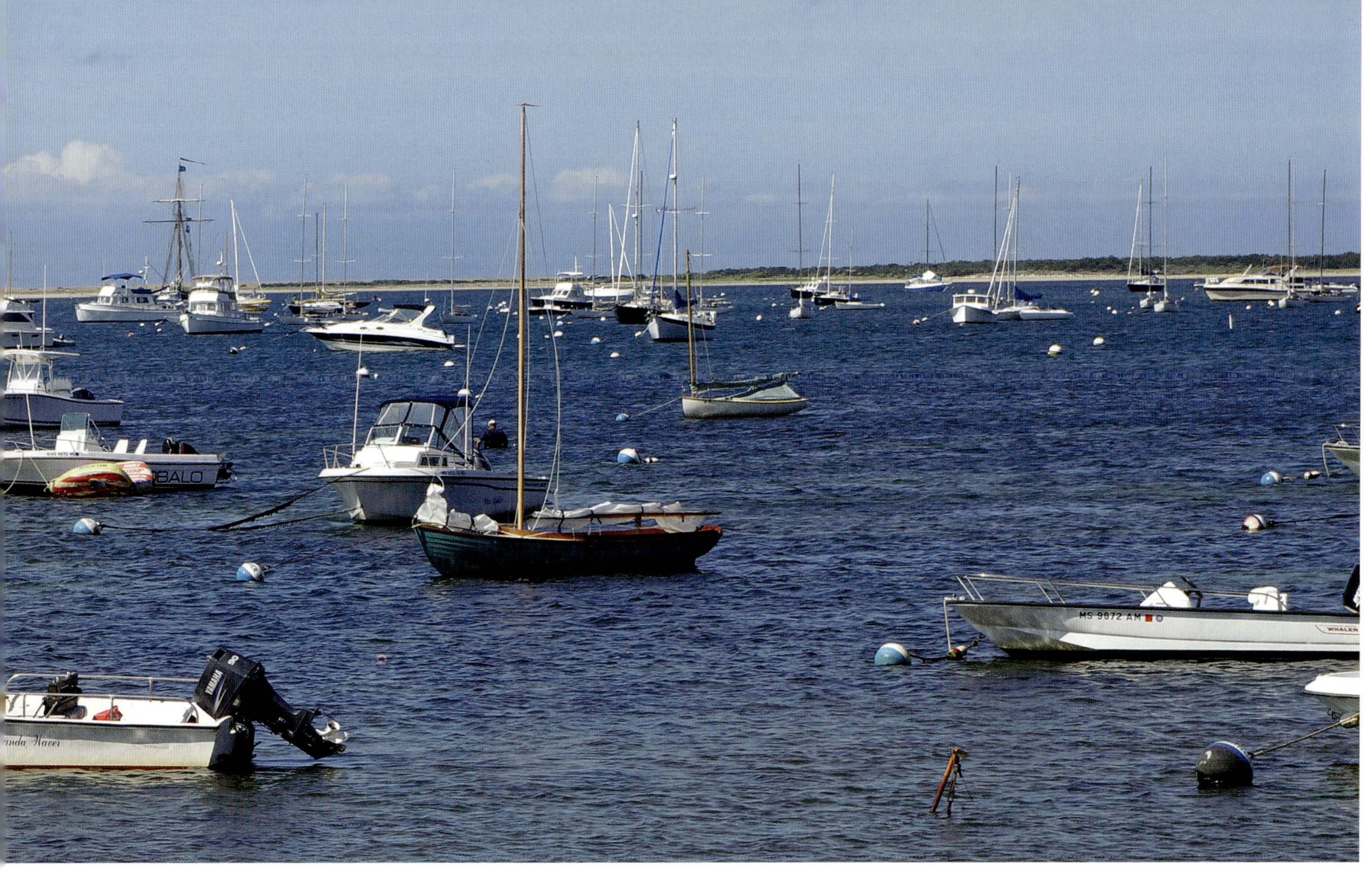

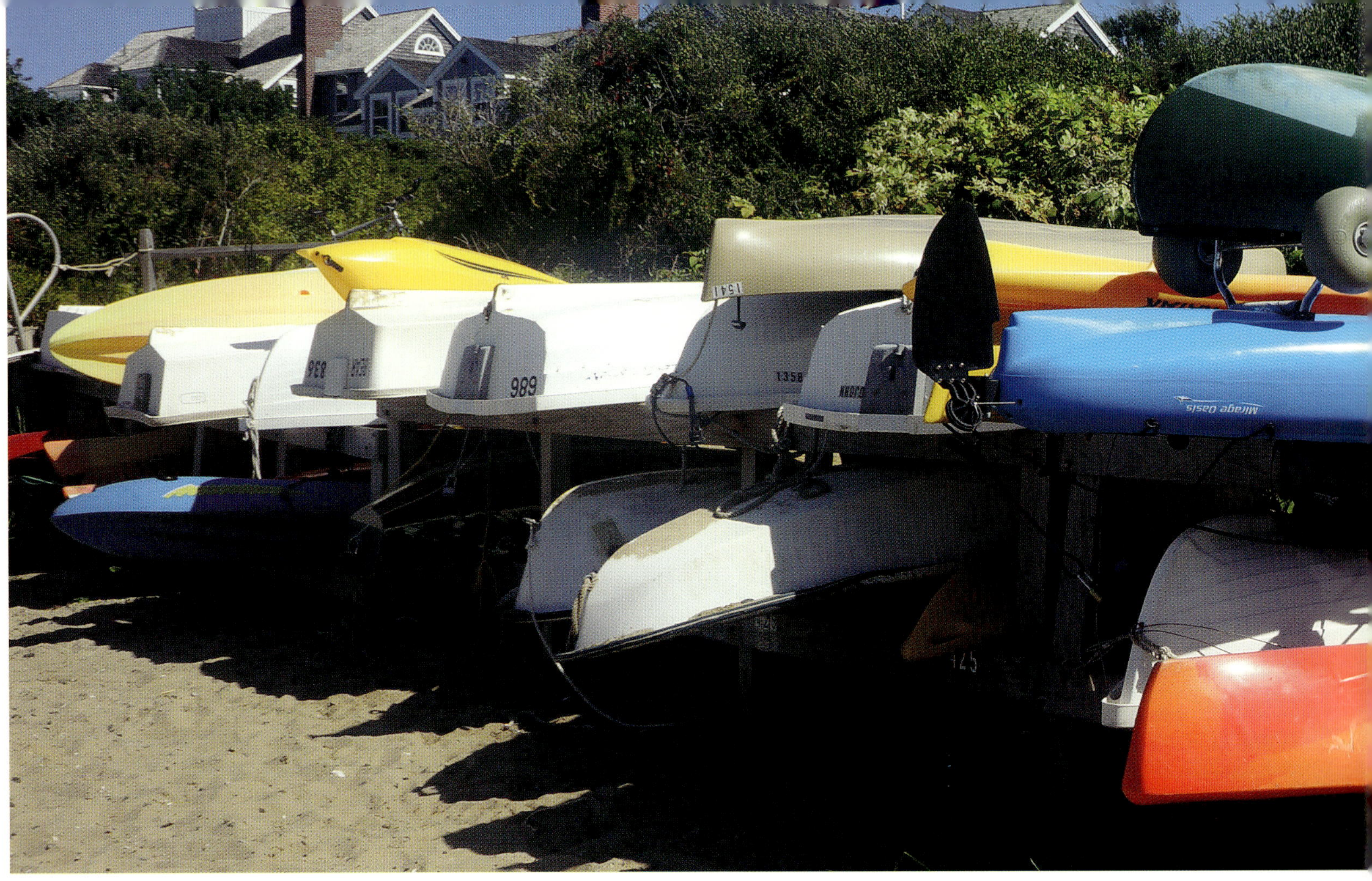

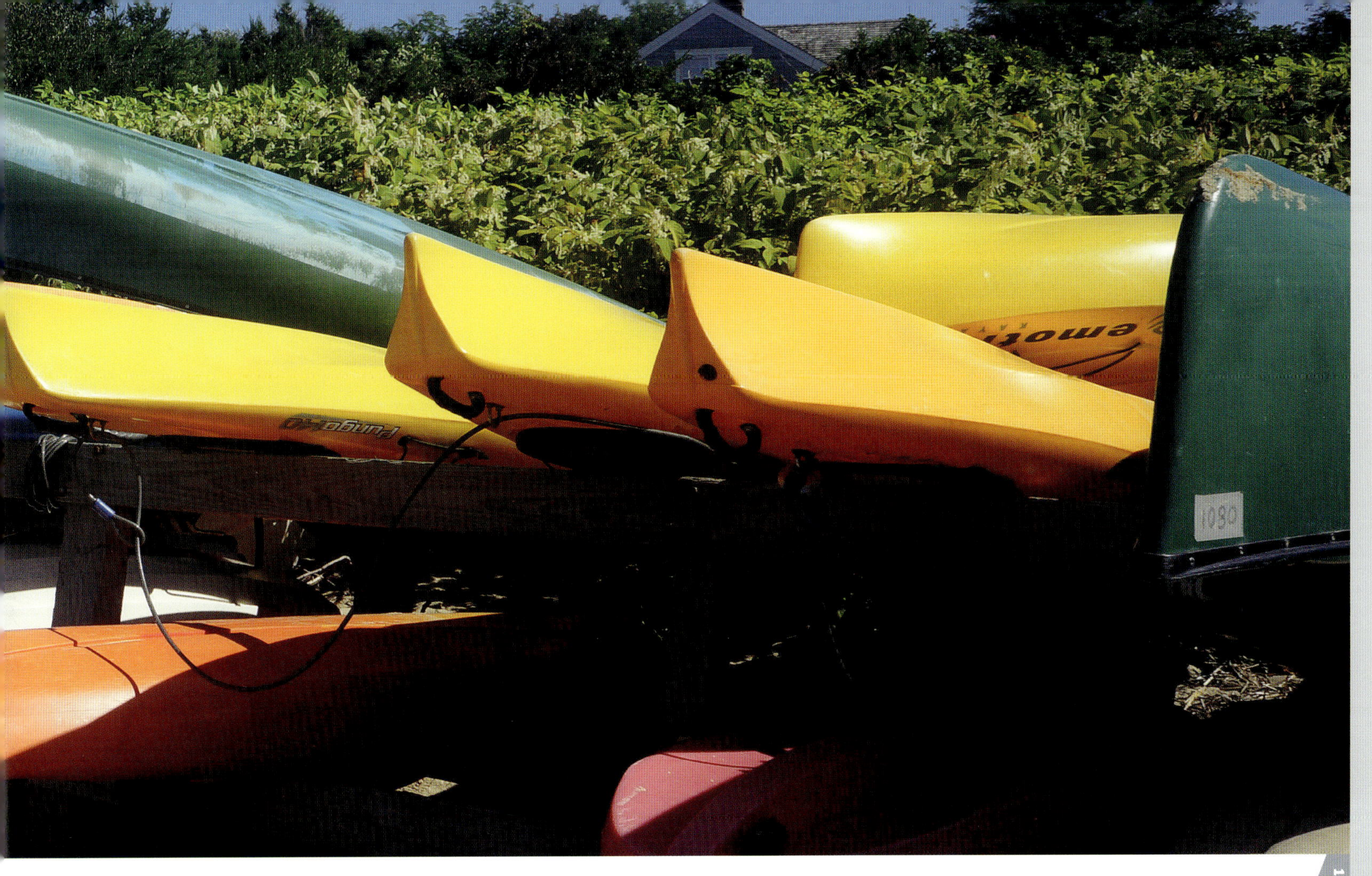

Kayaks and dinghies stacked along the shore.

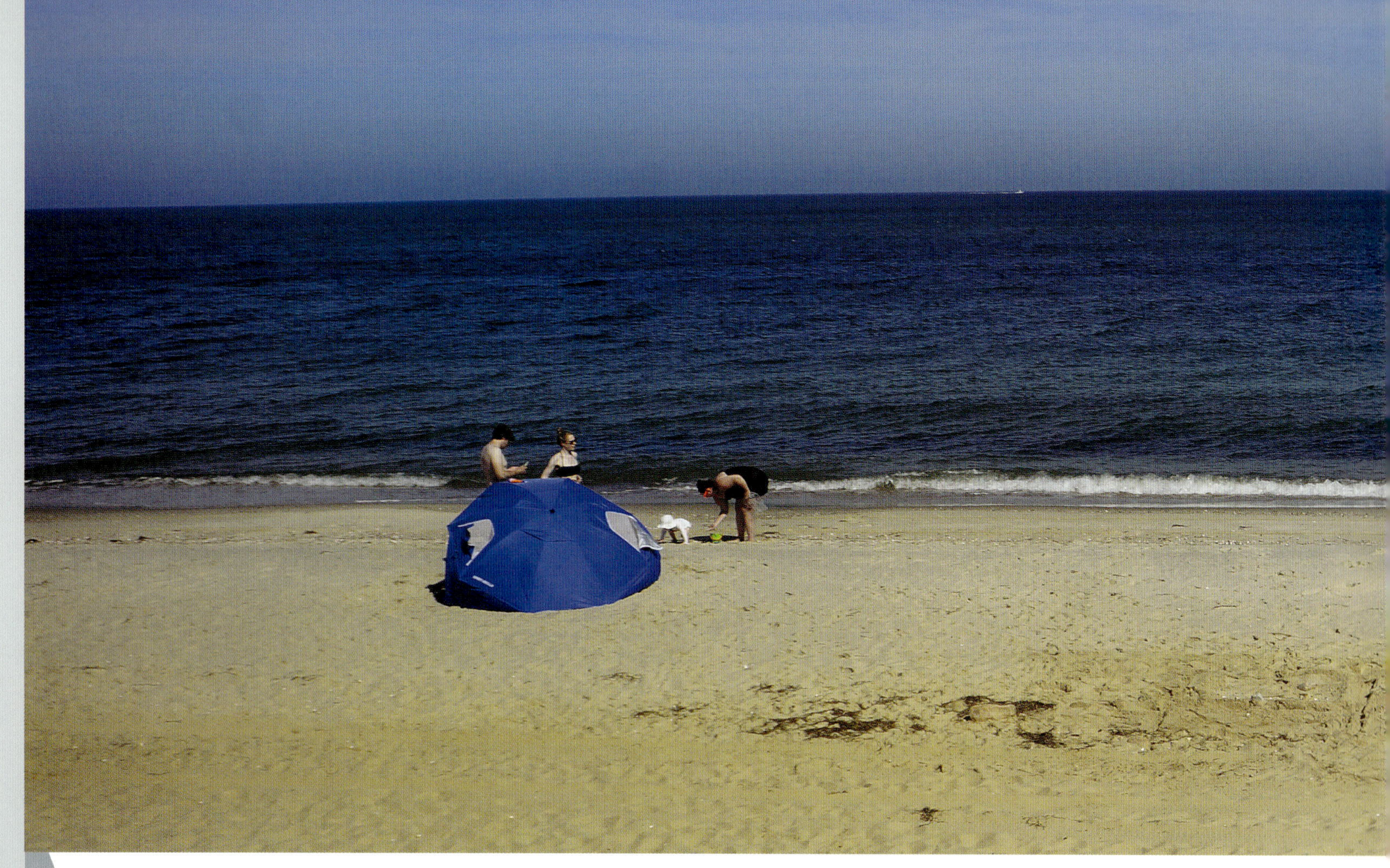

With the summer season over, the lifeguard stand at a popular beach is picked up for storage until next year.

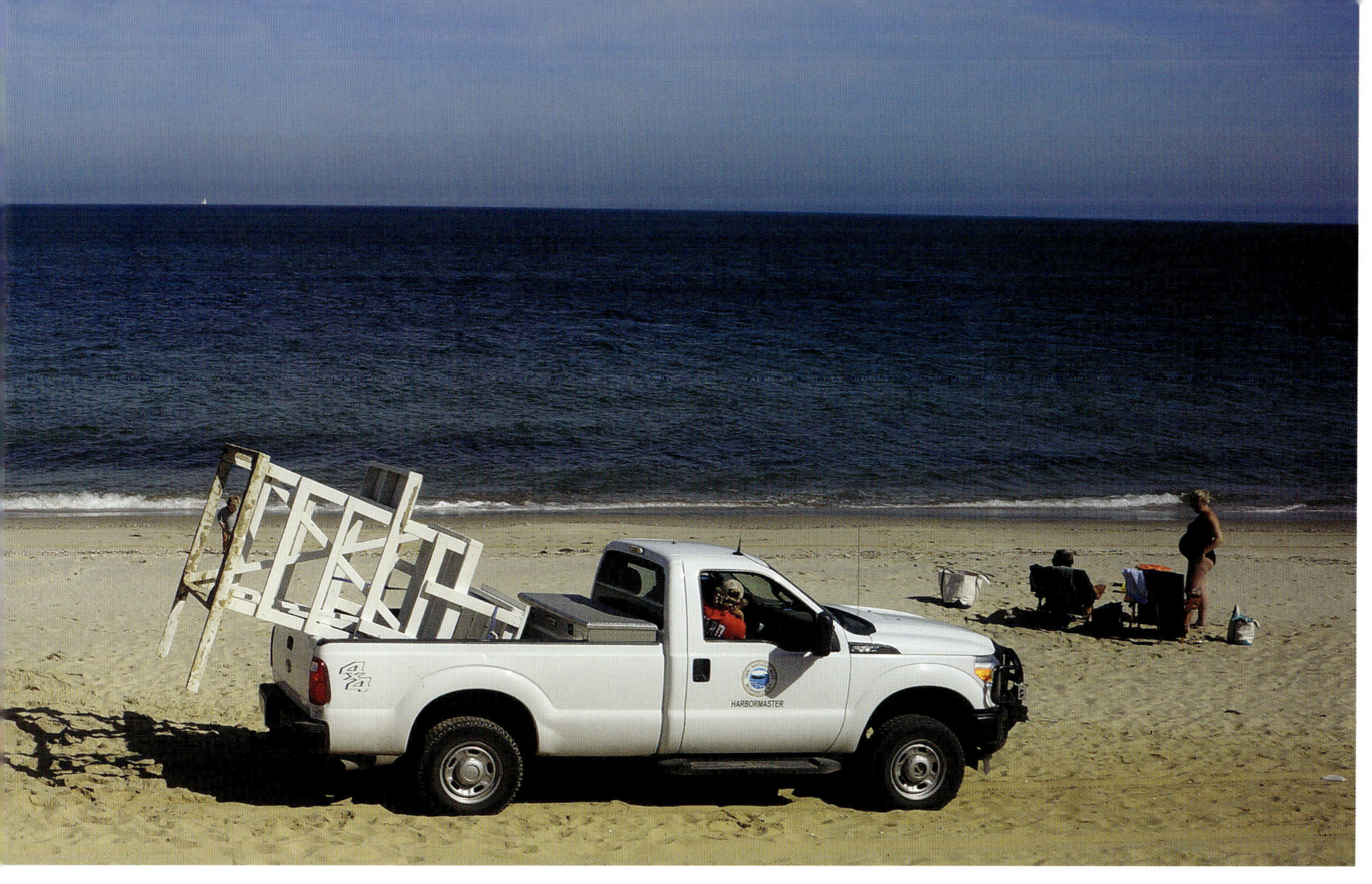

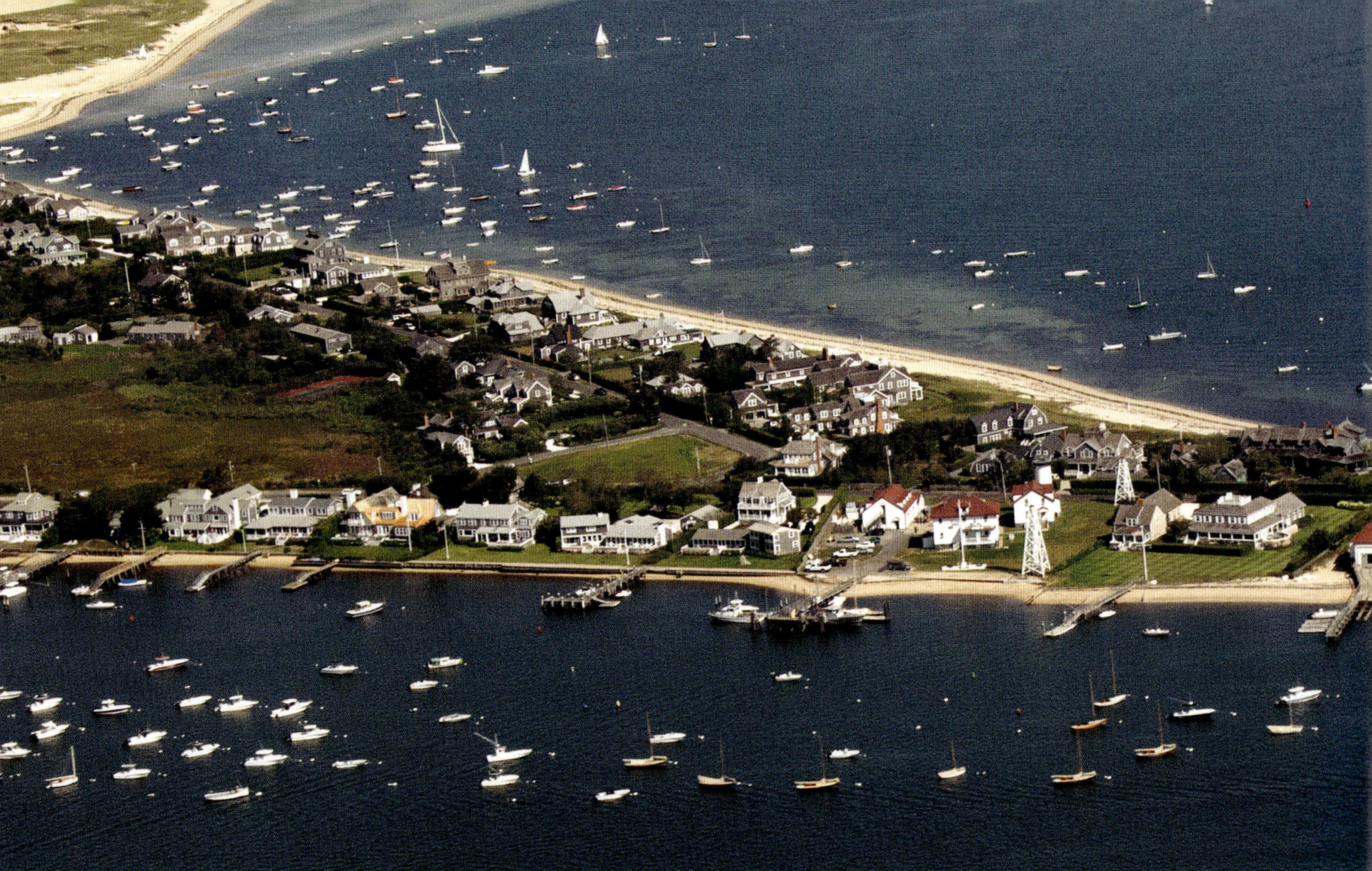

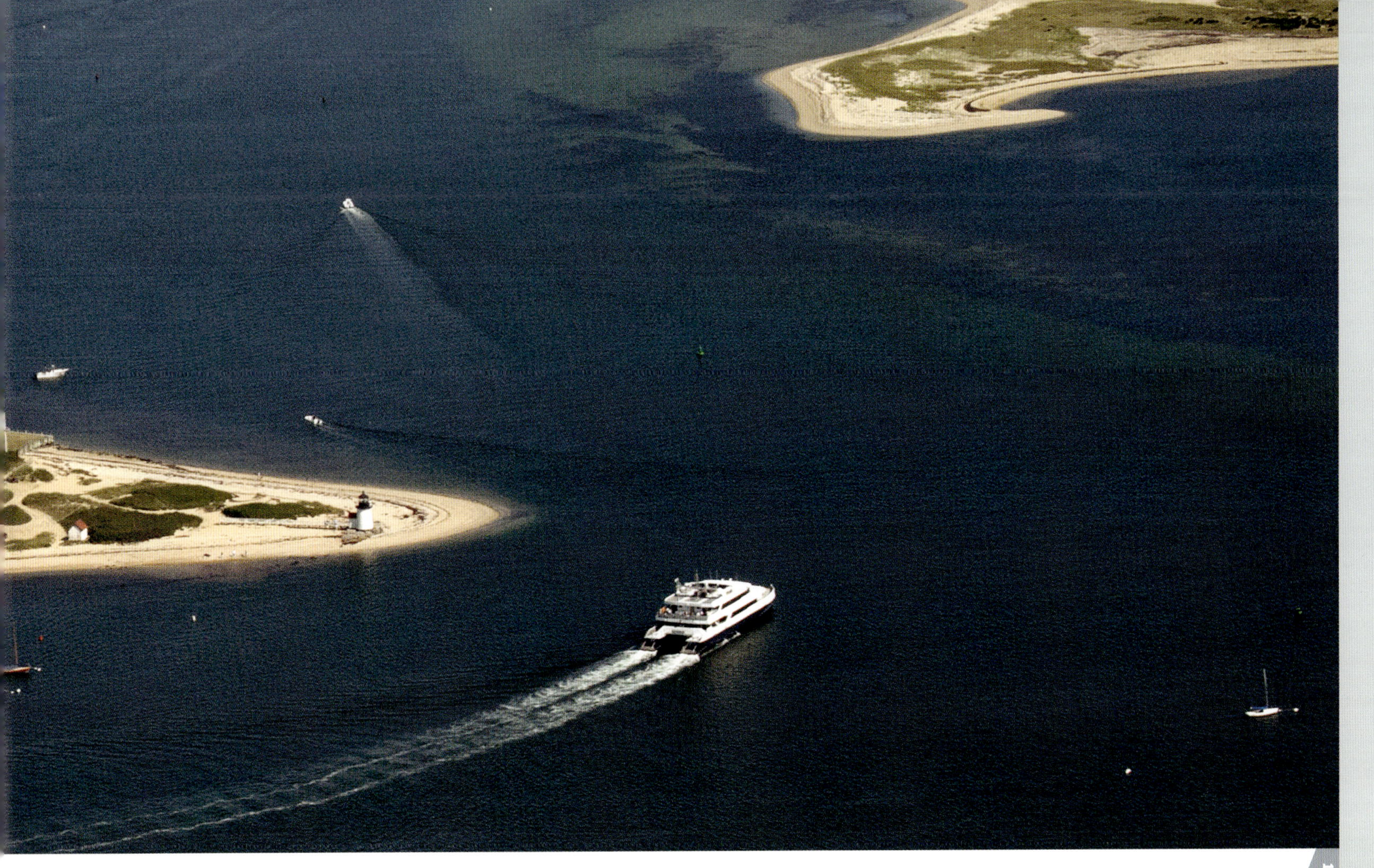

An aerial view of a ferry leaving the island and sailing past Brant Point Light.

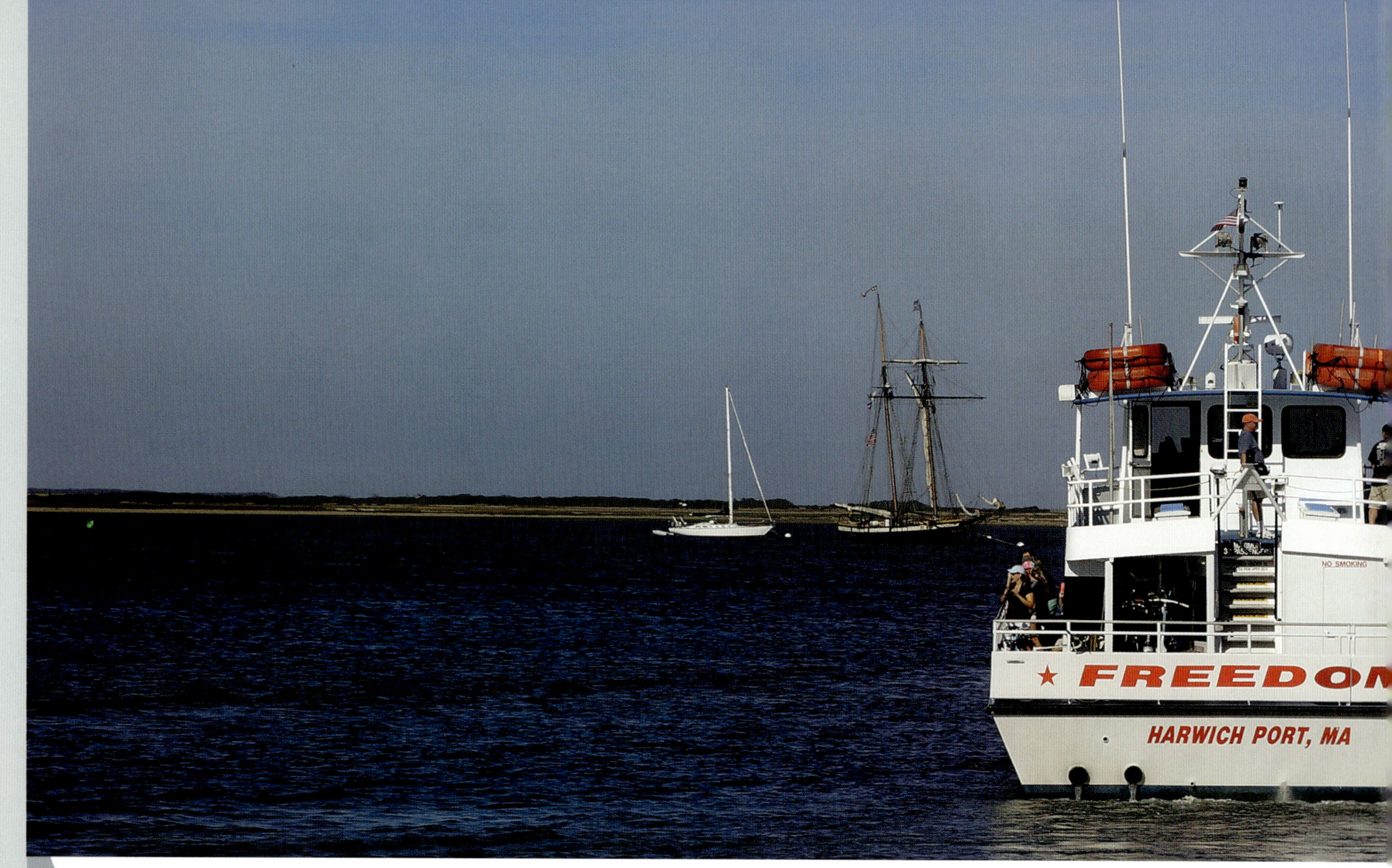

Ferries leaving the island and heading to Harwich port and Hyannis.

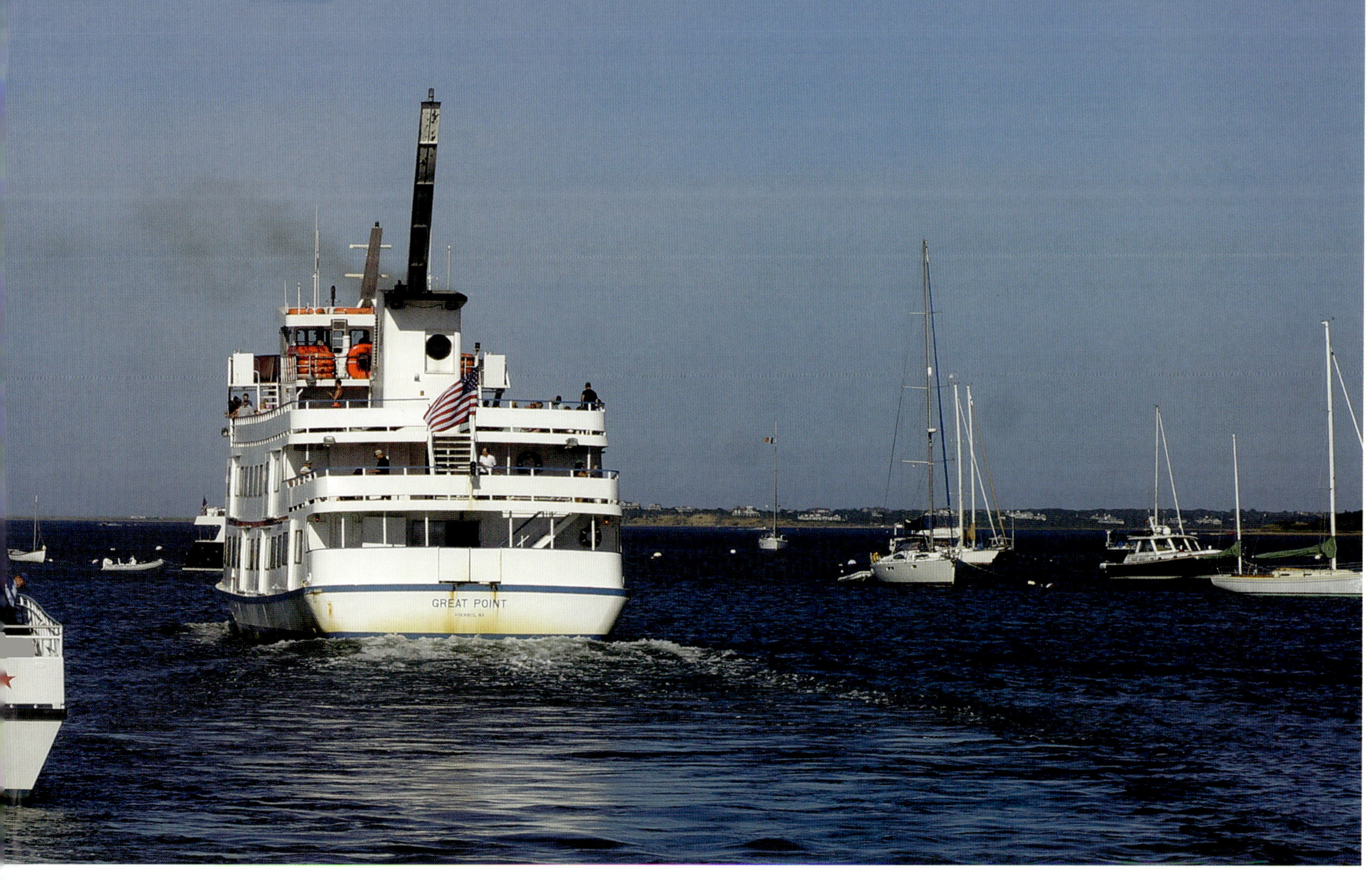
GREAT POINT
HYANNIS, MA

For Alexandra Paige

Published by Schiffer Publishing, Ltd.
4880 Lower Valley Road
Atglen, PA 19310
Phone: (610) 593-1777; Fax: (610) 593-2002
E-mail: Info@schifferbooks.com
Web: www.schifferbooks.com

For our complete selection of fine books on this and related
subjects, please visit our website at www.schifferbooks.com.
You may also write for a free catalog.

Schiffer Publishing's titles are available at special discounts
for bulk purchases for sales promotions or premiums. Special
editions, including personalized covers, corporate imprints, and
excerpts, can be created in large quantities for special needs.
For more information, contact the publisher.

We are always looking for people to write books on new and
related subjects. If you have an idea for a book, please contact
us at proposals@schifferbooks.com.

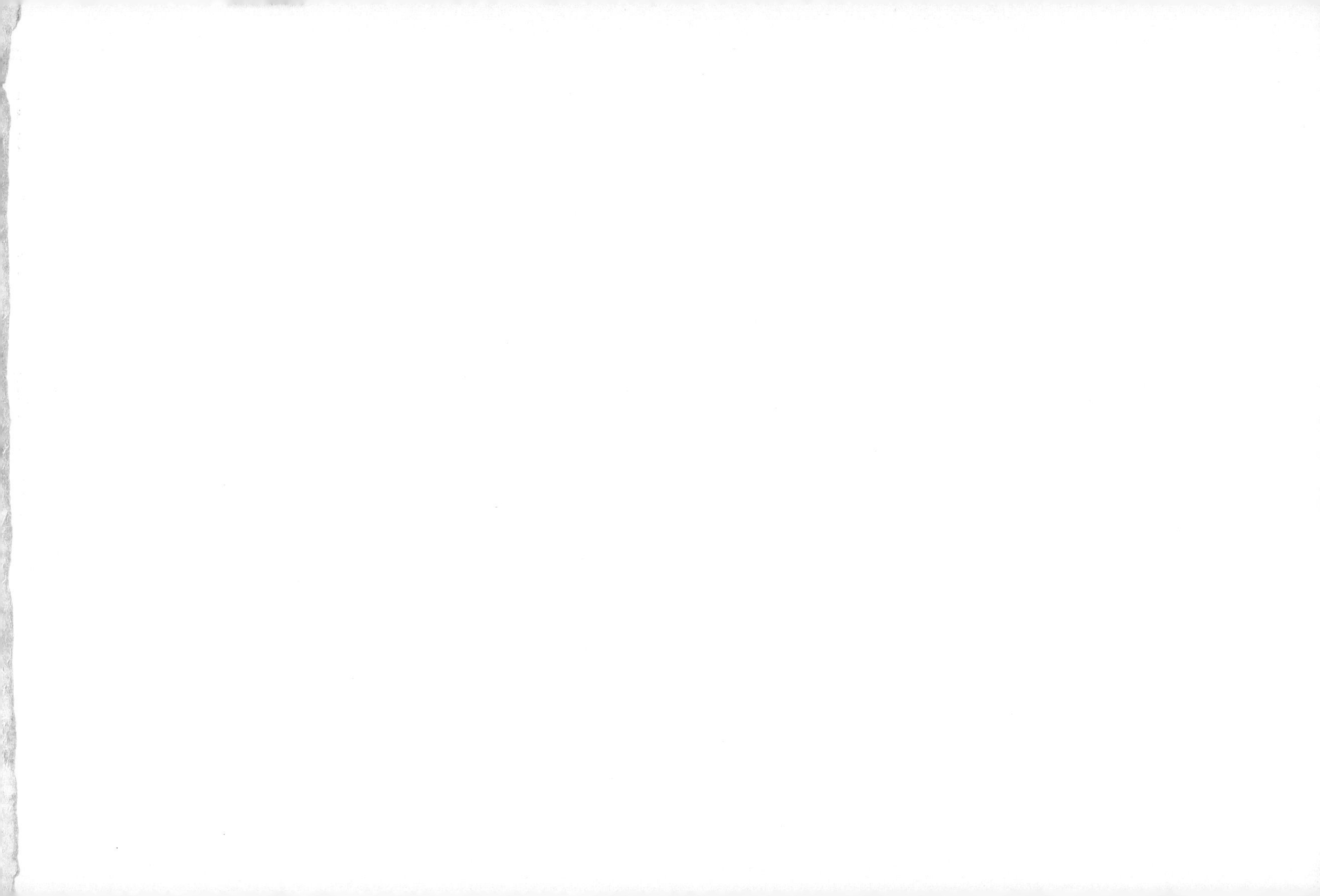